PROLOGUE

March, 1916

G *ujarat, India*

As THE SUN sank into the horizon, the man took his rifle from the cabinet near the front door and crept out of his house, taking care not to make more noise than necessary, although he had good reason to suspect he was not the only person awake.

A full moon had risen in the darkening sky. Bone-white, it silvered the narrow paths that ran between the rows of newly planted indigo seeds. He headed down the nearest path. Gathering speed as he strode along, he repeatedly stamped his heavy boots on the ground to send any snakes scattering.

Reaching the fringe of the jungle that bordered the far end of his plantation, the man deflected to the right and made for the track that cut off the corner of the jungle and led to the road linking the neighbouring villages. He paused a moment to remove his rifle from his shoulder and carry it in his hand, then ploughed into the dense foliage.

The earth on which he walked felt spongy beneath his feet. Sturdy bamboo shoots sought to block his way but he brushed them aside with the stock of his rifle. Thickets of thorn snagged his jodhpurs. Heedless of everything, he pressed ahead until he reached the road.

At the road he turned left and walked along the packed-earth surface to a nearby dak bungalow, long fallen into disuse, as were so many of the daks set up by the East India Company for the convenience of British officers.

When he reached the building, he stood in the road outside and stared in the direction of the indigo plantation that lay closest to his.

But no one stepped out of the gloom, and there was nothing to be heard other than the familiar sounds of the night, so he went across to the dak, climbed the few steps to the veranda that encircled the bungalow, sat down on a rickety wicker chair and stared towards the wall of jungle on the other side of the road, waiting.

He didn't have long to wait.

Moments later, he heard the approach of a motorcycle.

The man stood up, stepped from the shadows and went out into the road. He saw the person for whom he'd been waiting get down from his motorcycle, turn and untie a basket that had been fixed behind him.

Slipping his rifle back over his shoulder, he moved forward and then stopped.

The second man came up to him, the basket hanging from his hand.

'You brought it then,' the first man said, indicating the basket. 'You didn't change your mind?'

The second man shook his head. 'It's for the best. She can see that and she agrees.' He gave a twisted smile. 'Or it might be more honest to say that she'd no choice but to agree.'

A whimper came from the basket.

Both men glanced down at the source of the noise.

In the dim light, the face of a baby no more than a few days old was visible just above a lacy white shawl.

The two men looked back at each other.

'Have you made the necessary preparations?' the second man asked.

'Of course.'

For a moment, neither moved.

Then the second man held out the basket, and the first man took it.

The second man stepped back, wiping one hand against the other as if to clean them. 'That's it then,' he said. 'We'll never speak of this in our family or with anyone else. And you and I will never refer to this, should we meet again. Not that we ever will. You're not the only one who's leaving the area – we are, too.'

'Where're you going?' the first man asked.

The second man hesitated. 'It's better I don't say. We agreed that this transaction would end all contact between us, and that's what must happen. It's of no interest to either of us, therefore, to know where the other is going or what he's doing.'

The first man nodded. 'You're right.'

The baby whimpered again.

The first man looked down at the child, and then back at

the second man. 'I must be going. The child – my child now – needs to go home.' He hesitated. 'Thank you,' he said.

With a slight nod, he turned away, and holding the basket tightly in one hand and his rifle in the other, he walked up the road without looking back. A little way along, he crossed to the other side and struck out into the jungle, instinctively finding the track by which he had come.

He didn't bother to look for the footprints he'd earlier left in the muddy ground as he knew the mud would have already closed over them, just as it was rapidly closing over the new footprints he was making. Even before he reached his house, it would be as if no one had disturbed the life of the jungle that evening.

In the same way as all trace of his presence in the jungle that night would vanish, so, too, would all trace of the recent exchange. Only two couples would ever know what had passed, and with both couples keen to forget what had taken place, and unlikely ever to meet again, it would be as if the transaction had never happened.

1

___

September, 1934

*J*aipur, India

RISING high above the domes and towers of Jaipur, veiled thinly by loose dust thrown up from the surface of the streets, and by the smoke that curled upwards from the numerous cooking stalls throughout the town, the moon climbed slowly in the sky.

The glittering lights in the open-fronted shops sparkled more brightly and the salmon-pink walls of the old city were bathed in an ethereal glow. To the north of the town, a sheen of gold settled on Man Sagar Lake and on the fairy-tale palace that seemed to float on the surface of its water. Beyond the lake, the brown Aravali Hills that framed the upper part of the town melded into a purple silhouette that was stark against the darkening sky.

Amer Road, which ran from far north of Jaipur down the side of Man Sagar Lake and through the town, gleamed golden in the light reflected from the water.

So, too, did the houses in Victoria Crescent, a sweeping crescent that lay opposite the lake on a section of the extensive open fields that paralleled Amer Road, separating the road from the hills.

In the late nineteenth century, ignoring the fact that the fields had been deliberately left empty to create a wide gap between the hills, where wild animals lived, and the town, where people lived, members of the small British community in Jaipur, who'd wanted to live in a house that felt British, rather than Indian, which wasn't pale pink, divided up by small balconies bordered with intricately carved metal railings, had built the houses that formed Victoria Crescent.

For their convenience and comfort, they had ensured that the crescent opened at both ends on to Amer Road, and that all of the houses had an unimpeded view of the lake.

Each of the two-storeyed houses, which varied in size and slightly in style, was built of pale stone and had a portico that allowed horse-drawn tongas to unload their passengers protected from the elements. Each was fronted by a courtyard entered though iron gates, and boasted colonnaded verandas that ran the length of the ground floor and the upper storey.

On one side of the house, there was stabling for the horses and a small building that housed the family's tongas. Hidden at the back of the buildings were the servants' quarters and the kitchen where most of the food for the British family was cooked. Between the door leading from the tiny kitchen in the house itself and the servants' quarters, there was a vegetable garden. A modest lawn bordered by flowers and bushes ran from the vegetable garden around the back of the house.

As the moon climbed higher, darkness fell in the gardens, and they began to shimmer beneath a restless haze of fireflies and to rattle with the ceaseless chatter of the cicadas. Somewhere on the distant plains, above the nightly noises that rose from the town, dogs barked, jackals howled and birds squawked.

Inside one of the most imposing houses in Victoria Crescent, Philip Grainger sat at the end of a large teak dining table covered with a crisp white tablecloth. Drumming his fingers on the table, he stared at the three place settings of polished silverware, fine china and crystal glasses, which shone in the light from the sparkling chandelier above the table.

He was sitting behind his place setting. His wife, Julia, was sitting behind hers. The chair behind the third place setting, that of his daughter, Eleanor, was empty.

With a theatrical sigh, Philip raised his wrist and made a great show of looking at his watch.

'It's late, Julia,' he said. He lowered his arm and looked in annoyance at his wife. 'How much longer do you suggest I hold off dinner while we wait for your daughter to join us?' He glanced towards the wide archway that led from the dining room into the entrance hall and groaned in exasperation.

'She's your daughter, too, I believe,' Julia said mildly. 'I suggest we tell cook that we're ready to eat. If Eleanor misses her meal, so be it.'

'I'll do that,' Philip said, and he leaned forward and pressed the bell to summon the table steward.

Moments later, the *khitmutgar* appeared from a door at the far end of the dining room, and Philip told him he could start serving dinner. As the table steward left the room, they heard the sound of the front door closing, followed by voices, and then footsteps hurrying towards them.

Philip sat back in his chair and folded his arms as Eleanor rushed in and took her seat at the table.

'I'm sorry to be a little late, Papa,' she said breathlessly, 'but James came home just as I was about to leave Harriet's, and he started telling us something really interesting. Normally, James never has anything important to say so we only pretend to listen, but not this time. For once it was worth hearing, and I forgot all about the time.'

'Which means that you've not changed for dinner, and there's no time now for you to do so,' Philip said in irritation. 'You know how much I dislike the meal being delayed, especially when it's my favourite roast mutton, and I mean mutton, not goat.'

'Important though your stomach is, Papa, a delay is allowable if it's for an excellent reason. As this was,' Eleanor said brightly. 'You're going to be very pleased that I didn't leave before I'd heard everything.'

Glancing at her father with a pointedly self-righteous air, she picked up her starched white napkin, unfolded it and placed it across her lap.

'I'll be interested to discover if your idea of excellence accords with mine,' Philip remarked drily.

'It will, Papa,' Eleanor said, and she smiled at both her parents.

'Are you planning to tell us what James had to say,' her mother asked, 'or is this a guessing game? If we're to be held in suspense for the whole of the meal, we'll need something to preclude chronic indigestion.'

Eleanor laughed. 'No guesses are needed. No, it's that

James told us that a new family has moved into the crescent.'

Philip straightened up. 'New people you say? Are they British or Indian?'

'British obviously. No Indian would live in this road, in houses like these. It's far too English for them. James thinks they've moved into the empty house about five or six houses along from ours. It means they'll be about as far past us as we are from Harriet's in the other direction. And the most important thing is, he's certain they've got a daughter,' she added gleefully. 'Someone in his office told him.'

'In James's office?' Philip exclaimed in surprise. 'Why would anyone in the Department of Public Works know that we had new neighbours?'

Eleanor shrugged. 'I suppose our new neighbour might also work for the government. He could be going to work in James's department. James might not have met him yet, but his other colleagues could've done. Or he might be working in another part of the admin building and have bumped into someone from James's department.'

Philip nodded. 'You're right. Either is possible. Well, their timing's good in that they've missed the monsoon. They're going to see the city at its best, and at its driest.' He paused. 'I wonder where they've come from. I don't suppose James was able to tell you that?'

'I really would've been late for dinner if I'd badgered him for even more details,' she said with a sanctimonious air. 'Well, Papa? Was that sufficiently excellent for me to be slightly late and sitting here in a day dress?'

Philip laughed. 'All right. On this occasion, yes.'

The door at the far end of the dining room opened and the *khitmutgar* entered, followed by the cook's boy, who was carrying a tray with three bowls, a large soup tureen and a basket of naan bread. They came to a stop next to Julia's chair. The *khitmutgar* put the basket of bread in the centre of the table and started ladling creamy pea soup into the bowls.

'I hope the girl is of a similar age to you and Harriet,' Julia told Eleanor as a bowl of soup was placed in front of her. 'Oh, I can smell the sweet scent of garam marsala!' she exclaimed with pleasure. She smiled up at the *khitmutgar* and then turned back to Eleanor. 'It would be lovely for you and Harriet to have another friend. The two of you have spent so much time together over the years that you must feel in need of another companion.'

'It depends on what the girl's like,' Eleanor said, leaning back as her soup was placed in front of her. She waited for her father to be served and for the servants to leave the room. 'I wonder how old the girl is,' she continued. 'If she's the right age, James might be interested in meeting her.'

'Does Harriet think it's time that James got married, then?' Julia asked. 'After all, he's quite an old man. He must be all of twenty-five,' she added with amusement.

'I don't know about Harriet, but *I'll* be glad when he marries,' Eleanor said firmly. 'I'm sorry for Harriet, having such a bossy brother. But when he marries, he'll have someone else to boss around other than Harriet and me. He's always lecturing us, and he's unnecessarily strict when he chaperones us. He still sees us as babies. We much prefer being accompanied by one of our ayahs. At least our old nannies now see us as eighteen-year-olds who know how to behave.'

'Which is why your father and I are delighted that James is always willing to go with you if he isn't at the office and everyone else is tied up. He's a good brother. Not all brothers would be so solicitous of their sister and her friend.'

'So you agree he's bossy, then?'

Philip and Julia exchanged amused glances.

'To go back to the new family,' Philip said. 'It's good news that we're having another British family in Jaipur, even more so if he's in business or works for the government. Ours is still a very small community, despite a slight increase in size every year, and every newcomer makes us more of a force to be considered. And fresh faces at the club are always welcome.'

'I wonder how many fresh faces there'll be,' Eleanor mused. 'Maybe they've a son as well as a daughter. James didn't know if they had. But if they do, and he's good at billiards, he'd be welcomed by the men in the club with open arms.'

Philip nodded. 'You're right about that,' he said. 'It'd be interesting to know. Annoyingly, although it's Saturday tomorrow and the factory will be closed in the afternoon, there are things I need to do, so I'll have to be there for most of the day. If not, it would've been easy enough to see which house was theirs, call on them and leave our card. It's a shame I won't be able to do that. However, someone's bound to have told them that we usually go to the Royal Jaipur Club on Saturday evenings, so we might see them there.'

They stopped talking as the empty soup bowls were removed from the table, and then each was served with a plate of sliced mutton accompanied by potatoes and carrots that had been cooked with mustard seeds.

Julia picked up her knife and fork. 'I must say, I, too, am looking forward to meeting the new people. Like you and Harriet, I'd enjoy having another friend. And I'm sure Aunt Ivy would, too. Anyone who adds to our circle, and possibly to our book group, too, is very welcome.'

'If Aunt Ivy lets her, can Harriet and I go to the market

tomorrow, please, Mama?' Eleanor asked as she cut a piece of her mutton. 'The *durzi* will be in the area before too long and we need some material for him to make into dresses. The ones I wore last year are completely worn out. You said so yourself. I thought we could make a slight detour on the way home and have our lunch out. Meera could accompany us, or Harriet's ayah.'

Julia raised an eyebrow. 'Let me guess. You're thinking of a detour to the club?'

Eleanor laughed. 'It's only a small detour, but we might learn something about the new people.'

'Noble though it would be, there's no need for you and Harriet to inconvenience yourselves in such a way, Eleanor,' Philip said smoothly. 'We'll be going to the club tomorrow evening. That's quite soon enough.'

'Suppose you change your mind at the last moment, as you've sometimes done?' Eleanor said, and she looked at her mother for support.

'I won't,' he said. 'Maxwell Anderson is staying there. He's the exporter I told you about, Julia. He's been to the factory several times now, and I'd rather like to meet him in a social setting for a change. If the new people turn up at some point, someone is sure to tell us, and we'll introduce ourselves. Does that satisfy you, Eleanor?'

'It does, Papa, thank you,' Eleanor said with affected demureness.

They smiled at each other.

'I do hope James is right about there being a daughter,' she added.

Philip nodded. 'Well, you'll find out tomorrow if he is.'

. . .

'So, did you enjoy your day, Beatrice?' Frank Fletcher asked his wife, glancing at her across the table as he ran his finger around the rim of his glass of brandy.

Beatrice shrugged. 'It was all right. Even though we've been here for a couple of days, I'm still quite tired after our long drive and I spent most of the day on the verandah. An Austin Seven's not the most comfortable car for such a distance. When I've got some energy back, I'll go into the town.'

'We'll have to get a tonga for you to get into town. And for me, too. It'll be easier in the narrow streets than using the car. From what I've seen, all our neighbours have got their own buggy. It means hiring a syce to look after the horse and drive the tonga, of course, but we've got stabling in front of the servants' block, so we can manage. When you're able to get about more easily, I'm sure your energy will return. It'd be strange if it didn't. We're living in a town that's famous for markets, and you're a woman who likes to shop.'

'How would you know?' Beatrice snapped. 'There was nowhere to shop in Bayana, and you always said there was no spare money to spend anyway. You can't possibly know whether or not I like shopping.'

'So much for my attempt at a pleasantry,' he said, and he glared at his wife. He turned to look at his daughter. 'Did *you* enjoy your day, Alice?'

'Yes, I did, thank you. I've been sorting my things out and getting used to the house. It's not the most impressive house on the street, but it's so much better than the ghastly place we had in Bayana.'

She paused. 'You mentioned the markets,' she continued. 'Now we're living in a town like Jaipur, I'll need some clothes that are suitable for here. Can I have some money, please? I could get a tonga from in front of the lake and go to the market. I'd like to buy some material so I'm ready for when the *durzi* comes. There's bound to be a *durzi* who does the sewing and mending in this area. Sita can come with me if Mother doesn't want to.'

'I suppose I'll have to find some money from somewhere,' he said, scowling. 'We need to look successful now that I'm an exporter.'

'Thank you, Father,' Alice said, suppressing the gleeful smile that rose to her lips.

'How was *your* day, Frank?' Beatrice asked

He sat back and smiled. 'Very good, if not a little better than that. The advice I was given in Bayana proved to be excellent, and the purchases I made before we left have paid off. My modest showroom off Bapu Bazaar is going to be ideal for the moment. Prospective buyers can easily find me as I'm virtually in the centre of town and not that far from the railway station. And the showroom looks good as I've put some of the items I can export along the walls. I admit it's still a little sparse, but it's only a start. As I source products locally, I'll have more to display.'

'I look forward to seeing your premises,' Beatrice said. 'It's going to be very different for you from working on an indigo dye plantation.'

'It most certainly is. As for our new house,' he glanced around him with satisfaction, 'it's not looking too bad. Obviously, we need a few more furnishings as we didn't have much to bring from Bayana, but we'll get those in time. And we've certainly gone up a peg or two, having indoor plumbing and modern sanitation. That's an advantage of being in an area developed by British businessmen.'

'Father!' Alice exclaimed. 'You shouldn't talk about indoor plumbing. It's not nice.'

He laughed. 'D'you want me to say "flush toilets", then?' He laughed again.

Alice scowled.

'You're right about the house, Frank,' Beatrice said. 'I'm sure that once I've shed my fatigue I'm going to enjoy living here. At least I will if the social side of Jaipur lives up to its promise. And I'm full of praise for our servants. They did an excellent job of preparing the house for our arrival. It was such a relief that they wanted to come with us. I'd have hated to have had to train a new set.'

'And I'm very pleased that Sita came with us,' Alice said. 'No one could have a nicer ayah.'

'I agree, Alice,' Beatrice said. 'She'll make a trustworthy chaperone when I'm unable to accompany you. And when you don't need her, she can help me with the clothes and the house.'

'I hope I soon make friends,' Alice said, sitting back and gazing around the room. 'I wasn't sorry to leave Bayana. We were in such an isolated place that I didn't really have any close friends. I'm sure Jaipur will be better.'

Frank nodded. 'I'm sure it will,' he said. 'Better than you realise, in fact. Apparently, most of the British community, such as it is, go to a club on Saturday nights called the Royal Jaipur Club. It seems it isn't too far from here, which is very convenient. I've arranged to meet a fellow exporter there tomorrow evening. He's going to introduce us to everyone he knows. We couldn't have a better start to our new life here.'

Alice glanced anxiously at her mother. '*Can* I go into the town tomorrow morning and go to the markets? I want to get to know the place we're living in, and markets are as good a place to begin as any. Sita can come with me.'

'I'm not sure. I need Sita to help me sort out my clothes.

Some have got very creased in the journey and they need to be ironed or even washed.'

'Please?' Alice begged.

'I suppose I could defer the clothes till another day,' Beatrice said reluctantly, 'and she could go with you. Don't be out too long, though, in case I find I need you here. Also, we'll be going out in the evening, so you don't want to get overtired.'

'I'm almost eighteen, Mother, not eighty.' Alice stood up. 'I think I'll go to my room now and try to decide what to wear tomorrow evening. I want to look my best on our first social occasion here.'

'I'm sure with your fair hair and blue eyes you'll look fine in whatever you wear,' Beatrice said. 'You don't need to fuss so.'

Alice glared at her mother. 'Good night.'

When Alice had gone upstairs, Frank finished his brandy and stood up. 'I've one or two things to do in the room I'm making into a home office. As you claim to be tired, Beatrice, go up when you're ready. Don't wait up for me.'

And he left the dining room, leaving Beatrice sitting there by herself.

2

The Royal Jaipur Club,
The following evening

WEARING a pale grey silk dress that matched the colour of her eyes, Eleanor stepped down from their tonga and stood waiting for her parents. Then the three of them walked under the high stone arch which separated the club grounds from the parking area for the cars and tongas by which the members arrived, and turned right to walk up the drive flanked by a lawn on both sides to the wide single-storey building ahead of them.

At the end of the drive, a stone elephant stood on either side of the four terracotta steps leading up to the large paved patio that lay between the steps and a deep veranda that encircled the low white building.

Lights concealed beneath the sloping red tiled roof twinkled as night gathered around them, and the lamp in the centre of every table on the patio and on the veranda, the wick of each resting in ghee, shone beneath a halo of amber.

Most of the early arrivals were sitting at the clusters of cane tables spaced along the veranda, between which white-turbaned servants wove their way, each with a tray of drinks held aloft.

'Although we're still quite early, there's already a surprising number here,' Julia remarked, coming to stand next to Eleanor. 'Even the patio tables are filling up. And from the noise everyone's making, you'd think they hadn't seen each other for weeks,' she added with a smile. 'From the general tone, I can tell it's going to be an enjoyable evening.'

'I hope you're right,' Eleanor said. 'It's a pity, though, that the McKennas have had to go to dinner with James's boss instead of coming here. James can be quite entertaining. And Harriet's presence makes everything so much nicer.'

Julia raised her eyebrows. 'According to you not so long ago, James is boring and forever scolding you.'

Eleanor laughed. 'He is. But that can be fun.'

'Look, Julia!' Philip said suddenly, and he caught her arm. 'I do believe that's Maxwell Anderson.' Squinting slightly, he stared ahead at the veranda. 'He's sitting in the shadow, but it does look like him.'

Eleanor followed the direction of her father's gaze to a solitary man sitting at the back of the veranda, from which he'd have a good view of the people walking up the steps to the patio.

'I thought he might be here,' Philip said, a note of satisfaction in his voice. 'When he was at the factory a couple of days ago, he mentioned he was staying here. I told him in passing that we often come up on a Saturday evening. If I'm right that it's him, and he's on his own, we could suggest joining him. He's a pleasant young man, and seems to be successful at a relatively young age. I think he said he was thirty.'

Julia nodded. 'If you wish.'

'Apparently, in the past he's been in Jaipur for only two or three days at the most as this isn't his base. Like a lot of exporters, he travels around. But it seems that his business in Jaipur has developed to such an extent that he's set up a showroom at the town end of Amer Road and plans to stay here for longer. That could be good news for us. When he came to the factory this week, he indicated that he might put in a large order for our best quality paper.'

'Well done, darling,' Julia said, gazing at him with open affection. 'The quality of paper you produce is second to none, and it's to his credit that he realises it.'

'Thank you, Julia,' he said, quietly. He took her hand, raised it to his lips and lightly kissed it.

Eleanor pulled a face. 'You two are making me feel quite sick.'

'Nevertheless, Eleanor,' Philip said, turning towards her. 'If Anderson and I are going to be doing a volume of business together, it makes sense that you and Julia meet him, and there could be no better time than this. D'you think you could keep your sickness at bay?'

Eleanor made as if she was considering the request.

'Furthermore, I'd be grateful if you refrained from saying anything that could make him hesitate to do business with me, Eleanor,' he went on, a slightly more serious note in his voice.

'Silly me,' Eleanor said, lightly slapping the back of her hand. 'I thought we'd come here for purely social reasons this lovely Saturday evening, and to meet our new neighbours if they turn up. I didn't realise that the main purpose of the evening was to do business.'

'If a British man in Jaipur doesn't work for the British government and isn't attached to a military unit, he's probably in business – most likely an exporter or importer – so the social connections we make at the club are likely to have a business element, too, as you well know. And from which you profit.' Turning to his wife, he frowned questioningly. 'How much was the silk you wanted to buy for Eleanor's new dress, Julia?'

'Did I tell you how greatly I'm looking forward to meeting Mr Anderson, Papa?' Eleanor said serenely. 'I intend to ensure that he enjoys his time in Jaipur so much that he decides to stay even longer than planned, and then he can give you lots of orders.'

'I knew I could count on your selflessness, Eleanor,' Philip said with mock gravity. 'Well, now that we understand each other, let's go across and say hello to Mr Anderson.'

He offered his right arm to Julia and his left to Eleanor. They took his arm and went across the patio to the covered veranda.

'It *is* Maxwell Anderson,' Philip said quietly as he turned towards the table where the exporter was sitting, his eyes on a small piece of paper he was holding.

'I thought it was you, Maxwell,' Philip said heartily when he reached the table.

Maxwell looked up and smiled broadly. Thrusting the paper back into the pocket of his lightweight white suit, he rose to his feet. 'I'm delighted to see you, Philip. I'd rather hoped you'd be here this evening as you said you often came here on Saturdays.'

'Well remembered,' Philip said. 'May I introduce my wife and daughter?'

Maxwell Anderson took a step forward, and for the first time, Eleanor had a clear view of him.

Her heart missed a beat. He was tall and athletic in build, with a lock of his dark hair falling across his forehead. From a lightly tanned face, piercing blue eyes were gazing at her, full of open appreciation.

A wave of excitement shot through her, and heat rose to her face.

'I'd like you to meet my wife, Julia,' Philip said, lightly resting his hand on Julia's shoulder. 'Julia, let me introduce Maxwell Anderson, a fellow businessman.'

Maxwell Anderson promptly slid his gaze sideways and focused on Julia. 'It's a pleasure to meet you, Mrs Grainger,' he said, inclining his head towards her.

'And I'm delighted to meet you, Mr Anderson,' she said. 'Having heard Philip talk about you, it's an unexpected surprise to meet you in person. And a very pleasant one, I must say.'

'And this is my daughter, Eleanor.' Philip turned to Eleanor.

Eleanor put out her hand. Maxwell took it, and held it. 'I'm delighted to meet you, Miss Grainger,' he said. He held her hand for a moment longer, and then allowed it to fall.

Philip indicated the empty seats at the table. 'If these aren't taken, perhaps we could join you?' he suggested.

'I hope you will,' Maxwell said, turning his attention back to Philip. 'I'm expecting some friends, but as you can see they aren't here yet, and I'd enjoy your company. If necessary, when they arrive the waiters can bring us more chairs. Do please sit down.' He indicated the wicker chairs arranged around the table, and sat down again. Philip, Julia and Eleanor took the seats opposite him.

A waiter appeared at their table.

Both Philip and Maxwell ordered a chotapeg. He was sticking to two fingers of whisky while the evening was still young, Philip told Maxwell with a smile. Eleanor asked for a lemonade and Julia a gin gimlet.

The waiter left.

'I think you said this is the first time you've stayed here?' Philip remarked as they waited for their drinks to arrive.

Maxwell nodded. 'That's right.'

'How are you finding the accommodation?' Philip asked.

'It's fine,' Maxwell said. 'The room's comfortable and the club has all the amenities you'd expect in a British club, plus there's always someone to talk to if you feel like conversation. And it's extremely convenient for getting into Jaipur. In the future, if my business in Jaipur develops in the way I think it will, I'll look for a place of my own. But for the present, this suits me perfectly.'

'I can't imagine anyone having a dull moment here,' Philip said. He paused as the waiter put a drink in front of each of them, and in the centre of the table, a plate of samosas filled with spiced potatoes, peas and minced meat, and then left. 'You'll always find someone looking for an extra person to join in a game of cards or to play billiards,' he continued. 'And as I'm sure you've already discovered, they've an excellent bar.'

Maxwell nodded. 'It's why I opted to stay here rather than in one of the *havelis* in Jaipur that I've used in the past. Those old mansions are lovely, but I'd rather be somewhere like this for a longer stay.'

'Papa told us you'd been to his factory, Mr Anderson. Is paper the only thing you export?' Eleanor asked.

He smiled at her. 'If your parents have no objection, Miss Grainger, perhaps you would call me Maxwell? And if I may, I'd like to call you Eleanor.' He glanced at Julia. 'Would that be acceptable?'

Julia inclined her head. 'In an informal gathering like this,' she said, 'of course it would. And you must call me Julia. After all, you're Philip and Maxwell to each other, aren't you?'

'Indeed we are! I like to be on first name terms with all those with whom I do business,' Maxwell said. He smiled at Philip, and then turned back to Eleanor. 'To answer your question, Eleanor, no, it's only one of the items I export. Or hope to export. I haven't as yet exported paper, but if the first consignments go well, I shall certainly order more. Factories like your father's are rare, not only in India, but everywhere in the world. It produces handmade paper of a very fine quality.'

'So he keeps telling me,' Eleanor said lightly.

Maxwell laughed.

'I thought I recognised you, Mr Anderson,' they heard a voice say. 'And I certainly recognise *you*, Mr Grainger.'

'Why, Charles!' Philip exclaimed. 'This is a pleasant surprise! I wasn't sure you were coming this evening.' Both he and Maxwell rose to their feet, turning as they did towards the young man with light brown hair who'd come up to their table.

'You've met my foreman, Charles Davis, Maxwell?' Philip said.

Maxwell nodded. 'Indeed I have. He took me around the factory. It's good to see you again, Charles.'

'Hello, Charles,' Julia said warmly.

'And I think I'm going to get to know you even better, Charles,' Maxwell said as he sat down again. 'I've signed up for the proposed billiards tournament, and I recognised your name on the list.'

'That's excellent, Mr Anderson!' Charles exclaimed. 'We need more players, ideally people who play better than I do. I'm pretty poor, but I enjoy it.'

'That makes two of us,' Maxwell said ruefully. 'I'm sure the club has players who are far better than I am.'

Charles grinned. 'Now why do I have a feeling you're being modest, and that the truth might be otherwise?'

Maxwell laughed. 'I suppose I may have won the odd tournament or two. But as for what we call each other out of work, I think I can be Maxwell to you,' he said, 'especially as we're both billiards enthusiasts. Why don't you take a seat? Unless you've other plans.'

'Thank you. I'd be happy to join you,' Charles said, and he sat down on one of the last two empty chairs.

'Do you play any indoor or outdoor sports, or enjoy watching them, Eleanor?' Maxwell asked.

'A bit of tennis, and croquet,' she said. 'I'm always knocked out of the club's tennis tournaments fairly early on, but I like watching the remaining players. And I also like watching polo. We sometimes go to the polo club in town. Between the speed of the horses and the mallets being waved around in the air, it's hard to know what's happening, but it's always an enjoyable day out, nevertheless. And the divot stomping between the chukkas is tremendous fun. My friend, Harriet, and I try to outdo each other in the number of divots we stamp. Divot stomping is flattening the small mounds of earth churned up by the horses' hooves, if you don't know the term, Maxwell.'

'I do,' he said. 'I, too, like a good game of polo. If we go to a game together one day, I'll challenge you and Harriet as to who can stomp the most divots.'

Eleanor laughed. 'I'm sure Harriet won't mind me speaking for her, so on behalf of both of us, we'll take you up on that. But you'll probably have to include James in your challenge, too. He won't want to be left out. He's highly competitive so you'll need to take your stomping very seriously.'

'Who's James?' Maxwell asked.

'James McKenna,' she said. 'His father, Arthur McKenna, is one of the best-known exporters in Jaipur. I'm sure you've heard of him.'

'Indeed I have,' Maxwell said.

'My friend, Harriet, is his sister,' Eleanor continued. 'They live very near us. Harriet used to come to my home and study with me. She's almost a sister to me.'

Julia laughed. 'I'm afraid Eleanor is rather misusing the word "study", Maxwell. When we found a British governess for Eleanor, Ivy and Arthur, Harriet's parents, suggested that both girls be educated at the same time as they're similar in age. We'd thought that having company while they learnt would not only provide companionship for both, but would also generate a sense of competition between them. Each would be motivated to outdo the other in brilliance, or so we thought.'

'I'm picking up that it didn't turn out quite like that,' Maxwell said in amusement.

'Our hope that they would develop a friendship was more than delivered,' Julia said, glancing sideways at Eleanor. 'However, the motivation to do one's best in academic terms never seemed to materialise.'

Eleanor laughed. 'Don't believe everything Mama says, Maxwell. Harriet and I were model pupils. We had to be. Her brother didn't hesitate to tick us off if we did badly in our tests. He works for the government, and is based in the

British administration building close to Hawa Mahal. I'm not sure what he does, and Harriet isn't either. We think it's probably so uninteresting that James doesn't like people to know what a dull day he has.'

'I look forward to meeting him,' Maxwell said. 'If he's a billiards player, I suspect I'll meet him fairly soon. Aha!' he exclaimed, glancing towards the veranda steps. He rose to his feet. 'My friends have arrived. This is their first visit to the club as they're new to the town. They live quite close to you, Philip, I believe.'

Philip and Charles stood up and turned towards the new arrivals, a man, a woman and a girl.

Philip gave a sharp exclamation.

In grabbing the edge of the table, he knocked over his glass.

Julia glanced up at her husband's face and then at Maxwell's friends.

The friends had stopped walking and were standing still, staring at Philip in an unmistakeable mixture of horror and amazement.

A sound like a whimper came from Julia's throat, and the colour faded from her cheeks.

Maxwell's gaze moved from the Graingers to the new arrivals. Frowning slightly, he sat down again and watched the two families.

Alarmed at her mother's ashen face, Eleanor stared in bewilderment at the newcomers. The couple were no longer looking at Philip, but were staring intently at her.

How rude of them, she thought.

She glanced at their daughter. The girl, who had very fair hair and blue eyes, appeared to be similar to her in age, perhaps a few months younger. Delighted to see that, and knowing that Harriet would be, too, she shrugged off the unusual behaviour of both sets of parents, and stood up.

The fair-haired girl took a step towards the table, and stopped.

The two girls stared at each other. Then at the same moment, each tentatively smiled.

3

To Eleanor's disappointment, the girl, whose name she now knew to be Alice Fletcher, had been told by her father to sit between her parents, which was on the opposite side of the table from her. Biting her lip, she wondered whether she dared suggest that Alice come round the table and sit next to her.

It meant that her father's foreman, Charles Davis, would have to move along one seat, and also Maxwell and Mr Fletcher, but she couldn't see why any of them would mind doing so. It was fairly obvious that two girls of the same sort of age would want to sit together. She opened her mouth to make the suggestion, but at that moment Maxwell started to speak, and she bit back her words.

'Not so long ago I was sitting here all by myself, but look at me now,' Maxwell said, surveying the table with a satisfied air.

An indeterminate mutter came from everyone else at the table, followed by silence.

Eleanor took a deep breath, preparing to try again to make her request, but once more Maxwell forestalled her.

'The two of you appear to have met before, if I'm not mistaken,' he said, looking from Frank Fletcher to Philip.

Philip and Frank exchanged glances.

'That's right,' Philip said, and he attempted a smile. 'We didn't know each other before moving to Gujarat, but apparently we came over to India from England at about the same time. We met because we owned neighbouring indigo plantations. That was a long time ago, though.'

Maxwell stared at Frank in surprise. 'I didn't realise you'd lived in Gujarat before Bayana. If you've any connections in Gujarat, it could be useful.'

Frank shook his head. 'I haven't. Our Gujarat days were a long time ago. Beatrice and I moved from Gujarat to Bayana, and we were there for about sixteen years before we moved here.'

'I take it you met Frank in Bayana, then?' Philip asked Maxwell.

Maxwell nodded. 'That's right. I've business interests there, as does Frank. We met a couple of years ago. We were both visiting a cotton factory at the same time.'

'A cotton factory!' Philip exclaimed. 'So you didn't stay in indigo, either, Frank?'

'I did when we first lived in Bayana,' Frank said. 'But eventually I gave up and started an export business. By then, it had become blindingly obvious that the heyday for natural indigo was over. These days, it's hard to believe that it used to be one of the most profitable commodities traded in the European market. I stuck it out for longer than most planters in the area, but in the end, I'd had enough.'

'I'm not surprised. The system was unworkable,' Philip remarked.

'In what way?' Maxwell asked.

'Indian landowners and British planters could force

tenant farmers to grow indigo on a percentage of their land, regardless of the suitability of the land. The planters built the factories and agreed with their tenant farmers to advance them the money to grow the indigo,' Philip explained. 'The planter would then buy the crop from the growers at a fixed price. Unsurprisingly, the growers often thought the price too low and wanted to grow something more profitable, such as rice. And that's when the trouble began.'

'Don't forget the Gandhi effect,' Frank intervened. 'As soon as Gandhi returned from South Africa, he joined the movement to stop farmers from being restricted in what they could grow and then having to sell the indigo to the planter at a low price. After that, we didn't stand a chance.'

'I see,' Maxwell said. 'You left Gujarat before Frank, I believe, didn't you, Philip?'

Philip shrugged. 'I've no idea when Frank left. We lost contact with each other years ago. But I probably did. I'd seen the writing on the wall some time before we left. The final nail in the coffin had been when a German invented a synthetic indigo made of coal tar. With a synthetic dye, there'd no longer be a wide variation in the quality of indigo, and buyers wouldn't find particles of sand in the dye they'd bought. So who'd go for the real thing? So we moved to Jaipur and I changed direction completely.'

Maxwell nodded. 'A wise decision, and one that's obviously been made by many others, too. From what I've seen while travelling around, indigo plantations are shrinking and disappearing.'

'I'm certainly glad I finally realised that exporting was the future,' Frank said.

'It most definitely is,' Maxwell said with a smile.

Frank glanced at Philip. 'I imagine you're in export, too?'

'Not exactly,' Philip said. 'I make paper.'

Frank gave a derisory laugh.

'I know.' Philip forced a smile. 'But I enjoy the work. It couldn't be much more different from spending a day among rows of indigo plants and water-filled vats, though. Although, having said that, we use a lot of water to pulp the cotton scraps that form the basis of our paper.'

'How did you get into that?' There was a slight sneer in Frank's voice.

'We moved to Jaipur as I was confident I'd find work here. A former school friend who owned a paper factory lived here and I was sure he'd help. He was the one who found us the house we now live in.'

'You were lucky,' Frank said.

Philip nodded. 'I was luckier than you realise. My timing couldn't have been better. My friend had been unwell and wanted to cut back on his work. It meant he needed someone to help with the day-to-day running of his factory. And there I was, eager for work, so I became his foreman. A few years later, his health further deteriorated and he wanted to return to England, so he sold me the factory for a very low price. I hired Charles there,' he smiled at Charles, 'to replace me as foreman. He's doing an excellent job and we've gone from strength to strength.'

'I consider myself extremely fortunate to have a job I enjoy as much as I do,' Charles said. 'I think you'd be quite surprised at the way we make our paper. It's handmade, you know. If you ever want to visit the factory, Mr Fletcher, I'd be happy to show you around, just as I did Mr Anderson.'

'I may take you up on that,' Frank said. 'Thank you, young man.'

'I'd be interested in visiting the factory, too,' Alice said quickly. 'After all, I'm always writing letters or notes, so it'd be interesting to see how the paper I use is made.'

Charles coloured slightly. 'It'd be a pleasure to show you around, Miss Fletcher,' he said. She smiled at him gratefully. His hue deepened.

'Philip's factory produces excellent paper, Frank,' Maxwell said. 'You might want to consider suggesting it to buyers as I've started to do. There's a definite market for quality handmade paper.'

'That's kind of you to say so, Maxwell,' Philip said. 'It calls for another drink, I believe.' He indicated to the nearest waiter that he come to the table and take their order.

'How d'you like living in Jaipur, Alice?' Eleanor quickly asked before anyone else could start a topic of conversation.

'It's too soon to know,' Alice said. 'We've only been here a few days. I'm sure I'll like it, though. I intensely disliked living in Bayana, and from what I saw of Jaipur this morning, it's so much nicer. I went to the market and looked around.'

'Which market did you go to?'

'I don't know its name. How many markets are there, then?'

'Four main ones,' Eleanor said.

'Four!' Alice exclaimed. 'If he hears that, my father will be terrified.' She turned to Frank and laughed.

'What did it look like, the market you went to?'

'There were lots of open-fronted jewellery shops on both sides of the road. Then I came to a road on the right, again with open shops on both sides. There was a temple on the corner. I turned right into that. There were lots more stores down there. Many of them seemed to be selling textiles, but there were other things, too. There were so many different colours everywhere,' she said, her eyes shining. 'And so much noise and shouting. If it wasn't the vendors, it was the music. And people were calling to each other and laughing and being happy.'

'You probably went down Johari Bazaar and turned into Bapu Bazaar,' Eleanor told her.

'Bapu Bazaar!' Alice exclaimed. 'That's where your showroom is, Father, isn't it?'

'That's right. I'm in a turning off Bapu Bazaar.'

'What a lovely place to be, Mr Fletcher,' Eleanor said. 'That's the best market for textiles and they also sell really good handicrafts. The Tripolia Bazaar isn't as interesting, unless you like looking at brassware and things made out of metal.' She pulled a face. 'If you want carpets, quilts and pottery, go to Chandpol Bazaar, but my favourite of all is Johari Bazaar, the first of the roads you went along, Alice.'

'I didn't really look at the shops as they were full of gems,' Alice said.

'That's what they're famous for. They sell a bit of everything, like all the bazaars, but the things they're most famous for are their beautiful jewels. They've got emeralds and diamonds, gold and silver. And they've got intricately designed necklaces, bracelets and things like that. Harriet and I spend hours there, wandering from shop to shop. You'll love it, too.'

'You'll note that my daughter has yet to acquire an expensive taste,' Philip remarked drily.

Apart from Frank and Beatrice, they laughed.

'The next time Harriet and I go to the markets, you must come with us, Alice,' Eleanor said. 'It'd be easy to arrange as you live so close by. Harriet lives near us, too.'

Alice looked at her father. 'Can I go with Harriet and Eleanor, Father?'

Their faces impassive, Philip and Frank glanced at each other, and then both looked back at Eleanor.

Frank smiled, a smile without warmth, Eleanor noticed.

'Of course, Eleanor,' he said. 'It's a kind suggestion. I'm sure Alice would enjoy that.'

'That's decided then,' Eleanor said, turning back to Alice. 'And after we've done the markets, we'll visit some of the important places in Jaipur, where the tourists go. Everyone calls it the Pink City, and you'll soon see why. Harriet and I will tell you all we know about the places we visit. After all, if you live in a town, you ought to know about it.'

'That's just what I told Father yesterday,' Alice said, smiling at everyone around the table.

Julia cleared her throat. 'We brought Eleanor's ayah, Meera, with us, Beatrice. Did you bring your ayah from Gujarat with you?' she asked.

'Most definitely,' Beatrice said. 'Neither Alice nor I would want to be parted from Sita, who's been with us since before Alice was born. Fortunately, Sita had no reason to want to stay in Gujarat, or in Bayana for that matter.'

Julia nodded. 'Then we won't have any difficulty in finding chaperones for the girls. Harriet's ayah, Lakshmi, can always accompany them, too. Also, James, Harriet's brother, has helped in the past when none of the ayahs or mothers have been free to go with the girls.'

'Listening to you makes me feel ashamed, Eleanor,' Maxwell said, glancing across at her. 'Despite the fairly frequent occasions I've been in Jaipur over the past two or three years, I've never taken the time to explore the town. I've been too busy meeting prospective customers and suppliers, and going to factories and craft workers and outlying villages, to visit the places for which Jaipur is known. Hearing that you intend to show Alice the town, I'm thinking I'd do well to lurk unseen behind you and listen.'

Eleanor laughed. 'There's no need to lurk unseen. If you want to join us on any of our outings, just say.' She turned back to Alice. 'If you agree, Alice, we could make a start on Monday and go to Hawa Mahal in the morning? It's also known as the "Palace of the Winds".'

'I'd love that,' Alice said, smiling with happiness.

'Harriet's bound to agree, so that's decided then. You could come, too, Maxwell,' she added lightly.

Maxwell inclined his head to her. 'I might just do that,' he said, smiling at her.

Her heart jumped. Blushing, she picked up the fresh lemonade that the waiter had put in front of her and took a sip.

Philip glanced around the table. 'It's about time to think about going in for dinner. Have you made plans, Maxwell, or would you care to join us? Everyone else is very welcome too,' he added hastily.

'I spoke to the staff earlier and they've kept a table for me,' Maxwell said. 'It's large enough for us all. You must join us, too, Charles.'

'Thank you, sir,' Charles said.

'Shall we go in, then?' Maxwell asked, and he stood up.

As they rose to their feet, Eleanor noticed that Charles, with studied casualness, moved towards Alice and hovered near her. She saw also that Alice had witnessed that and didn't seem at all displeased. On the contrary, Alice moved a couple of steps closer to Charles as they went through an open doorway from the veranda into the lounge, and thence to the dining room.

A waiter in a simple white turban and wearing a crisp white button-down shirt with long sleeves and well-fitting black trousers showed them to the table reserved for Maxwell.

'We're not only being informal with names this evening,' Maxwell said, positioning himself next to Eleanor, 'but also with the table seating, so please, everyone, sit where you wish.' He pulled out the chair behind which Eleanor was standing, and indicated she should sit.

One of the waiters moved forward and pulled out the chair next to Eleanor's and held it for Maxwell.

Charles held out the seat on the other side of Maxwell for Alice, and then sat down next to her.

'I wonder if you'd be good enough to sit next to me, Charles,' Frank called to him from the other side of the table. 'I'd like to ask you a couple of things about the factory.'

'Of course, sir,' Charles said, and he promptly got up and went and sat on the chair beside Frank's. The smile he sent across the table to Alice was tinged with regret.

Eleanor glanced at Alice's face and saw her disappointment as Philip took the chair that would have been Charles's. She gave her a sympathetic smile, and then turned to look at Frank, who was directly opposite her.

Despite asking for Charles to sit beside him, he was again staring intently at her. Abnormally so, she thought, and almost with a degree of hostility.

A frisson of fear shot through her.

She glanced at Frank's wife, Beatrice, who was sitting next to him, but she was looking down at her plate. Venturing again to look at Frank, she saw that he and Charles had started talking, and his posture was more relaxed.

She mentally shrugged.

She must have imagined that his stare had been icy,

almost accusatory, she decided, and turning to Maxwell, she asked him if there were any places in Jaipur that he'd managed to visit.

As he began to answer, she felt Frank's eyes on the side of her face, and she turned to look at him.

Although ostensibly listening to Charles, he smiled at her. The smile didn't quite reach his eyes, and she felt cold inside. Wondering why he seemed to dislike her so much, she turned away, and tried to concentrate solely on what Maxwell was saying.

4

T*hat same evening*

JAMES MCKENNA LOUNGED on the red velvet sofa facing the fireplace in the library, his sister Harriet next to him. Opposite them, Arthur and Ivy McKenna sat facing each other in floral-upholstered armchairs that flanked the hearth.

At the side of the room there was a large window, in front of which stood a large mahogany desk where Arthur worked on the days when he chose to stay at home and leave the overseeing of his showroom in the capable hands of his manager.

A row of labelled trays lined the front of the desk. At one end of the row there was a wooden clock, and at the other, a marble-framed sepia photograph taken about five years earlier. In it, Arthur and Ivy were sitting down. James was standing next to Arthur and Harriet next to Ivy.

Whenever he looked up from his work, he had an unimpeded view of Man Sagar Lake and Jal Mahal, the palace that stood in the lake.

To the side of the desk, a glazed mahogany bookcase fixed next to the wall ran from the floor almost to the ceiling. In the bookcase there were a number of books relating to aspects of exporting, and a larger number of novels that had been old favourites since his childhood days. The feet of the bookcase stood in small bowls of water intended to deter the ants.

Both Arthur and Ivy had a snifter of brandy on the small mahogany table next to them, and James had a brandy on the occasional table next to his sofa. Harriet was holding a pineapple juice.

'What a dull evening that was!' she said with a pout. 'I bet Eleanor had a really lovely evening and didn't have to sit next to an ancient whiskered bore. I thought he'd never stop going on about his past exploits. I felt quite sorry for you, James, having to work for such a man.'

'Don't waste your pity,' James said. 'He's more of a nominal boss than anything else. I don't have a lot to do with him.'

'Then you're lucky. How I managed to look interested, I don't know.'

'I suppose it might have been helped by Father's promise that if you were a credit to us this evening,' James said smoothly, 'the next time you went to the markets, you could choose some material for two new dresses.'

Harriet gave a little giggle. 'I suppose that did help. But I'd still rather have been at the club with Eleanor. For a start, the new people might've been there. I can't wait to meet them. Well, not the parents – I doubt they'll be interesting – but the daughter. I know that Eleanor, too, was keen to meet her. Just think, she might have been doing so while I was struggling not to yawn while listening to your boss.'

She glared at James.

He grinned back at her.

'I think it's time for you to go upstairs, Harriet,' her mother said.

Harriet tossed her auburn hair over her shoulder. 'I'm not a baby, Mama!'

'I know you're not. It's just that you look tired and I thought you might be anxious not to have bags under your eyes tomorrow. It wouldn't surprise me to see the new family at All Saints' tomorrow morning. They're bound to have been told by now that Sunday morning worship is one of the most fertile places for businesses deals. Isn't that so, Arthur?'

'I think that's a touch cynical, my dear,' he said.

She raised her eyebrows in surprise. 'I'm mistaken, am I, in thinking that you've made some of your best deals in front of the church after the service?'

He chuckled. 'No, you're not. You're right as always.'

They smiled at each other.

'But that was a silly comment I made just now about bags under your eyes tomorrow, Harriet,' Ivy said, turning back to her daughter. 'I wasn't setting you the best of examples. It doesn't matter what we look like when we go to church. It's our interiors we should be thinking about improving, not our exteriors. If you want to stay up a little longer, that's fine.'

Harriet stood up. 'Actually, I do feel a little tired, and I think I'll go to bed now. Goodnight.' She smiled at her parents and brother and left the sitting room.

When the door had closed behind Harriet, and they'd heard her footsteps going up the stairs to the landing, Ivy stood up. 'You know, I think I'll follow Harriet's excellent example,' she said, and she bid her husband and son goodnight.

James made a move as if to get up.

Arthur McKenna shifted his position to face James. 'What about another brandy, James?' he asked. Without waiting for a reply, he got up and went across to the cocktail cabinet on the wall opposite the bookcase.

James settled back in his seat. 'Thank you, Father. I'd like that.'

Arthur poured some brandy into James's snifter, sat back down in the armchair and poured some into his glass. Then he put the decanter on to the table next to him.

'Your health,' James said, raising his glass. 'It doesn't hurt to say it again.'

'Yours, too, son.' Arthur took a drink and then returned the glass to the table next to him, sat back and crossed his legs. 'I do have a degree of sympathy with Harriet,' he said with a wry smile, 'though I wouldn't tell her so. Reginald's a prize bore. But these things have to be done, as we both know. And it was quite a compliment that your boss invited us to dine at his home this evening. It shows how highly he thinks of you.'

'He's an important man, so I hope you're right.' James paused. 'But I assume that the reason you've engineered a conversation in the absence of Harriet and Mother isn't to do with the tedium engendered by as much as two minutes with Reginald,' he added drily.

Arthur gave a slight laugh. 'You're right,' he said, and he shifted his position to better face James. 'No, it's William Campbell I wanted to ask you about.'

'William?'

'That's right. This evening was the first time we've met him.'

'That's because he hasn't been here for long. He's with the India Office and was transferred to Jaipur to deal with a project that needed more manpower, which is in my territory.'

'For an Oxford graduate, which I believe he said he is, India's an unusual place to end up, isn't it?' Arthur remarked. 'And Jaipur even more so. People active in the British Raj refer to Jaipur and the other princely states as the Great Sloth Belt. It's not where you'd expect to find someone with William's educational background.'

'I don't know that you're right about that.'

'But the maharaja rules Jaipur, the British government doesn't. He appoints his own ministers and negotiates matters relating to Jaipur's waterways and railway system. It's the maharaja who works out the state's budget and copes with requests for roads, schools, post offices, hospitals, and so on. The British are responsible for Public Works and Revenue, and only get involved in other matters if there's a clear case of misrule. Not surprisingly, elsewhere they think that the Resident is little more than a ceremonial position, and that the rest of the British government here has a very easy lifestyle.'

'Funnily enough, I asked William a similar question. I wondered why he'd chosen to come to India. He said that India offered the prospect of an outdoor life, of doing things that were interesting and varied, and above all, of having responsibility at an early age. If he'd gone to Whitehall, for example, he could have been confined to a desk for years, and he'd have had to wait ages to be in a position of control. Whereas, at twenty-six, he's now already seen and done so much more than if he'd stayed in England.'

'That's fair enough,' Arthur said. 'And as a person, you think he's a good man?' he asked.

'Most definitely!' James exclaimed. 'He's good at his job, is pleasant to talk to, and is an excellent billiards player, or so I believe.' He paused, frowning. 'Why d'you want to know about William?'

'You probably didn't notice how taken with Harriet William appeared to be, given that Reginald's wife claimed your interest for much of the time.'

'Interest is a slight exaggeration,' James said in amusement. 'If only that were so. She spent the entire evening listing all the aches and pains that were besetting her. It would've had more point if I'd been a doctor and not a member of the government, so the best I could do was every so often make what I thought were suitably sympathetic noises.'

Arthur laughed. 'Considering the way she continued to clamour for your attention, those sympathetic noises paid off and you proved yourself a pleasant dinner table companion. Reginald obviously noticed his wife's approval of you as he remarked when we were leaving what a very pleasant young man you were, and that you'd be going far. But to come back to William and Harriet.'

James looked at him in surprise. 'Are you sure he was as interested as you say? If that's so, I'm surprised that Harriet didn't mention it when we got home.'

'I don't think she noticed how much he was watching her, claimed as she was by Reginald and his lengthy, pompous accounts of past military successes. But if we see William again, which we're sure to do as you're working together, she's bound to notice then.'

'I don't think you need have any fears about William. I like him enormously. He's bright and has an excellent career ahead of him. Every instinct tells me he's honest and reliable. Harriet would do well to have such a husband.'

Arthur gave a slight nod. 'Well, that's good to hear, very good.' He paused. 'You say he hasn't been here for long, so perhaps it'd be friendly to invite him to a Sunday lunch in the not-too-distant future. What d'you think?'

James burst out laughing. 'I think you're nothing if not subtle,' he said. 'Go ahead. I'm sure William is strong enough to withstand the parental inspection, even though he hasn't declared any intentions, hasn't walked out with Harriet, and hasn't directly spoken to her at all. And even though she hasn't even noticed him.'

Arthur smiled. 'Hopefully, we'll change that situation before too long. There aren't a lot of suitable young men in Jaipur. From what you say, William is most definitely eligible, and as he already seems to like Harriet, it's something to build upon.'

'Then you'll be happy to know that you can start building tomorrow. William mentioned he'd be going to All Saints'. But don't make me cringe at any obvious matchmaking, I beg of you,' he added, and he put his hands together in a mock plea.

5

L *ater that evening*

SITTING ON THEIR UPPER VERANDA, enjoying the balmy night air, Eleanor having gone to bed, Philip and Julia stared across the open space in front of their house to the road, and across the road to the distant lake, a shining expanse of black in the middle of which seemingly floated a palace. Vivid against the black water, each of the storeys of the palace was traced by a series of small golden lights.

From the city came the strains of music played on traditional Indian instruments, the sound of people singing what they assumed were local folk songs, and the clamour of revellers laughing and shouting their farewells at the end of the day.

As the cacophony of noise slowly died away, they heard more clearly the calls of late-trading vendors in the bazaars trying to entice the last few customers to buy their wares, and the fifth and final call to prayer that day, which issued forth from the tall minarets.

Finally, the sounds tapered off.

In the absence of noise from the town, they heard more clearly the rustle of leaves as the night breeze whispered its way through the branches of the apple and mango trees that had been growing in their garden since the house had been built, and through the wide-spreading neem tree that shaded the house.

From the depths of the undergrowth at the rear of the garden, the insistent chirping of the cicadas grew louder and the scrabbling of the flying foxes swelled in noise as they frantically foraged for food. Every so often a twig snapped as it took on the weight of an unseen raccoon or red fox or badger.

High above them an owl hooted.

'The sounds of a typical Indian night, you might say.' Julia glanced at Philip. 'In a way it's somewhat settling, don't you think?'

He shook his head. 'Not really, though I wish it was. We never expected Frank Fletcher and Beatrice to appear in our lives again. There was nothing I wanted less.'

'Nor me,' she said quietly. 'I was so sure we'd never see them again. But now we have. And what's more, they're living close to us. I know they've got another daughter now, and that Eleanor was given to us as Frank didn't want a reminder that Beatrice cheated on him. But suppose they decide they want to get to know her better, or worse still, become a part of her life. It doesn't bear thinking about.'

Philip nodded. 'I couldn't agree more.'

'So what are we going to do?' she asked, a catch in her voice.

'I don't know that there's anything we *can* do,' he said

morosely. 'It all happened a long time ago, and everyone agreed to the arrangement. Surely he can't want to dig it up again.' He looked at her anxiously. 'But I saw the way that Frank looked at Eleanor tonight, didn't you?'

She nodded. 'Yes, I did.'

'He was like a coiled spring all evening,' Philip went on. 'And the looks he gave her verged on hostile. I'm not sure why that should be, unless seeing Eleanor, the product of Beatrice's adultery, reminded him of what had happened. But whatever the reason, I can't see what we can do about it.'

'We can ignore them,' Julia said firmly. 'We never had a close friendship with them. Frank wasn't a very pleasant man and I found Beatrice rather cold as a woman. There weren't that many British families in the area so we socialised with them out of convenience, not because we liked them.'

'All that's true,' he said.

'But it's different here,' she went on. 'The number of British-born families is steadily increasing, so we don't need to be close to them. I don't think we should call on them or invite them when we have friends to dinner. And we must try to keep the two girls apart. Beatrice won't want them to be friends any more than we do. Eleanor has Harriet, she doesn't need Alice. Alice can make her own friends. Don't you agree?'

He shook his head. 'I'm afraid I don't. Apart from the fact that it'd be impossible to keep the girls apart with them living as close to us as they do, our community here is a hotbed of gossip, probably because we all regularly meet each other at the club. Everyone has a pretty good idea of what everyone else is doing, and it would arouse real curiosity if we treated the Fletchers in the way you suggest.'

'Would anyone really notice?' she asked.

He gave her a wry smile. 'Yes, they would,' he said. 'The women here have servants to run their homes and ayahs to look after their children. They've plenty of time on their hands to interest themselves in what other families are doing. Being curious by nature, they could well try to discover why we're ignoring the Fletchers. And that could lead them to finding out that we aren't Eleanor's real parents.'

'Of course, we are!' Julia retorted. 'We've loved her from the moment Frank gave her to us. She's ours in every way that matters and always will be. But like you, I'd hate her to learn what happened. It could be very distressing for her and rather confusing. So what d'you suggest we do?'

'Treat them like any other neighbours or customers. Invite them to our house, and go to their house if they ask us to. We can do that without forming a close friendship with them, which I'm sure neither family wants.'

'I suppose that makes sense, but I know I'll never feel comfortable with them.'

'It might help if you reminded yourself that Anderson looks like being an excellent customer, and that he was quick to recommend us to Frank. Such a person is good to have as a friend, but my instinct says he'd be bad to have as an enemy. He's known Frank for a while now, and they clearly get on and like each other. If we were visibly inhospitable towards the Fletchers, Anderson might well turn against us.'

Julia put her hand to her mouth. 'You're right. I hadn't thought of that. No, awful though it'll be, we'll have to be on good terms with them.'

'If they let us,' he said drily. 'Frank hardly seemed well disposed towards us this evening. They were clearly no more pleased to see us than we were to see them.'

. . .

'D'YOU WANT lemonade or anything, Alice?' Frank Fletcher asked as Alice stood on the veranda, hovering by the wicker table and chairs where he and Beatrice were sitting.

She shook her head. 'No, thank you. I'm quite tired. I think I'll go to bed now.' She paused. 'You could've let me sit next to Eleanor,' she added sullenly. 'You know I need to make friends. Her house is so close to ours that she's an obvious friend to make.'

'I'm sure she isn't the only girl of your age around,' he said curtly. 'She mentioned someone called Harriet. Harriet could be a friend.'

'Harriet's friendly with Eleanor. I could hardly be friends with Harriet but not Eleanor,' Alice said accusingly. 'I can't see what you've got against Eleanor. You don't know her.' She glared at Frank.

'I'm not overly keen on seeing more of the Graingers than we have to, and that's that.' Frank clamped his lips in a firm line.

'I thought they seemed nice,' Alice grumbled.

'Oh, do stop going on about them, Alice, and get to bed,' Beatrice snapped.

Scowling at both of her parents, Alice turned and stormed from the veranda into the sitting room. A few minutes later, they heard her run up the stairs and her bedroom door slam shut.

Frank got up, went into the sitting room and crossed the room to his teak cocktail cabinet. He poured himself a whisky and went back to the veranda with it.

Beatrice glanced up at him. 'Don't I get a glass of Marsala this evening?' she asked.

'If you want it, you know where to find the bottle,' he said tersely, and sat down again.

Her heart pounding with sudden anxiety, she got up, went into the sitting room, poured herself a drink, returned to the veranda and sat down.

He picked up his glass and went across to the edge of the veranda. With his back to her, he leaned against the balustrade and stared up at a black sky studded with diamond-like stars. The range of hills to his right was silhouetted against the night sky.

She sipped her drink and waited.

An owl hooted.

'That bloody owl again!' he exclaimed. 'What with the coppersmith barbet going beep beep all morning, and the owl every night, not to mention the dogs, there's never a moment's peace.'

He went back to the table and sat down. He took a drink of his whisky, put the glass on the table, and leaned back staring towards the black shapes of the hills, with lines of anger etched into his face.

Beatrice picked up her wine and took a sip. 'I wonder if the Graingers are sitting on the veranda like we are.'

'If they are, I can just imagine what they're saying about the evening,' he said icily. 'They'll say what an unpleasant shock it was to see us again. Which is exactly what I thought when I saw them. I was tempted to turn and walk away, and to have nothing at all to do with them, not in business, not socially. If it hadn't been for Maxwell, I'd have left there and then.'

'Everyone there must've realised we weren't pleased to see each other again.' She paused a moment, and then, clearing her throat, gathered her courage about her. 'I'm wondering why you're as set against them as you obviously are,' she remarked, her gaze on her glass. 'They didn't force us to do anything. It was agreed by both sides.'

'You lied to me, didn't you,' he said, his voice ice-cold. 'A bare-faced lie. But it was only this evening that I found out.'

The blood drained from her face. 'What d'you mean? Found what out?' she stammered, pulling her shawl more tightly around her.

He stared at her with contempt and dislike. 'You told me the bastard resulted from a short affair with a businessman working in the area at the time I was frequently away.'

'That's what happened,' she said, her voice wavering.

'No, it wasn't,' he spat, and he leaned forward. 'The girl Eleanor,' he sneered her name, 'looks exactly like her father, Philip Grainger. He's more than the man who adopted her, he's the man who got into my wife's bed and cheated on me. When I was with a delegation, taking part in protests at Gandhi's ashram, hoping to stop him from attacking indigo plantation owners, and trying to keep him from taking an active part in India's freedom movements, you were getting into bed with my neighbour. Again and again.'

'I wasn't,' she said weakly.

He thumped the table hard. 'Don't lie to me! Not only did you betray me, but you lied to me afterwards. If I'd known it was Grainger who'd fathered the brat, I'd never have given her to him. She'd have gone to an orphanage. And I'd have made you pay.'

'If you *had* known, you might've killed him. Would you really have wanted to end up in an Indian prison? I saved you from that. As for making me pay,' she said, her words clipped. She leaned forward. 'You've made me pay every single day since then. How would you describe the act of brutally forcing yourself on me when you got back from giving the girl to Philip?'

He made as if to speak but she went on regardless.

'Neither of us had ever wanted a child, but your rape ended up in us having Alice. For almost eighteen years she's been a daily reminder of your attack on me. And in all those years, you've never shown me any warmth. It's been a dismal life. You may not have known that the father was Philip, but you couldn't have made me pay any more if you *had* known.'

He glowered at her. 'If you hadn't made me so angry by your action, and then by having to hold the physical result of your betrayal in my hands, that wouldn't have happened. But if your life was so bad,' he said with a sneer, 'you could have left me any time you wanted, with or without Alice. I wouldn't have held you back.'

'And where would I have gone?' she asked bitterly, throwing her shawl on to the chair next to her. 'We'd lost contact with our families in England long before then. And you've always controlled any money you made. I didn't have the wherewithal to go anywhere.'

'You could've made some money for yourself. You could've charged for what you gave Philip for free. Though perhaps that wouldn't have been a good idea,' he said, pretending to give his suggestion some thought. 'You might've starved.'

'I was stuck with you and our miserable life, Frank, and you know it,' she said.

Silence weighted the air between them.

'So what are you planning to do?' she asked at last. 'The Graingers will always remind us of something that's better forgotten. Are we going to have to move somewhere else?'

'No,' he said bluntly. 'We're staying put. I've no intention of losing the contacts I've made, or the chance to meet the importers that Maxwell wants to introduce me to. My business could really take off, thanks to his help. We're here now and it's in our interests to stay here. But I intend to avoid seeing the Graingers. And I certainly won't be exporting any of his damn paper.'

'You might be making a mistake,' she said hesitantly.

He glanced impatiently at her. 'What's your point? The more we have contact with them, the more likely it is that the girls will be friends. Surely you don't want that. Or do you?' he asked in sudden suspicion.

'Of course I don't! And Julia won't either. She's bound to want to keep us at a distance, even though from her manner this evening I'm sure she's no idea of the role that Philip played in all this.'

He nodded. 'You're probably right about her not knowing. I can't see Grainger telling her. And when you're with someone all day, as she's been with the girl, you're less likely to see facial features and mannerisms in the same way a stranger would.'

'There's a risk, though,' Beatrice went on, 'that Julia might be sufficiently uncomfortable about us being here that she tries actively to turn the people round here against us. If we appear to be shunning them, that's more likely to happen. They're well known here, and we aren't, so we'd be the losers. But if we mix with them socially, we reduce the chance of that happening.'

'For once you've said something sensible,' he said slowly. 'But thinking about it, the reason you gave isn't the only consideration. Being estranged from them could damage my business. As you say, Grainger's been here for years now and is well established. It was clear from what Maxwell said that Grainger's a highly respected businessman, so I wouldn't want to antagonise the man in case he decided to make negative comments about me as a businessman. It takes time to build up a good reputation, but only a matter of moments to get a bad one. And if you got a bad reputation, it'd be no easy matter to correct it.'

'And another thing, if we stay away from them,' she went on, 'they could say whatever they wanted about us and we wouldn't know what they were saying. Whereas if we go where they go, including into each other's homes, it'd be much harder for them to spread any unpleasantness about us.'

'Again, you might be right.'

'It's only Philip who's likely to be unhappy about us being here, for obvious reasons,' she continued. 'Although Julia might prefer it if we weren't here, she's every reason to be grateful to us. After several miscarriages, it was obvious she was never going to be able to carry a child, but we gave them one. So there's no reason for her not to be friendly, and there's every reason for her to want to keep the arrangement a secret between the four of us.' She paused. 'I think we should try to make them believe we genuinely want to be friends.'

'The girls mustn't be friends,' he said flatly. 'We'd end up with Eleanor coming round here and Alice going to her house. It'd be rubbing our noses in it.'

She gave him a scornful smile. 'That's going to happen anyway. D'you really think we could keep them apart, living as close as we do? Did you see Alice's face when Eleanor offered to be her guide? We'd already lost a battle we hadn't even begun.'

He slumped back. 'I suppose you're right. And we wouldn't want the girls to start wondering why we were dead set against what anyone else would think a most acceptable friendship. Heaven knows what explanations they might come up with. But there's one battle we won't be losing,' he said. 'I saw the way Grainger's foreman looked at

Alice. That must be nipped in the bud. I'm not having her with someone that close to Grainger. And awkward though the girl is, just as we're doing better for ourselves, she should aim higher than a mere foreman.'

'I agree with you there.' She paused. 'So we're going to be friends with them, are we?'

'Not exactly. We're going to *appear* to be friends with them,' he told her. 'We'll make a start tomorrow morning. I heard Grainger tell Maxwell about All Saints' Church in the town. Apparently, the Sunday morning service is quite a social event. So we, too, will be there tomorrow morning, a smile on our faces, a pleasant word for everyone. But you're to keep your distance from Grainger,' he added nastily.

She nodded. 'It was over years ago, not that it was anything much to begin with. It's only your twisted mind that made it what it wasn't.' She stifled a yawn. 'I think I'll go up now. It's been a long day.'

'You do that.'

She finished her drink, rose to her feet, picked up her shawl and went back into the house.

He stared in anger at where she'd been sitting.

So she thought the matter of Grainger's betrayal was over, did she? Now that she'd seen him explode in justifiable anger, she thought the issue dealt with.

Well, she was wrong.

So far, Grainger had been lucky in getting his daughter, and also his house and job. But luck could run out. And if ever he found himself in a position to punish Grainger for betraying him, and for lying to him, he'd grab it with both hands. And the more severe the consequences on the man, the better.

· · ·

ALICE STOOD motionless on the upper veranda, just outside her bedroom door.

As soon as she'd reached her bedroom, she'd gone outside to enjoy the fragrant air as she did nightly, and she'd been standing there when her parents had started to argue on the lower veranda beneath her, unaware that she was hearing their every single word.

Paralysed by misery, she'd stood through it all, unable to move, unable to hide from the way her parents thought about her, and she'd continued to stand on the same spot long after they'd gone inside the house and up to their rooms, oblivious to the tears that were streaming down her cheeks.

6

The following morning

SHE HAD COMPLETELY FORGOTTEN to roll down the bamboo mat that covered the bedroom window the night before, and the room was brightening early.

Cold with anger and grief, Alice lay in her bed in the pearl-grey light of dawn as she'd done throughout the night, hour after sleepless hour, her sheet pulled up to her chin, her eyes on the ceiling above her, a tight knot in her stomach.

That explains it, she told herself bitterly, as she'd told herself over and over again in the long, never-ending night. It accounted for why she'd had such a lonely, unhappy life, a life throughout which she'd felt unloved, unwanted.

She *had* been unloved and unwanted.

Her father hated her mother because she'd cheated on him, and out of a hatred that had turned violent, she'd been born. They didn't love each other, and it sounded as if they never had. The only reason her father hadn't thrown her mother out of the house must have been that he needed someone to run the house while he worked in the plantation. Living in such an isolated place, there wouldn't have been anyone to replace her mother.

And her mother had stayed with her father as she'd no money of her own, no place to go, nor any family.

Neither of her parents had ever wanted a child, and the sight of a little baby, first Eleanor and then her, hadn't changed a thing.

But now, with her eyes wide open to what had happened all those years ago, she could see how their dislike of each other, and of her because of what she stood for, had been actively present every day of her life. She'd never been any more than an encumbrance to them. To her mother she was the unwanted outcome of violence inflicted upon her as a punishment for her sin. And to her father she was a daily reminder that his wife had betrayed him.

She'd felt their rejection all her life, even though she would never have been able to put that awareness into words, it hurt too much.

Oh, why hadn't Philip Grainger been *her* father, not Eleanor's! If he had, *she* would have been the baby given away, not Eleanor. It would have been Eleanor who'd grown up unwanted, with loneliness as her daily companion. She, Alice, would have grown up with the Graingers, feeling cherished and loved.

From the few hours they'd all been together the previous evening, she'd seen the way in which Eleanor's family talked to each other, teased each other. Anyone could see that they loved Eleanor deeply and that she loved them.

Furthermore, not only had Eleanor been loved, but

she'd also had a life full of comfort, which was very different from her life in Bayana, where her father had increasingly struggled to make any money from the indigo trade, and what he'd made he'd kept for himself, and where he had regularly vented his rage and frustration on her and her mother.

Eleanor's father had a respected job and earned good money. Eleanor had always had friends she liked, especially Harriet, and she'd had a governess who would have given her and Harriet a proper education. It was worlds away from the indifferent teaching in the small out-of-the-way school in Bayana where she'd gone, and where she'd more or less had to teach herself from the few educational books she'd been able to get her hands on.

Her classmates had been either children of businessmen trying to get a foothold in the exporting trade or of struggling plantation owners beset by the same troubles as her parents.

Being in school hadn't been much fun, but it had been better than being at home, where her mother was so completely wrapped up in herself, and had frequently taken one drink too many, that she had never once stood up to her husband when he was being harsh and unfair.

How different it had been for Eleanor!

She'd walked past the house in which Eleanor had lived for almost all of her life. It was a lovely house, clearly well-tended by servants, and set in an attractive garden.

Eleanor had never known what it was like to live in a single-storey building that was little more than a dak bungalow, set at the back of a dank plantation. And Eleanor hadn't just grown up in a better house, but it was a house from which it was easy to get into town. In Bayana they'd lived some way out of the town so had rarely ventured there.

It wasn't that there was nothing at all in Bayana – it was historic and there was an old fort there. Also, important battles had been fought there years before. But if you weren't enthusiastic about that sort of thing, and she wasn't, there was little reason to go there. The Bayana shops were uninteresting.

But Jaipur was so different, so exciting.

Tourists flocked there, understandably. The short amount of time she'd been in the town had been sufficient to show her that with all the terracotta-pink buildings in the centre of the old city, it was really attractive.

And exuberant.

Everywhere there was noise. Vendors called out from the shops and the markets, and people laughed and talked to each other as they made their way along the streets or gathered around the cooking stalls. And it was so colourful, with the brightly coloured saris and dresses that the women wore, and the bright turbans wound around the heads of the men. The town was bursting with life.

Even at night the town was vibrant. She'd been so excited to hear the buzz and hubbub every evening, and the music and singing and shouting, that she'd stood every night in the dark on the veranda and drunk in the sounds of people enjoying themselves.

It was a different world from the world she'd known all her life.

Even her father had seemed to feel it was going to be a good place to live.

In the first few days after they'd moved there, he'd defi-nitely been much less angry, much less nasty and much more relaxed than he used to be.

He was confident his business would do well, helped as he was by Maxwell Anderson, and he was pleased with the house Maxwell had found him. He clearly liked Jaipur in a way he hadn't Bayana, and the atmosphere in their home had verged on pleasant on several occasions. And then he'd seen Eleanor!

His anger had returned with a vengeance, as she'd so clearly heard the night before.

And now that she knew the reason behind it, she couldn't see how it could ever disappear. He was certain to see the Graingers on a regular basis, be it at the club, in the town, at the church, in the homes of the people they'd get to know. Eleanor, with her likeness to Philip, would be a permanent reminder of the past.

So not only had Eleanor had a much better life than she'd had, in a much nicer town, Eleanor's presence was going to mean that she, Alice, who surely deserved some happiness at last, wasn't going to have it. Her father, back to his bad-tempered ways, had told her mother that Philip Grainger's attractive foreman wasn't going to be allowed to court her. Of course, he might not have wanted to do so, but she very much hoped he would have done.

Her father had also said that he wasn't keen on her being friends with Eleanor.

But if she didn't get close to Eleanor, how would she know when there was something she could do that would hurt Eleanor?

She gave an inward gasp.

She hadn't realised she was thinking that way. But yes, that's what she intended to do.

It was because of Eleanor that she'd had such a rotten life. And now, because of Eleanor, the happiness she might have enjoyed was being snatched away from her. Eleanor's father had caused the trouble, but only she, Alice, had suffered, and she was going to continue to suffer. But

Eleanor wasn't. Well, it was time that Eleanor learnt what it was like to be constantly unhappy.

It was only fair.

She'd been so miserable before they'd moved to Jaipur that had it not been for her ayah, Sita, she would have run away.

She threw back her sheet and sat up.

Sita!

Sita must have known the truth about her birth. She'd been with her parents since before she'd been born. If she was careful about how she approached the subject with Sita, she might learn more about what had happened at that time. It wouldn't make any difference to anything, but it'd be interesting to know.

The only other people apart from Sita and her parents who'd know what had happened all those years before were Philip and Julia Grainger.

Or perhaps not Mrs Grainger, she thought.

Philip Grainger was unlikely to have told his wife the truth as there'd have been no need for him to tell her that he was Eleanor's real father.

She got out of the bed and went across to the door leading on to the veranda.

The people she'd like to see suffer were Philip for starting it all by his actions, her mother for cheating on her father, Eleanor for having been born and for being as lucky as she, Alice, had been unlucky, and her parents for making her pay for something for which they'd both been responsible, but which hadn't in any way been her fault.

If ever there was a way of promoting the suffering of any of them, she'd take it.

7

L ater that day,
    Outside All Saints' Church

PHILIP, Julia and Eleanor strolled out of All Saints' Church and stood at the side of the wide patio in front of the church, waiting for Arthur and Ivy McKenna and Harriet to join them. As soon as the McKennas appeared, they went up to the Graingers. When the two sets of parents were engaged in a conversation, Harriet and Eleanor moved away from them.

'Where's James?' Eleanor asked.

Harriet shrugged. 'He's somewhere around. He caught sight of someone he knew and disappeared as soon as the service was over. So how was last night? I was so annoyed that we had to go to that boring dinner instead of the club.'

'I don't blame you. It was a really enjoyable evening. It's such a shame you missed it. The big news is, I met the new people,' she told Harriet in excitement. 'The girl's about our age, maybe a bit younger, but not much. They were in church this morning, so as soon as they come out, I'll introduce you. Her name's Alice. There isn't a son.' She glanced back at the entrance to the church. 'Look, there she is! Come on!'

With Eleanor slightly ahead, they threaded their way through the groups of people standing and chatting. As they neared Alice, she saw them. Smiling broadly, she left her parents and went up to them.

'Hello, Alice. This is my friend Harriet,' Eleanor said.

Harriet and Alice smiled at each other and both said hello.

'I haven't yet told Harriet,' Eleanor went on, 'that our parents apparently knew each other years ago. They all used to live in Gujarat, Harriet, but they lost contact.' She turned back to Alice. 'It makes us almost sisters, Alice,' she said lightly.

Alice managed to laugh.

'It's lovely to meet you, Alice,' Harriet said warmly. 'Welcome to Jaipur. Eleanor and I were really excited when my brother told us a new family had moved into our road, and he thought they had a daughter. I'm so glad he was right. That's my brother, James, over there.' She pointed to where James was standing. 'He's talking to someone he works with, whose name is William. William's the one in the pale grey jacket. We met him at the dinner we went to last night,' she added.

As Alice glanced round at the two men, she saw a third man go across to James and William and start talking to them. Colouring slightly, she turned back to Harriet and Eleanor.

'The man who's just joined them was at the club last

night,' Alice said. 'I think he said his name was Charles. That's right, Eleanor, isn't it? He sat at our table and seemed very pleasant.'

'That's right. It's Charles Davis, Papa's foreman.'

Eleanor turned to look at Harriet. 'It's funny, Harriet,' she said, 'and I'm sure it's entirely coincidental, but last night, when Alice heard that Charles worked at Papa's factory, she expressed a great interest in visiting the factory and seeing how paper was made.'

They both laughed.

Alice went a deeper shade of red, and then started laughing, too.

'They're coming over to us,' Harriet hissed. 'We'd better change the subject.'

James was the first to reach them. 'Your conversation looks a lot more fun than our discussion about the growing momentum of the Indian nationalist movement, so we thought we'd join you,' he told them cheerfully. He smiled at Alice. 'It isn't difficult to guess who you are. Welcome to Jaipur. I hope you and your parents will be very happy here.'

Alice glanced over her shoulder at her parents. Frank Fletcher was talking to Philip, and Beatrice was engaged in a conversation with Julia.

'Thank you. I'm sure we will,' she said turning back to him. 'Harriet said your name was James. I'm Alice Fletcher.'

'It's a pleasure to meet you, Miss Fletcher, or Alice, if I may?'

'Of course.' She gave a shy smile to Charles. 'You, too, Mr Davis. You must call me Alice.' Charles smiled at her in delight, and edged closer to her. 'We met Mr Davis last night,' she told James.

James put his hand on William's shoulder to pull him slightly forward. 'I don't think either of you, Eleanor and

Alice, have met my friend and colleague William Campbell yet. William's staying in the same *haveli* as I am, and he, too, was invited to dinner at my boss's house last night. He's with the India Office, but more importantly, he plays billiards.'

'He attempts to play billiards,' William corrected.

They all laughed.

James performed the introductions.

'It's lovely to see you again, William,' Harriet said.

'I was just about to say the same to you,' William said, and they smiled at each other. Then he turned back to the others. 'I'm quite overwhelmed by the warm welcome I've received since getting here, both in the office by James and by the rest of the people I've met.'

'I hope Mr Anderson felt similarly welcomed last night,' Eleanor said, 'especially as he's decided to spend more time here. I don't know if you've met him yet, William. He's an exporter, like just about all the British businessmen here. He's decided to make Jaipur his base.'

'I've heard of him,' he said, 'but not yet had the pleasure of meeting him. Is he here this morning?'

'I haven't seen him, so I don't think so.' She turned to James. 'You missed an excellent evening at the club, James. It's such a shame you couldn't go. Maxwell Anderson, the exporter I mentioned just now, was at the club when we got there and we joined him. And later we all had dinner together. He's really charming, and quite successful, too, I believe. He's going to buy some of Papa's paper, so he's discerning, too,' she added cheerfully.

James laughed.

'And I believe you said he's quite good-looking, didn't you, Eleanor?' Harriet asked with an innocent air.

'Not that I remember.' Eleanor laughed with embarrassment.

'May we join you?' a voice asked.

Turning, Eleanor saw Arthur and Ivy McKenna standing just behind William.

At the sight of her parents, Harriet rolled her eyes at Eleanor, who smothered a giggle behind her hand.

'Only we saw that there was a new young lady in your midst,' Arthur went on, 'and we wanted to make ourselves known to her, and to tell William how much we enjoyed meeting him at dinner last night.'

William nodded. 'It was a most enjoyable evening, sir.' The smile he gave Arthur and Ivy encompassed Harriet, and lingered on her.

She smiled back up at him.

Eleanor glanced from William to Harriet, then raised her eyebrows in Harriet's direction.

Harriet pretended not to see her.

'Of course you may join us, Father,' James said, and he introduced Alice and his parents to each other.

'It's a pleasure to meet you, Miss Fletcher,' Arthur said. 'There was a lot of local excitement when we learnt that a new family had moved into the crescent. Your father's in the export business, I believe, as indeed am I.'

Alice nodded. 'That's right. But don't ask me the fine points of what he does because I don't really know them. That's him over there. And that's my mother next to him.' She indicated across the courtyard, where her parents were talking to the Graingers.

James turned to his parents. 'I suggest that Charles, William and I leave the girls to their discussions, and that you and Mother go across to the Graingers. They'll introduce you to Mr and Mrs Fletcher.'

'Good idea, James,' Arthur said.

'It was a pleasure to meet you again, Mr and Mrs McKenna, albeit briefly,' William said.

'Please do call us Arthur and Ivy, William,' Arthur said with a warm smile. 'I hope we'll be seeing more of you.'

William nodded. 'Thank you, sir.'

Harriet beamed at her father.

'Well!' Eleanor exclaimed to Alice and Harriet when James and William had left, with Charles reluctantly following them, and the McKennas were heading for the Graingers. 'So that's the way it lies with both of you. Your father's obviously in favour of William, Harriet, and so are you judging by the colour you went. Uncle Arthur's never normally so informal this early on. And as for Charles, Alice. He obviously likes you.'

'I've no idea what you're talking about,' Alice said, blushing.

'And I don't know either,' Harriet remarked, dragging her gaze away from William's retreating back.

'Of course you don't,' Eleanor said airily. 'Right, Harriet,' she went on. 'I told Alice yesterday that we'd take her around Jaipur and tell her all we know about each of the important places. It's not much, but it'll give her an idea of the town. I thought we could start tomorrow by taking her to Hawa Mahal. What d'you think?'

Harriet smiled. 'I think it's a really good idea. It'll be fun.'

At the same moment, she and Alice glanced over their shoulders to see where the men were standing.

Eleanor laughed. 'The two of you,' she said, and she shook her head in amusement.

'It's a shame you missed what was a very pleasant evening

at the club,' Philip told Arthur and Ivy when the McKennas joined him and Julia and the Fletchers.

'We were delighted to meet up with Maxwell and to join him for the evening,' Philip continued. 'As you weren't there last night, you won't yet have met Frank and Beatrice Fletcher, our new neighbours. Let me introduce them.'

With smiles all round, Philip made the introductions.

'It was a huge surprise to see Beatrice and Frank last night,' Philip said. 'We last saw them about eighteen or nineteen years ago in Gujarat, and we'd never expected to see them again. I think it's true to say that they were as stunned as we were. It turns out that Maxwell got to know Frank and Beatrice in Bayana, and knowing they'd just moved into Jaipur, had invited them to the club.'

He smiled briefly at Frank and Beatrice.

'That must have been quite a reunion,' Arthur remarked.

Philip nodded. 'It was. We'd completely lost contact so we spent much of the evening catching up on old times. Frank and I have been doing a bit more catching up this morning, and so, I imagine, have Julia and Beatrice.'

'Indeed we have,' Julia said. 'Beatrice has been telling me about living in Bayana. It's been most interesting. And it's made me extremely pleased that you abandoned indigo when you did and moved us here, Philip.'

They all laughed.

'Are you another in the export business, too, Frank?' Arthur asked.

He nodded. 'That's right. I made a modest start in Bayana, which is a popular destination for businessmen as it's easily reached from both Jaipur and Agra. Over time, I'd got to know some of the importers and exporters who passed through the town, including Maxwell Anderson, and when I decided to become an exporter myself, I received a lot of advice and encouragement from him. With his help I made some good contacts in Jaipur, so it made sense to move here.'

William smiled. 'Then if I ever decide to do a little exporting as a sideline, I'll know where to go, Mr Fletcher. It'll be to you and Mr Anderson.'

James looked at him in surprise. 'Would you ever want to do that, d'you think?'

William shrugged. 'We'll see. I'm more office-based at the moment than I like, and it could be fun to have an interest that isn't confined to four walls.'

'Well, if you do decide to spread your wings more widely, son, don't hesitate to come to me,' Frank said.

'That's very kind of you, Mr Fletcher. Thank you.'

'And I, too, would be happy to help you,' Arthur quickly said.

JULIA AND BEATRICE moved slightly away from the men.

'I won't pretend it's not been difficult seeing you and Frank again, because it has,' Julia began. 'And I think the best thing is to try to forget about what we did all those years ago and start with a clean sheet. You have a daughter and we have one, too. Living as close to each other as we do, in such a small community, our two families are likely to meet a lot, and the girls will probably be friends.'

'I'm sure you're right,' Beatrice said.

'But before we leave the past completely behind us, Beatrice, I want to thank you from the bottom of my heart for giving us Eleanor. She's brought us such pleasure. It's not an exaggeration to say that she's greatly enriched our lives and given us a degree of happiness we could never have had without her.' Her voice shook. Clearing her throat, she made an effort to steady herself. 'Philip and I will always be deeply grateful to you and Frank,' she continued, a tremor in her voice, 'and if you ever need any help, you mustn't hesitate to come to us.'

Beatrice nodded. 'Thank you, Julia. I'm glad it's worked out so well for you. I think having Alice so soon afterwards helped Frank to put my transgression, if I can call it that, behind us.' She paused. 'Last night was difficult for us, too, and Frank and I had a long talk about it when we got home. Fortunately, Alice seemed unaware of anything being out of the ordinary. She was much too interested in your factory foreman to notice anything else.'

Julia smiled. 'Was she indeed? Well, she could do far worse than Charles. He's a good worker and a kind man. Philip thinks very highly of him. I'm sure he'd make someone an excellent husband.'

'But not Alice, if we have any say in it,' Beatrice said a trifle sharply. 'I'm sure he's everything you say he is, but at the end of the day, he's only a factory foreman. There's no possible promotion from that. Philip doesn't look the sort of person to give up working when he doesn't have to, so I imagine a foreman Charles will stay for a very long time.'

'That's true about Philip,' Julia said quietly. 'But if Alice loves Charles?'

'How can she? She doesn't know him,' Beatrice said tersely. 'They've spent a few hours in company together, but that's all. She obviously likes his appearance, but she knows nothing about his interests, background, ambitions, and so on. And she's not going to be given the opportunity to find them out. We intend to keep them apart.'

'I see,' Julia said slowly. 'That could be a problem. I've issued invitations to some of our friends to come to lunch with us next Sunday, including Maxwell Anderson. Charles will be there, too. I was planning to invite you and Frank to join us. Either we or the McKennas often host a lunch after church to which we invite our friends. Both of us always invite Charles as his family is in England.'

'Philip invites his foreman to his home?' Beatrice asked in surprise.

Julia nodded. 'That's right. He doesn't bother with hierarchy. He likes Charles and finds him good company. And Charles is also often a dinner guest in the evenings when we invite friends or business colleagues, such as Maxwell. It would be impossible to stop inviting Charles to events to which he would normally have been invited without it reflecting badly on him. People would wonder what he'd done to fall out of favour. But he obviously isn't invited every time we have friends for dinner. Would you prefer us to invite you only on the occasions when Charles won't be with us?'

Beatrice hesitated. 'It won't be necessary to restrict our invitations in such a way,' she said at last. 'I imagine there'll be other occasions, too, where we'll be guests as well as Charles. Upon reflection, trying to stop them from being in the same room together does sound rather ridiculous. Perhaps, though, you'd seat Alice as far from Charles as possible.'

'Of course,' Julia said, and she smiled. 'We look forward to you joining us for lunch next Sunday. I can tell you then about our small book group. It's just for the ladies. I seem to recall you were a keen reader, and that on one or two occasions we swapped our books in Gujarat. We'd love to have another member and you'd be very welcome to join us.'

· · ·

As PEOPLE STARTED DRIFTING BACK to their homes, Julia and Philip said goodbye to their friends, and followed Eleanor to where their tonga-wallah was waiting for them.

'I told Ivy that Beatrice showed an interest in the book group when I mentioned it,' Julia said as they walked, 'and Ivy's invited her and me to tea on Tuesday afternoon so we can explain how it works.'

'Why ask her to join your group? I thought you were only going to see her when necessary,' Philip remarked in surprise.

'I'd much rather she didn't join us, but I knew she'd hear about it from Ivy or one of the others, so I felt I had to mention it.'

'It was probably the right thing to do,' Philip said. 'We want them to feel the past has been forgotten, and if we deliberately hid things that might interest them, it would give the opposite impression.'

'But you should've seen her face when the subject of Charles came up,' Julia said, tucking her arm into Philip's as she told him what she'd said about inviting them to their house. 'I could see her mind going round and round about whether, in the interests of their friendship with Maxwell and business, she should forget about not wanting Alice to be put in the position of meeting lowly foreman Charles. What might she and Frank lose, I could see her wondering, if their invitations were limited solely to the occasions when Charles wouldn't be there.'

Philip grinned at her. 'That was inspired.'

She laughed. 'I thought so, too! In the end, she decided that they'd risk losing too much, and she capitulated. I think the reference to Maxwell and Charles in one sentence did it. She's such a silly woman. Charles is so much nicer as a person than either she or Frank. So that's the first battle won.'

He glanced at her in alarm. 'I don't like the sound of that, Julia. We need to get on with them, and not think in terms of battles. The most important thing is to make sure we don't antagonise them, or do anything to make them decide to tell Eleanor the truth.'

She nodded vigorously. 'You're right. Forget I said that. Fortunately, I did say that they should come to us if they needed help.'

He smiled. 'That's more like it. Don't rock the boat.'

'WELL DONE, William. I think we can call it a successful morning, don't you?' James said as he and William headed for his car in which his syce was going to drive them to the club.

William grinned. 'I most definitely do. We've now got something to build on. My next step is to practise billiards. Being able to pocket every ball without the opponent getting a look-in would be an obvious entrée into the world of the people we've got our eyes on.'

'Good luck,' James said with a smile.

'I wondered if I'd be meeting our Mr Anderson today,' William remarked as they walked along, 'since most of the British around here seem to attend All Saints', if only to further their business interests, but not so. With luck he'll be at the club. If he isn't, you'll have missed a family lunch for nothing.'

As they reached the car, the syce opened the door for them.

'I was watching you mingle today,' James said as they slid into the back seat. 'The powers that be in Madras certainly knew what they were doing when they sent you here. But perhaps we'd better talk about something more general now.'

'Agreed.' William leaned back against his leather seat. 'Have any of the eligible women here caught your eye?'

'That's not general,' James said with a laugh. 'That's specific.' He paused. 'But maybe one has,' he added, and he smiled to himself.

8

M*onday morning*

'WELCOME to the area known as the old city, Alice,' Eleanor said, as she, Harriet and Alice stepped down from the Graingers' tonga and stood at the side of the dusty Hawa Mahal Road, staring across at the salmon-pink building that rose up in front of them.

Behind them, the horse that had been pulling a second tonga from which the two ayahs, Eleanor's Meera and Alice's Sita, were getting out, whinnied loudly.

Smiling in excitement at the loud noise made by the horses and pedestrians around her, and by the stallholders, Alice glanced at the road and at the steady stream of rickshaws and horse-drawn tongas, plus the occasional car. Laden carts drawn by oxen trundled by, and a cow and a goat walked unhurriedly down the centre of the road, impervious to the noise and vitality in the street.

Her gaze moved to the open shops on both sides of the road.

The shops closest to her were selling trinkets that the vendors hoped would appeal to tourists: brightly coloured bangles; earrings in pearl and gold and coloured paste; rings and metal necklaces, intricate in design.

Clothes hung from the front and the sides of shops further back, or were piled high on wooden tables: cotton and georgette saris in magenta red, daffodil yellow, and a deep pink shot through with gold; there were collarless shirts and dhotis, pieces of material worn by Hindu men that tied around their waist and extended to cover most of their legs; there were piles of loose trousers that tied at the waist by a drawstring.

Other stalls were piled high with items made of wood and stone and pottery and leather, with woven rugs and souvenirs.

Everything shone brightly in the sunlight; everything exploded with colour.

Sighing with pleasure, Alice turned back to the pastel five-storeyed building in front of them. 'It's like something from a fairy tale,' she said. 'The pink building against the blue sky is so dramatic. Jaipur is really wonderful.'

'Then let the lesson begin,' Eleanor said with a smile. 'Our governess said that the old Jaipur city, the part the people call the Pink City, was founded in 1727 by Sawai Jai Singh II. "Pur" means city, so the name means Jai's city. He was a very clever man, who was interested in absolutely everything, and before the city was built, he sent teams of people out across the world, looking at the layout of different cities. It was the plan of Baghdad that became his main inspiration for Jaipur.'

Between her and Harriet, they explained how the town

had been laid out according to a grid. It had been divided into nine sections, each with a wall around it and fortified gates on the corners. The streets ran parallel to the city walls and were wide and very straight. They met at right angles to each other, and where the important streets met, there were vast open squares. Master craftsman and traders had then been invited to settle there and create a trading hub.

'But why did the city need to be pink?' Alice asked.

'It's a colour of hospitality,' Harriet said. 'Also, a lot of buildings were built in red and pink sandstone. Everything was painted pink in 1876 when Prince Albert Edward, the oldest son of Queen Victoria, came to town, and it's been pink ever since then. At first the decorative white lines on the walls were etched with white marble, but the supply of marble ran low, and became very expensive, so the maharaja said that from then on the lines should be painted with white paint.'

'Both of you know so much,' Alice said, her tone envious.

Harriet and Eleanor looked at each other and giggled.

'It's because whenever we were bored with mathematics or any of the other dry subjects,' Eleanor said, 'we'd ask our governess a question about the history of one of the places in Jaipur. We always had a number of questions planned in advance for any emergency occasion, such as one of us starting to fall asleep from acute boredom.'

Their governess had loved history, they explained, and no matter how many times they'd been to the place before, she'd taken them to wherever they'd asked about, and had again narrated its history. Being out of the house had been so much more fun than being at home that even though they'd had to listen to historical facts they'd heard several times before, it had been worth it.

'So be warned, Alice,' Harriet said, wagging her finger. 'When we go to Amber Fort, you'll be weighed down by a barrage of information. It's a few miles to the north of the town, and we liked going there so much that we plied our governess with questions about it more than about any other place.'

Alice shook her head in wonder. 'This is so different from Bayana, both in the number of places of interest here and in the way the town's set out. It's going to be simple to find my way around Jaipur. Bayana was full of narrow, winding alleys and you could easily lose your way.'

'Not so in Jaipur,' Harriet said.

Alice looked up at the pink building in front of her. 'Hawa Mahal looks a bit like a pyramid.'

'You're right, it does,' Eleanor said. 'It was shaped to look like the crown worn by the god Krishna. It's probably the best-known building in Jaipur, and this is the most famous view of it. But this is actually the back of the palace. We have to go round to the other side to see the front. It was built in 1799 by the grandson of Sawai Jai Singh II. "Hawa" means air, and "Mahal" means palace, hence the Palace of the Winds. The best time to see it is in the early morning sun when it has a lovely orangey-pink glow. Perhaps we'll come here at sunrise one day.'

'I'd like that,' Alice said, looking up at the tall building. 'It's very impressive, with all those windows. But why the Palace of the Winds? It doesn't seem unusually exposed to the weather.'

It was because of the number of windows and the way in which they caught the breeze, Eleanor told her. The building was really only a façade. Although very tall, most of it was only the depth of a single room. This was because it didn't need to be more than the width of a person.

It had been built so that the maharaja's wives and concubines, all of whom were in purdah, which meant that they mustn't be seen by strangers or any man other than their husband or the men in their immediate family, could look out at what was happening on the street but not be seen by anyone. They were able to watch, unseen, the many processions, for example.

The windows, screens, balconies and arches had all been designed to catch the breeze, and when the women were looking out through the windows, they could hear the wind making a low humming noise.

Their governess had a keen interest in architectural styles, and she had pointed out that each tiny window had its own arched roof with a hanging cornice that had been beautifully modelled and carved with intricate latticework.

'Well, shall we cross the road,' Eleanor said when they'd finished explaining everything, 'and go round to the entrance?'

Followed by the two ayahs, they crossed the wide road and turned to their left to walk the short distance to Tripolia Bazaar Road.

When they reached a small silver-coloured temple that stood at the corner of the two roads, they turned right into a large open space backed by shops. Walking diagonally across the space, they came to Tripolia Bazaar Road and turned down it.

'The entrance is just off here,' Harriet told Alice a little way along the road. She glanced back at the ayahs as they walked. 'I'm surprised at how well the two ayahs get on with each other,' she remarked, seeing that Meera and Sita were absorbed in conversation. 'They're like old friends. Did they know each other when your families lived in Gujarat?'

'I don't think so,' Alice said, frowning. 'D'you know if they did, Eleanor?'

'I doubt it,' Eleanor said. 'Mama once told me she'd had an ayah before Meera, but as she'd lost the baby before it was born, she'd let her go. I expect she hired Meera when I was on the way. But there wouldn't have been any reason for our ayahs to meet as our families didn't meet, from what I understand.'

'I don't know when my mother got Sita,' Alice said. 'She's been with me forever, and that's all I know.'

'Eleanor!' At the sound of Eleanor's name being called, the three girls stopped abruptly and looked round.

'James!' Eleanor exclaimed in pleased surprise as they saw James getting down from a tonga that had pulled up alongside them.

'I've been at the Residency this morning,' he said coming up to them. 'I was on my way back to admin when I spotted the three of you. I guessed you were heading for the entrance to Hawa Mahal and decided to say hello. The tonga-wallah is happy to be paid for just sitting there till I want to get going again, so here I am.' He smiled broadly. 'Have they been doing a good job, Alice? Do you now know all there is to know about this famous building?'

'I do, or rather I did,' Alice said with a laugh. 'When Eleanor told me the first fact about the building, I remembered it. But when she told me the second fact, it seemed to push the first fact out of my mind, and I could only remember the second fact. And then she told me a third fact, and so on.'

He nodded sympathetically. 'I know what you mean. There's only so much you can take in at any one time. That's unless you have a notebook with you.' He glanced down at her hands. In them she held a handbag, but nothing else.

He looked back at her face and gave her a rueful smile. 'If you had something to write with and on, you could jot down everything Eleanor and Harriet tell you. Then you'd have it to look at later. You could even make it into a sort of diary. I think women like doing that.'

'Of course!' Alice exclaimed. 'It's the obvious thing to do. And I could also do a small drawing to put with it,' she added excitedly. 'I don't know why I didn't think of that myself.'

'Careful,' warned Eleanor. 'You'll make him even more big-headed than he already is.'

James grinned at her.

'Perhaps the next time we go out, you could repeat what you said this morning. If you both don't mind, that is. I could then jot it down,' Alice suggested. 'Then I could come here again one day and do a drawing to go with the writing.'

'Of course, we don't mind,' Eleanor said. 'I think it's an excellent idea. And I've an even more excellent idea. Instead of you drawing a picture of each place we visit, you could take a photo. You could borrow my camera if you haven't one. When it's really hot, it's uncomfortable to sit and draw, and also the glare from the sun can tire your eyes. Or you could be knocked over by an elephant or a camel as you sit there, or we could be knocked over as we waited for you. And the monkeys can be a pest. Also, people might come and stare at your drawing and they'd kick up dust, which could cover your paper and also your paints.'

'I hadn't thought of any of that,' Alice said, biting her lip.

'Some time ago, Papa gave me a box Brownie camera,' Eleanor went on, 'thinking I might like photography, but I've never really used it. I'm sure he said there are a hundred exposures. I doubt you'd need any more than that.'

'Well, if you really don't mind?' Alice said hesitantly.

Eleanor waved her hand dismissively. 'Of course I don't. It's better for it to be used than for it to sit untouched on a shelf in my room. What's more, Papa will send the film away for processing if I ask.'

'That's very kind of you. Thank you,' Alice said. 'It would be better than having to draw things everywhere we went. And you wouldn't have to wait around for me.'

'That's decided then,' Eleanor said firmly. 'As for what we've already told you about Hawa Mahal, we could go for a pineapple juice when we've finished here and tell you it again. There's a *haveli* between here and the Residency that has a café in its courtyard, and Harriet and I often go there in the morning. Then all you'll need to do is take a photograph, and you can do that on another day when we pass it.'

'And you wouldn't mind?' Alice said anxiously.

'Not at all. It'd be easier for you than trying to write when you're walking around. James's briefcase will be in the tonga. He's bound to have paper and a pencil that you could use. You have, haven't you, James?'

'As a matter of fact, I do,' James said. 'You could come and get it. I wanted a quick word with you anyway. I imagine you could take Alice into the courtyard, Harriet, and show her the maharani's entrance and what there is to see of the palace, and do it just as well as Eleanor, couldn't you?'

'Of course,' she said. 'Come on, Alice.'

He indicated to Meera that she should approach them.

'For appearances' sake, we should have a chaperone with us, Eleanor. Also it would allay any concern you might have that I might be about to fling myself upon you,' he added.

Eleanor burst out laughing.

She was still laughing as, trailed by Meera, she and James went up to his tonga.

'Meera doesn't look at all pleased to have been separated from the other ayah, who must be Alice's, I assume,' he remarked as he helped Eleanor up into the tonga, and sat down next to her.

Meera positioned herself at the side of the road, where she could see them both, but not hear what they said.

'It's funny you should say that,' Eleanor said, 'but Harriet and I remarked on the fact that the ayahs are like old friends. But they couldn't have met each other before.'

James shrugged. 'They're probably just two women who've been starved of companionship with people of the same cultural background and are now making up for it. Or they could even have come from the same village.'

She nodded. 'That would make sense.' She paused. 'So what did you want to talk to me about?' she asked.

He shifted to a different position. 'It's a bit delicate,' he began, his voice reflecting a sudden discomfort. 'And perhaps it's not entirely appropriate that I should say it.'

'Since when has that ever stopped you?' she said with a half-smile. 'Since the day we first met, you've been bossing poor Harriet and me around and saying a million things that weren't entirely appropriate. You'd started before you'd even left for school in England. I long ago developed a protective shell against anything you could say, so feel free to speak away.'

Smiling, she sat back and waited for him to begin.

'It's about your feelings for Maxwell Anderson,' he said, hesitantly.

She sat bolt upright.

'I don't have feelings for Maxwell,' she said sharply. 'Not like I think you're implying.'

'I hope that's right,' he said quietly.

'And if I *did* find him interesting and attractive, why

would that matter to you?' she asked in obvious annoyance. 'You've never even met him. How can you know anything about him?'

'It's true that I haven't met him yet, which is something I hope to remedy soon, but I believe I've heard his name mentioned in the admin building. And not always for the best of reasons. Given what I've heard, my instinct says it'd be better if you didn't get too close to him.'

She glared at him. 'And my instinct tells me that this is none of your business, James. And even if it were, I'm hardly going to take notice of things that might or might not have been said,' she added sharply. 'I've met him. You haven't. As far as I'm concerned, he's very polite, considerate and charming. So the subject is closed.'

She folded her arms and stared ahead.

'I'm not going to apologise,' he said, 'for being anxious about you, Eleanor.'

'There's no need for any such concern. I'm no longer in the school room. I've grown up. Harriet's your sister, not me, so your concern must be for her alone. Now, you'll have to excuse me. I want to get back to the others,' she said, and without waiting for his help, she jumped down from the tonga and ran towards the large salmon-pink arch that marked the entrance to the palace buildings.

STANDING a little way down Tripolia Bazaar Road, Maxwell Anderson stood half hidden by a cooking stall, surrounded by people buying samosas and pakoras. Seething with frustration, he realised that he'd wasted a morning.

It had only occurred to him the evening before that Eleanor's visit to Hawa Mahal presented him with an excellent opportunity to ingratiate himself with her.

From the first time that Philip had mentioned his daughter, he had thought it might be worth meeting her and showing an interest in her. An attachment with Philip's daughter could lead to a closer relationship with Philip, he'd reasoned, and that could be good for at least one aspect of his business. Furthermore, it wouldn't be long before he bought a house, and for that he needed a wife at his side, ideally a woman with some social standing.

So he had been looking forward to meeting Eleanor, and had been predisposed to like her when he did. The interest she'd seemed to show in him on the Saturday had been a most welcome surprise, and was certainly something to build upon.

Accordingly, he'd decided to turn up at the palace that morning, but not approach them until they'd got the basic information out of the way. He wasn't interested in any of that. When he was pretty sure that the worst of the educational stuff was over, he'd hurry up to them, blame business for delaying him, and express the hope that he wasn't too late to join them for the last stage of their visit.

He'd got there early to be sure that they wouldn't have arrived yet, and had waited a little way along on the opposite side of the road from the building, certain they'd want Alice to first see the palace as it appeared in so many pictures.

Before long, the three girls, followed by a tonga with two women who must have been their ayahs, had pulled up not far from where he was waiting and they'd all got out.

Eleanor looked very attractive, he thought, in a pale yellow cloche that matched her pale yellow cotton dress. Although she wasn't his type, being too young and too recently out of the school room, her pleasant appearance would make courting her more enjoyable.

As soon as the three girls and their ayahs had crossed the road, walked along to Tripolia Bazaar Road and had turned into it, he had moved swiftly across Hawa Mahal Road and followed them, intending to reach them just before they got to the arch that led to the courtyard behind Hawa Mahal.

As they'd neared the arch, he'd speeded up his steps to get close enough to hail them, when he saw a tonga pull up next to them and a man jump down and go up to the girls.

He stepped swiftly behind the stall next to him and watched them.

They obviously knew the man as they'd stopped and were talking and laughing with him.

Surely he would soon bid them farewell and continue on his way, he thought impatiently. But the man didn't. On the contrary. When the other two girls and one of the ayahs went under the arch and into the palace courtyard, the man and Eleanor stayed outside, sitting in his tonga, talking.

He stared at Eleanor. She was clearly displeased at what the man was saying, and was looking increasingly annoyed. This would not be a good time to talk to her, he realised in irritation. Apart from the mood she now appeared to be in, the day was getting hotter and when they'd finished their visit, the man would quite likely invite the girls to join him for some refreshment or the girls would either go home or go somewhere by themselves.

His moment had passed, and there was no point in him hanging around.

But since he was in the town, he might as well salvage something from the morning, and he could do that by going to Bapu Bazaar and seeing how Frank Fletcher was settling in. Still annoyed at having wasted so much time, he turned and started retracing his steps.

9

L*ater*

'THIS IS CALLED SUKHA HAVELI,' Eleanor told Alice as they sat down at one of the small round tables shaded by a large umbrella that was near the stone-edged pond in the centre of the courtyard. Arched colonnades ran round three sides of the paved courtyard, above which rows of carved balconies lined the upper storeys. '"*Sukha*" means happiness, and a *haveli* is a really grand house, a sort of manor, if you like. But you might know what a *haveli* is from being in Bayana.'

Alice shook her head. 'I didn't.'

'William has rooms in a *haveli*. He's in the same one as James,' Harriet chipped in. 'It's between the old city and the Residency.'

'If it's anything like this one, they're lucky. It's a lovely building,' Alice said, looking around her again.

Harriet nodded. 'Eleanor and I really like it here. There's always so much noise and bustle everywhere in the town that if we want to talk or relax over a juice, we come here as it's so peaceful and pleasant.'

'It's unusual to find such a place,' Eleanor said. 'The people who own this *haveli* were struggling to maintain it and then they had a brainwave. They realised that serving refreshments in the courtyard would bring in some money, especially as they're not far from the Residency. There really aren't many places like this, if any, so people who live in the Residency buildings, and even those who work in the admin building, which is the other side of Hawa Mahal, often come here. Ah, here's the waiter! What are you having, Alice?'

When all three had ordered a fresh lemonade, and had asked that their ayahs, who were sitting together at a table on the other side of the courtyard, be brought refreshments, Eleanor gave Alice the paper and pencil she'd got from James, and while they were waiting for their drinks to arrive, she repeated the salient points of what she'd told Alice earlier in the morning. Harriet filled in the rest of the facts.

Just as Alice finished writing everything down, the waiter returned with a tray holding three glasses of lemonade, two cups of chai and a plate of small disc-shaped cakes. He put a lemonade in front of each of the girls, and the cakes in the centre of the table, and then went across to the ayahs' table and put a cup of chai in front of each of them.

''I think the next place we visit should be Jantar Mantar,' Eleanor said. 'It's almost opposite Hawa Mahal. You could take a photograph of Hawa Mahal on the way there.'

'What's Jantar Mantar?' Alice asked.

'An observatory,' Harriet told her. 'It's to do with astronomy. The instruments can tell the position of the moon and movement of the stars and planets, and how strong the next monsoon will be, and they can tell the time. It's amazing. The tall sundial calculates the local time to within two seconds.'

Alice wrinkled her nose. 'To be honest, it sounds a bit boring to me.'

'You ought to visit it, though,' Eleanor said firmly. 'All the tourists go there. It's more interesting than it sounds.'

Alice smiled. 'All right, you've convinced me.'

Eleanor nodded with satisfaction. 'Then I think it's time to move on to a subject that we'll all find interesting. Harriet wasn't there on Saturday, so she won't have seen the way you looked at Charles when you were introduced to him, Alice, and the way he looked at you.'

Harriet looked questioningly at Eleanor. 'Charles Davis? D'you mean your father's foreman?'

Eleanor nodded. 'That's right. You didn't see the sparks fly when he and Alice met at the club and the looks they exchanged at the church yesterday, but I did.'

'Maybe not.' Harriet gave Alice a knowing look. 'But come to think of it, they did seem very pleased to see each other when they met after the service.'

Alice went red. 'You're making something out of nothing,' she said. 'I've met him twice, that's all. I don't know him and he doesn't know me. And from something I overheard my father tell my mother, my father's no intention of allowing me to have a friendship with Charles.'

Eleanor opened her mouth to make a comment, but Alice got there first.

'And talking of men who interest us, Eleanor,' she said archly, 'what about you and Maxwell Anderson? If there were any sparks flying on Saturday, it was between the two of you. And from the expression on your father's face, he's no keener on you being with Maxwell than mine is on seeing me with Charles.'

Eleanor flushed. 'I'm sure you're wrong about that. Maxwell's a successful businessman and I know Papa respects him. He's attractive, I'll admit, but I haven't given him any thought.' She turned slightly to face Harriet. 'What about you, Harriet?' she asked. 'You and William seemed to be getting on extremely well after church, and you'd met him the night before, too. What would you like to tell us?'

Harriet shrugged. 'Nothing. To say "extremely well" is a gross exaggeration. Although I'd met him at the tedious dinner with James's boss. I didn't really speak to him there. He seems very pleasant, but there's nothing else to say. And as there isn't,' she added firmly, 'what about going to Bapu Bazaar? It's not too hot to do that, and if we go as soon as we finish our drinks, we'll avoid the crowds who converge there later in the day.'

SURROUNDED by the excited noisy chatter, and by the pungent aromas and vibrant colours of Bapu Bazaar, the three girls, closely followed by their ayahs, pushed their way along one of the narrow colonnaded walkways that flanked the road, passing as they went an unbroken line of open-fronted stores selling traditional Rajasthani fabrics and handicrafts made by local artisans.

In turn, they were pushed by marketgoers who were forcing a way in the opposite direction.

On both sides of the road, fabrics were piled on every stall, and brightly coloured clothes hung from the rafters. Vendors everywhere were urging potential customers to examine the tie-dye fabrics, block prints and cotton and silk fabrics, many of which were hand-woven or dyed using traditional methods, or to rifle through lines of ready-made Indian clothes, some for daily wear, and some that had been skilfully embroidered or woven with patterns and were meant for ceremonial purposes.

'I'm sure the Bayana bazaars were the same as the ones here,' Eleanor said, pulling a pair of silver sandals from a pile of shoes heaped on a table and studying its stitching. 'Never pay them what they ask. You must haggle.'

'I've never seen such a collection of clothes together,' Alice said in awe as Eleanor put the sandals back and they continued walking. 'There's so much to see, you don't know where to begin.'

'Beginning is easy,' Harriet said with a laugh. 'It's stopping that's difficult.'

'I'm not surprised my father is so pleased to have a place in a bazaar like this,' Alice said. 'There's so much going on here.'

'Of course, his business is in Bapu Bazaar, isn't it?' Eleanor exclaimed, stopping and turning to Alice.

Alice nodded. 'He's got a showroom here, and a small office, also a storeroom on the upper floor. The office is only small, he said, but it's all he needs. He's using a room in our house as his main office.'

'Papa, too, has an office at home,' Harriet said. 'It's actually the library, but he's got a desk in there and a lot of files.'

'How did your father find a place here?' Eleanor asked. 'It's a very sought after bazaar so it can't have been easy?'

'Mr Anderson found Father the premises. He said that Father should be where he was likely to be seen by textile importers and other buyers, and where he'd get to know a number of craftsmen. He knew that Father wanted to buy from craftsmen who were skilled in block printing and tie-dye. Also from those who wove high-quality carpets.'

'That was really kind of Maxwell,' Eleanor said, smiling broadly. 'I thought he seemed a very pleasant person, and I was obviously right.' She hesitated. 'As we're so close to your father's showroom, Alice, shall we go and visit him? D'you know where his business is? If he was busy, though, we wouldn't stay,' she added quickly.

'We've not long passed the road he's in,' Alice said after a moment's hesitation. 'He told me the turning down which he had his showroom. But we must leave at once if he's in the middle of a transaction.'

'Of course, we will. You lead the way then,' Eleanor said.

They turned round and Alice began to walk back up the road with Eleanor and Harriet following her, and the ayahs following them. A few minutes later, Alice turned left up a side road and came to a stop in front of a showroom on the right. A sign above the premises said: "Frank Fletcher, Exporter".

'Here we are,' Alice said. 'I don't think there's a lot of room inside, so Meera and Sita had better wait outside.' She went up the single step and into the showroom, and glanced around.

To one side of her, bales of textiles and handmade goods were displayed on painted shelves that lined the walls. On the other side, carpets and rugs hung from the walls.

At the far end of the showroom there was a desk with a chair on either side, and on the right in front of the desk, there was a low table around which a few chairs had been arranged. At the very back of the showroom, behind the desk, there was a door in front of which hung a bead curtain. Next to the door, a metal staircase led to the floor above.

Alice hesitated a moment, then went across to the desk on which a hand bell stood and rang the bell. Harriet and

Eleanor followed her inside and went straight across to the corner in which an electric fan was whirring around. They positioned themselves in front of it, and Alice went and stood next to them while she waited for her father to appear.

'Being in the cool air is very welcome,' Eleanor said, easing her damp dress away from her back. 'It's not normally very humid in Jaipur, apart from during the monsoon, that is, but there is some humidity today. I hadn't realised how much till I came in here and felt the contrast.'

At the rattling of the bead curtain being pushed aside, they all stared towards the doorway.

Alice swiftly moved forward.

'Alice!' Frank exclaimed in surprise as he came into the showroom. 'What are you doing here?' Annoyance fleetingly darkened his face. Seeing Eleanor and Harriet, it swiftly passed. 'So you thought you'd come with your friends and see me, did you?' he said jovially. The smile he gave the three of them widened.

'I hope we're not interrupting you, Mr Fletcher,' Eleanor said, 'but we were in the bazaar and when Alice mentioned that your premises were here, we persuaded her to show us where you were. I hope that's all right.'

'It certainly is,' he said warmly. 'It's probably time we had a break. I've a cold box in the back. Why don't we all have something to drink?' He turned towards the back of the showroom. 'You're not in a hurry, are you, Maxwell?' he called over his shoulder.

Eleanor straightened up. Her hand went to her straw hat and she made its angle slightly jauntier.

'Not at all. I think it's an excellent idea,' they heard Maxwell reply. A hand pushed aside the bead curtain and he appeared. 'Good afternoon, ladies,' he said with a broad smile. 'Having a drink is a good idea, Frank. I'll go to the cold box and get what everyone wants.'

'That's good of you, Maxwell,' Frank said, coming from round the desk and starting to arrange the chairs in a circle.

'What can I get you ladies?' Maxwell asked.

'A lemonade, please,' Eleanor said, and Alice and Harriet both asked for the same. 'Our two ayahs are outside,' she added, 'and they're bound to be thirsty.'

'I'll see what they want,' Harriet said. A moment later, she returned and said that they, too, would like a lemonade.

Maxwell glanced at Frank. 'I assume it's a beer for both of us, is it?'

Frank nodded. 'It is, thank you. While you get those, I'll bring down two more chairs.'

'Perhaps you'll give me a hand, Eleanor,' Maxwell said with a smile. 'I'll leave the door open so everyone will be able to see us from where they're sitting, apart from the ayahs. Even the most vigilant of mothers would be satisfied, I'm sure,' he added, and he laughed. 'Let's go, shall we?'

With a quick smile at Harriet, she followed Maxwell through the door at the back of the shop to a small room where there was a cold box next to the wall.

'Am I right in thinking from that last remark that you don't really believe chaperones are necessary?' she asked.

He stood still and looked down at her. 'They're essential for a young woman's reputation, but they can make it difficult when a man wants to say something for the woman's ears alone,' he said, his voice suddenly serious.

She swallowed hard.

'Aren't you going to ask me what I want to say?' he asked.

She shook her head in denial.

'Well, I'll tell you anyway. I was going to say that the moment I saw you standing on the veranda on Saturday, I knew that I wanted to spend the rest of my life with you. That's what I wanted to say.'

She stared up at him, frowning. 'But you don't know me,' she said in bewilderment.

'Sometimes a person's instinct comes into play, and should be listened to. As you say, I don't know you yet, Eleanor, but I hope I'll soon be given the opportunity to do so. Of one thing I'm sure, however, whatever I felt on Saturday will only be increased by knowing you better.' He paused. 'I know I'm a few years older than you,' he said, losing some of the gravity in his tone, 'but I hope I'm not so old that you consider me in my dotage.'

She giggled.

'Those few years between us,' he went on, seeing a pink haze spread across her cheeks, 'means I'm now established in business and in a position to follow my heart. I hope that in the months to come I'll be able to convince you of the strength of my feelings. And perhaps you'll come to feel something as strong for me. I do hope so.' There was a loud crash as Frank dropped one of the chairs. 'Hmm,' he said with a rueful smile. 'This isn't the most romantic of places. Hopefully, when I next speak to you, it'll be more so. Right,' he opened the cold box door, 'now where are the lemonades?'

SITTING around the low table on which they had put their drinks, with a bowl of curry puffs produced by Frank, Eleanor's heart beat fast, acutely aware of Maxwell sitting next to her, their arms occasionally touching.

Every so often, when he was talking to the others, she glanced at his profile. He was certainly a very handsome man. James was very good-looking, too, of course, but he lacked what she thought her father would call a certain rakishness, but that made Maxwell so attractive.

But why was he interested in her, she wondered.

She glanced surreptitiously at Alice. Alice had been there when she and Maxwell had met, and Alice and he had met on other occasions, too, both in Jaipur and in Bayana. Alice had blonde hair and blue eyes, a look men seemed to favour, and was very pretty, so why wasn't he setting his sights on Alice?

And why wasn't she as bowled over with excitement as she should be at the thought of such an attractive man expressing the feelings he had for her?

It was because she felt uncomfortable at such an emotion uttered by someone who didn't really know her at all, she realised. It had all been too fast.

While there were countless stories of people falling in love at first sight, and perhaps Maxwell was one of those people, she thought she probably wasn't. She knew that she found him very attractive, and looked forward to getting to know him better, but she hadn't fallen in love with him. Not yet, anyway.

It was flattering, though, being chosen by someone whom any woman would find attractive. And sitting there, sipping her lemonade and idly listening to Frank give the backgrounds of two interesting people he'd met that day, who were thinking of putting in an order for rugs, she felt a warm glow spread through her that was nothing to do with the heat of the day.

10

T*hat evening*

ALICE SAT at her dressing table and stared into the mirror.

So that was the way things were going for Eleanor, was it? On the Saturday, she'd seen Maxwell and Eleanor's instant interest in each other, but it had been nothing compared with that afternoon at the bazaar, where Maxwell had made a blatant beeline for Eleanor, and she had succumbed without a moment's hesitation.

Harriet had noticed it, too, and had teased Eleanor on the way home. She, too, had joined in. But from the one or two looks she'd exchanged with Harriet behind Eleanor's back, it was clear that Harriet felt a degree of genuine concern at the speed with which things were moving between Eleanor and Maxwell.

So, too, had her father as he'd sat in his showroom,

drinking his beer, although he'd refrained from making any comment.

But he had seen them together at the club when they'd met, so she wasn't surprised that he'd glanced intently at Maxwell when they'd come back with the drinks. Seeing a blushing Eleanor beside Maxwell, his eyes had narrowed and he'd stared hard at them.

From a fleeting expression of dislike that had crossed his face, she knew that he wasn't pleased. He hadn't said anything, though, but then he wouldn't have done. Apart from the fact that he was already heavily indebted to Maxwell for the start that Maxwell had helped him to have, he clearly liked him and wouldn't have wanted to offend him by speaking out about a matter so personal.

But that didn't mean he'd sit back and do nothing about it. Not at all.

She knew her father well enough to predict that he would be violently against Maxwell, whom he frequently met for work and with whom he'd relax over a drink, marrying a woman whose real mother was his own wife.

Apart from the fact that he wouldn't want to be put in the position of regularly seeing Eleanor, who'd be a constant reminder of the fact that he had been betrayed by his wife, if ever Maxwell were to discover that not only was Eleanor illegitimate and adopted, but that she'd been adopted by the man who was her real father, he would have some hold over her father. And her father wouldn't want to be put in that position.

Illegitimacy had a stigma. If information like that got out, it could damage her father's business as well as Philip Grainger's. The British community in Jaipur wasn't large enough for a scandal that involved two businessmen based in Jaipur and the wife of one of them, to be tucked away and forgotten about.

Her father would know that.

So what would he do about the obvious attraction that Maxwell and Eleanor felt for each other, she wondered. He would do something, she was sure.

And if he did something that negatively affected Eleanor, would she mind?

Yesterday, she would have said that she didn't mind at all, that she'd welcome it, in fact. Today she wasn't so sure.

All the years she'd been more or less alone in Bayana, she'd longed to have a close friend. There just hadn't been anyone with whom she'd had anything remotely in common. One of her first thoughts when she'd come to Jaipur had been that at long last she might make some friends.

She and they would go out to places together, she'd thought, and they'd gossip about who they'd seen, what they'd said and what other people had worn. They'd swap books, and talk about what they thought of the stories in them, something she'd never been able to do with anyone other than her mother, and they'd discuss what they were going to wear to the next dinner or dance.

Well, she now *did* have friends like that. Before she'd gone home on the Saturday evening, she'd been certain that she and Eleanor would become good friends. And she was hopeful about a friendship with Harriet, too.

Then she'd overhead her parents talking, and until that morning, she'd thought that learning the truth about Eleanor's birth, and the envy she'd felt for her, had killed any desire to be friends with her.

But that day she'd found she'd been wrong.

She didn't think of Eleanor as a half-sister, but it was

difficult not to like her as she had been so very friendly and welcoming, and was including her in everything she and Harriet did, rather than trying to keep Harriet to herself. And she'd been very kind in saying she'd show her the most famous places in the town, and then lending her a camera so she could take photographs. You couldn't not like such a person.

But at the same time, Eleanor was the person she'd become because she'd had a comfortable childhood full of love, a childhood so very different from her own.

Nevertheless, she *did* like her and she liked Harriet, too, and she was looking forward to visiting Jantar Mantar with them.

And when they went to Jantar Mantar she'd be better prepared for the sort of day it would be as she'd know what to expect, unlike when they'd set off that morning.

The day had seemed never-ending to her, unused as she was to spending time with girls of her age. It was a long time to be with two other people, no matter how pleasant they were, and she wasn't used to keeping a conversation going for such a period of time, and to listening and responding to the range of topics they covered. When they'd left Sukha Haveli, her head had been spinning, and she'd been ready to go back home.

Instead, they'd gone to Bapu Bazaar.

By the time they were halfway through the bazaar, she'd been on the point of suggesting they go home when Eleanor had asked to see where her father worked. She'd heard her request with dismay. But she could hardly say no, so she'd had to pin her hopes on her father being so displeased at seeing them that they wouldn't be there for long.

But Maxwell was with him, and the short visit she'd envisaged had become a much longer one. However, having to keep smiling and be involved in the conversation had helped her to get over her peak of tiredness, and she'd be better prepared for the next trip.

And one other good thing had come out of the day. She'd seen her father's displeasure at Maxwell's interest in Eleanor, and she knew he'd do whatever he could to prevent it from developing into anything serious.

At the end of her day with Eleanor she was no longer sure that she wanted her to suffer for the easy life she'd had. After all, it hadn't been Eleanor's fault that things had turned out the way they had, and she was very pleased, almost relieved, in fact, that she no longer had to decide if Eleanor, whom she genuinely liked, was to be made to taste unhappiness.

The matter was now out of her hands.

'YOU SHOULD HAVE SEEN THEM,' Frank said bitterly. 'Whatever it was that Maxwell said to the girl when they went into the back, it'll have been of a romantic nature from the colour she was when she returned.'

Beatrice looked up from her book. 'Couldn't that be a good thing? If Maxwell's attracted to someone in Jaipur, he'll spend even more time here than he would have done, and that can only be good for your business.'

'That's true,' he said impatiently. 'But it's not that he's with someone, it's *who* he's with. The more time he spends with the girl, the more likely it is that the truth will come out. Truth has a way of doing that. Neither Grainger nor I would come out of this well. No, the idea of Maxwell with Eleanor is unacceptable.'

'But what can you do about it?'

'I can stop him from marrying her, if that's his intention,' he said bluntly. 'Don't ask me how. I've not yet given it much thought. But rest assured, I'll find a way.'

Beatrice frowned. 'I agree that the less we see of her the better. I never wanted her, and she doesn't feel like my daughter. She's a reminder of something unpleasant. But I can't see how you could stop Maxwell marrying her, if that's what he wanted to do.'

'You can sometimes achieve what you want by going round a back way.' He paused and sat back. 'D'you think Maxwell could be persuaded to show an interest in Alice?'

Beatrice stared at him in surprise. 'No, I don't. He saw Alice on a number of occasions in Bayana, but he never exhibited the slightest romantic feelings towards her.'

'Then perhaps he should be encouraged to do so,' Frank said tersely. 'It could kill two birds with one stone. If someone successful like Maxwell took an interest in Alice, she'd soon forget the lowly factory foreman.'

'This isn't something you can organise, Frank,' she said sharply. 'You can't make Maxwell feel what he doesn't.'

'We'll see,' he said, and stood up. As he turned to leave the sitting room, he stopped and looked back at Beatrice. 'Julia Grainger's a good-looking woman, so you must have used some feminine wiles to get her husband into your bed. Perhaps you should share your secrets with Alice. She's pretty enough that with a few womanly tricks, it's not impossible she might draw Maxwell's attention away from Eleanor.'

PHILIP STARED at Eleanor in exasperation. 'You were distracted all though dinner this evening and hardly said a word. Your mother and I wanted to hear about your day, and how you got on with Alice. But we don't even know if you enjoyed it.' He paused. 'Well, did you?'

Mentally sighing at being forced to stop thinking about Maxwell and what he'd said, Eleanor smiled at her father. 'I did enjoy the day, thank you. I'm just tired.'

'Did you like Alice?' Julia asked. 'When we met her on Saturday she seemed very pleased to meet you, and that was true on Sunday, too. From what she said, and from what she didn't say, I got the impression she'd had a lonely childhood.'

'She did. She didn't like Bayana very much. But she seems all right, and she got on well with Harriet. When we were at Hawa Mahal, James gave us some paper and a pencil so Alice was able to make notes of what we were saying, so she was obviously interested in what we were telling her.'

Julia looked at Eleanor in surprise. 'What was James doing there? Don't say he was listening to your account of the history?' she added with a laugh.

Eleanor shook her head. 'He wasn't. He was going along Tripolia Bazaar Road when he saw us, and he stopped. Alice needed paper, and he had some.'

'How kind of him,' Julia said. 'And what else did you do?'

'The usual,' Eleanor said. 'We had a juice at Sukha Haveli and then went to Bapu Bazaar.'

'Should I be nervous?' Philip asked with a smile. 'Did you buy anything?'

'Not a thing.' Eleanor paused. 'We went to see where Alice's father works. His showroom's in a road off Bapu Bazaar.'

'You went to see Frank!' Philip exclaimed. 'And he didn't mind you interrupting his working day?'

'He didn't seem to,' Eleanor said, and fell silent.

Philip and Julia exchanged glances.

'What are you not telling us, Eleanor?' Philip asked in a tone of exasperation. 'And don't say nothing. Your mother and I know there's something. Every time you've been out with Harriet, you've returned full of what you've seen and done. We haven't needed to ply you with questions as the words have just flowed from your mouth... what you enjoyed, what you didn't enjoy, who said what, who did what. This evening it's been like drawing teeth to get anything out of you. So what aren't you telling us?'

Frantic to avoid any mention of Maxwell, Eleanor gave a deep sigh and looked at her father in feigned anxiety. 'I'm afraid you're going to be very annoyed with me, Papa,' she said, allowing a slight tremor to wobble her voice.

'Annoyed about what?' Philip asked impatiently. 'What is it, Eleanor?'

'Well,' she said, looking at the dining table as she drew a design on the white table cloth with her index finger. 'It's what I promised Alice.'

Philip and Julia exchanged worried glances. 'What was that?' he asked.

She looked up at him. 'You know you were really kind and gave me a Brownie camera? Well, I haven't used it yet, and I said that Alice could borrow it. It doesn't mean that I don't like it, because I do,' she added hastily. 'It was a really lovely gift. It's just that I haven't yet had much use for it, and Alice would find it helpful. She's making a little book about Jaipur with notes and photographs, you see. I hope you don't mind me lending the camera to her.'

She remembered to nibble her lower lip.

'Of course I don't,' he said, sending a quick smile of relief to Julia. 'I know you've not had many occasions to use it yet. If Alice has a need for it, then by all means she should borrow it. That was a kind thought.'

'Thank you so much, Papa,' Eleanor said, her wide smile intended to convey relief. 'Taking a photograph will be so much quicker than her having to draw a picture of every place. Harriet and I would have been stuck there, waiting for her.'

'Your father's right. It's a good idea to help Alice like that,' Julia said.

'Actually, there's one other thing,' Eleanor went on. 'I hope it's all right, Papa, but I told Alice that you were extremely kind, and would send the film away for processing.'

He gave a dramatic sigh. 'All right, then.'

'Thank you,' she said tremulously.

'What's the next place you're taking Alice to see?' Julia asked as she folded her napkin.

'Probably Jantar Mantar. We might go on Friday. We thought to leave Amber Fort till next week. I think she'll love the fort.'

'That sounds a good plan,' Julia said with a smile. 'I shall be seeing her mother tomorrow. Beatrice and I are going to tea with Ivy, and we're going to tell Beatrice about the book group.'

'That's a good idea,' Eleanor said. 'Alice said something about her mother liking books.' She feigned a yawn. 'We walked for miles today, and it got surprisingly hot for October. I feel quite tired, so I think I'll go up to bed now.'

She stood up, bade her parents good night, and left the dining room.

As she went up the staircase to her room, she wondered why she was so certain her father would be against her growing friendship with Maxwell.

But since she had no more to go on than instinct, which could always be wrong, and since she wanted her father to become accustomed to the idea that she liked Maxwell, who might turn out to be the person she'd want to live with for the rest of her life, she resolved to start introducing his name into the conversation, and if she, Alice and Harriet met Maxwell again as they'd done that day, she would tell her father.

If she didn't have to combat any hostility towards Maxwell, it would help her to know what she felt about him. It didn't mean that she assumed she'd feel the same way about him as he seemed to feel about her, it just meant that she'd like the chance to know one way or the other.

It was a shame that James was so against Maxwell, she thought as she opened the door and went into her bedroom. There was no one with whom she'd rather discuss what Maxwell had said that day than with James, but after James's comments that morning, it was impossible to do so.

11

T *he same evening*

SUNSETS WERE VERY BEAUTIFUL, but they didn't last long, Maxwell thought as he sat on the club veranda watching the crimson-red sun streak the sky with purple and gold as it slid into the hazy horizon. A dusty purple twilight lingered, but in a matter of moments it had been consumed by the black of night.

Drawing deeply on his cigar and intermittently sipping brandy from the snifter that the waiter had placed on the glass-topped wicker table in front of him, he gazed up at the sky as one glittering star after another broke through the blackness, small pinpoints of sparkling light that fell as a shower from the heavens.

He allowed his breath to escape in a long, drawn-out sigh of satisfaction.

What a day, he thought.

After such a disappointing morning, it had ended in an extremely satisfying way, and in a matter of hours, he'd gone from uncertainty and frustration to a state of quiet confidence.

He shook his head in wonder.

His frustration had been brought about by his disappointment at failing to join Eleanor at Hawa Mahal that morning, and at the time he'd wasted. That afternoon, though, he'd unexpectedly seen her at Frank's showroom. And better still, he'd managed to separate her from Frank and the other two girls so the two of them had been able to talk together for a few minutes.

Certain that someone as pretty as she, of an age to have a head full of romantic thoughts, would be thrilled to think he'd fallen in love with her at first sight, he'd seized the moment with both hands and declared how strongly he felt about her.

The giggling and the blushing with which she'd heard his words had made him confident that it wouldn't be too difficult to get her to reciprocate his feelings, and if he'd had any qualms about making an effort to marry a girl he liked but didn't love, they had been swept away at the thought of the benefits of marrying Eleanor, the daughter of a respected businessman with contacts throughout Jaipur.

It had, indeed, turned into a very promising day.

The future with Frank looked good, too. He knew he had done so much to help Frank set up his business that Frank was bound to feel obliged to do the small things he soon intended to start asking of him on a regular basis.

He just had to understand Frank a little better before he did so.

Surprisingly, although Frank clearly liked money and was desperate to get more of it, he had not yet picked up on the oblique feelers he'd been putting out, and he was beginning to wonder if he'd read Frank incorrectly. From the time he'd met Frank, he'd assumed that he would be prepared to undertake some illegal activities in order to augment his funds, but Frank's failure to pick up on the hints he'd thrown down had made him no longer quite so sure.

But he was going to have to decide about Frank before too long.

With the supply of stolen gems now so great, and the demand increasing all the time, it was necessary for him to have a second company exporting them, too. There was a limit to how many export orders he could ship from his company in any week before the authorities became suspicious, and not all the customs officers were willing to turn a blind eye for a suitable weekly payment, although a satisfying number were.

From the outset, he had intended Frank's business to be that second company.

The plan had been to give Frank the details and addresses, and Frank would ship the consignment, the gems concealed within, to the warehouses overseas, from which they'd be distributed to those who'd purchased the gems or they'd be sold in clandestine auctions or through established gem dealers operating in cities like London, Paris, or Amsterdam.

Being able to use Frank's business as well as his own would mean that he could double the number of gems he smuggled. Both he and Frank would benefit as Frank would be handsomely paid for the part he'd played in this.

He just had to get Frank's agreement, and ideally, it

should be a whole-hearted agreement, and not a grudging willingness borne out of the feeling that he owed a debt of gratitude to Maxwell. Having a reluctant participant could be risky.

But on the whole he didn't think he could have been so completely mistaken about Frank, which would have meant that he'd wasted a whole lot of time. No, the future looked bright. He smiled up at the star-spangled sky.

It had looked bright since the day he'd met Paul.

He'd met Paul when they'd gone to the same school in Assam, both their fathers having decided there was no need for them to be sent to a school in England, the local education being sufficiently good.

Paul's father was an exporter, and Paul had to help in his showroom when he wasn't in school. It was expected he would work full time at the company when he left school, and eventually take it over when his father retired.

Maxwell's father owned a tea plantation, and Maxwell, too, worked with his father in his spare time. Like Paul's father, Maxwell's father clearly expected him to help run the plantation when he'd completed his education, and eventually take it over.

Neither boy had any intention of doing what was expected of them.

Sensing a kindred spirit, they'd gravitated towards each other, and over the years had shared their resentment at the hours they were having to put in to help their fathers, for which they received little or no recompense, and their horror at the thought of being stuck there for the rest of their lives and never knowing any other part of India than Assam.

On the day they both left school, Paul's father was in

Sualkuchi, putting in an order with local weavers for traditional Assamese silk, and Maxwell's father was in the train accompanying chests of tea on the way to Calcutta, where they were to be auctioned.

The two boys went home, helped themselves to the money they felt their fathers owed them for their years of hard work, left without anyone other than the servants realising they had been there and met up at a prearranged place.

Neither wanted to stay in an area full of tea plantations, so they immediately headed south, making their way from town to town by whatever means they could, stopping for periods of time in places where they could get a few hours of work, at all times trying to conserve the money they'd taken from their fathers by spending only what they could earn by casual labour.

They knew that when they found a place where they'd like to settle, a town with a bit of life and something other than tea bushes for neighbours, they'd need the wherewithal to start a business.

In the back of their minds they had the idea of setting up as exporters.

Paul already knew a fair amount about exporting, and while he hadn't wanted to work for his father, the idea of using his knowledge while working with a friend with similar ideas to his, in a place they both liked, for a company that the two of them owned, that gave them a great deal of freedom, was very appealing.

As the months passed, they'd realised one day that they'd been staying longer in the town they were in than they had in any of the other places they'd passed through, and because of that, they had got to know the craftsmen in the local villages in the area. Consequently, they'd decided there and then that the time and place were ripe for setting up their own export business.

They'd used some of their money to open a showroom, in which they'd displayed items of interest to attract passing importers. Knowing the local craftsmen well, and having watched the transient exporters bargain for a good price, they had become adept at bargaining themselves and were able to get good prices for the display goods they'd initially bought, and later for the orders that the importers started to give them.

Soon they were receiving a steady stream of modest orders, and they were making money, but not a lot of it. They were impatient to make more, and when, a few months after they'd started their business, Maxwell had been approached by one of the village men who was in charge of a group of weavers, he'd listened to the man with interest.

The man had asked him if he'd like to slip a few stones into the next batch of carpets that he and Paul would be exporting. If so, the man would give him the address to which the goods should be sent.

Nothing more was said by the man, but it had been pretty obvious from what he and Paul had heard on the grapevine about the man that the gems had been stolen. He was aware, too, that real money was made by smuggling stolen gems. He wasn't surprised, therefore, that as the man was speaking, he was putting a pile of rupees on the table in front of Maxwell.

It would have taken a considerable amount of time, and a lot of hard work, for him and Paul to have equalled that sum through legitimate means, he saw at a glance, and he'd told the man he'd think about it overnight and would return to the village the following day with an answer.

He'd started to get up and walk away from the money. But the man had pushed the money closer to him and told him to take it. He could always return it the next day if he didn't want it, he'd said. So Maxwell had picked it up.

As soon as he'd got back to the small hotel where he and Paul had rooms, he'd put the money in front of Paul, telling him what the man had said and asking him what he thought they should do. Paul had picked up the money, kissed it and then looked back at him, grinning. That was all the answer he'd needed.

Their business was about to take off, both had realised at the sight of the rupees, though perhaps not along quite the same path as they'd originally envisaged. But as the ultimate aim of their business was to be a financial success, only a fool would have turned down the opportunity to make some easy money, they'd reasoned.

That was the first major decision they'd made. The second was that each of them should take on a different role in the company. They agreed that Maxwell would build on the contacts they'd been making with gem suppliers and local weavers, buy the items to be exported and organise their delivery.

Paul, who'd been feeling a little restless by that time, would move to Bombay and take a position in a British trading house. Once there, he'd focus on gems as well as textiles and handmade goods, and he'd build up a range of contacts in Bombay and in the port area.

Over time, Paul's contacts had proved invaluable, and he had learnt where the searching of consignments was the most lax, and was thus able to oversee the passage through customs of numerous shipments in which stolen rubies, sapphires and emeralds were concealed. He and Maxwell had quickly built a reputation for being the safest hands in which to place stolen jewels.

Furthermore, having established connections with foreign buyers, Paul had been able to pass on information to Maxwell about which stones were in greatest demand in Europe, information that Maxwell had passed on to his suppliers.

The other sensible decision they'd made was that Maxwell should make Jaipur and the surrounding area the main focus of the business, rather than the area between Bayana and Agra, as they'd been doing. And long before Maxwell had made the actual move to Jaipur, he'd started working on the changes in transport he intended to make, and on setting up details for a number of fictional importers.

By making Jaipur the centre for his business, he was no longer forced to rely on the covert illegal overland trade routes that meant he'd had to collude with local criminals, racketeers, corrupt officials and other smugglers to ensure that bribes were paid. In future, he'd be able to take advantage of the Rajputana–Malwa Railway, which connected Jaipur to the port of Bombay, and would export solely through Bombay.

Switching away from the overland routes also had the bonus that he'd now removed himself from being too close to a situation in which coercion and violence were often used to ensure that the local networks were successful in continuing to bypass official channels and tariffs.

He'd never been comfortable with the use of violence. He and Paul were businessmen with slightly irregular ways of making money, but no worse than that.

Furthermore, being able to send the goods by train to Bombay speeded everything up, and once the consignments reached Bombay, they were rapidly shipped from there to ports such as London, Marseille, Rotterdam and other important markets. Paul dealt with that side of the business.

But it wasn't just information about gems that Paul had passed on to him.

Jaipur was a thriving centre for handicrafts as well as textiles and gems, and as they felt it would be prudent to widen their range of exports so they could secrete gems in places other than in textiles and carpets, it was helpful to know what else was in demand.

The most sought after exports, Paul had told him, were block-printed fabrics, tie-dye textiles, woven fabrics and carpets and rugs. As a result, Maxwell had spread his net more widely, taking the precaution of ensuring that not every shipment included gems.

The effort and caution shown by him and Paul had helped their business to go from strength to strength.

So, all in all, he thought as he finished his brandy, this was the right time to take a wife. He felt fairly confident about securing Eleanor's affections, so all he had to do was get Philip's agreement to let him court his daughter. With luck, a large order for high-quality paper, accompanied by the promise of more such orders in the future, would do the trick.

'We thought it was you!' a voice hailed him.

Maxwell turned in surprise and saw James and William coming out of the club building towards him. Stubbing out the remains of his cigar, he rose to his feet. 'What are you two doing here?' he asked.

'We came up earlier,' James said, sitting down at Maxwell's table. 'We had a game of billiards, and then had dinner. With the cooler weather almost upon us, and the high season for sport about to begin, we thought we ought to knock our billiard skills into shape. If we'd known you were out here, we would've come and asked you to join us, both for billiards and dinner.'

'I've been in the town today,' Maxwell said, sitting down again. 'I had a bite to eat before I returned. I came back in time for pudding, though.' He indicated his empty brandy snifter. All three laughed.

'William and I were going to have a drink before we left,' James said. 'If you don't mind us joining you, we could get you a second pudding similar to the first.'

Maxwell laughed. 'I'll take you up on that.'

James turned and indicated to the hovering waiter that he'd like to give their order. When all three had ordered a brandy, the waiter left.

'So you were playing billiards, were you?' Maxwell commented, offering them a cigar from the wooden box on the table next to him. They declined, but Maxwell took another one.

'That's right,' William said. 'I wanted James to realise how bad I am before the rest of you saw it for yourselves.'

'I'm sure you're being modest,' Maxwell said, slicing off the head of his cigar.

'He's not,' James remarked, grinning. 'We were also saying that we might go to watch a polo game at the polo club, now the high season's beginning. My family and the Graingers usually go to a game at least once in the year. Charles always comes, and you'll come, too, William, won't you? And the Fletchers are sure to be invited to join us. Does polo interest you, Maxwell?'

He paused while the waiter gave them each their drink, put a plate of small deep-fried pastries filled with spicy lentils in the centre of the table, and left.

'Generally, no,' Maxwell continued. 'But if the maharaja's

team was playing, I'd go like a shot. When they went to England last year, his team won every major tournament they participated in, including the Open Championship. And they won the Indian Polo Championship in Calcutta at the end of the year. No one's ever seen such a team before. All four players are tremendous, but as for Hanut Singh, well what can you say? It's no wonder the team's had the Polo Crown since 1930 and doesn't show any sign of losing it. So I'd willingly go to see them play. I'm not sure about other teams, though.' He paused. 'Have you ever played polo, William?'

William nodded. 'Occasionally when I was in Madras. I used to sit in an office all day and I felt I was starting to get unfit. Polo's a great way of keeping in shape, so I joined a team. But I didn't last long. You need to practise regularly, and to be disciplined about keeping fit if you're going to be any good, and you've got to be a good team player. With only four players in a team, they've all got to be up to the job. And quite simply, I wasn't.'

'It means you probably didn't like it that much,' Maxwell said. 'If you'd really wanted to be good, you'd have put in the work that made you the equal of the others.'

William gestured helplessness. 'I was building a career and I just didn't have the time. The others in the team were either wealthy in their own right or sons of wealthy men. They didn't need to earn a crust each day, but I did, and I couldn't afford the time it required. You're probably right, though, that although I quite enjoyed playing, I didn't have the all-consuming passion that the others had. As a result, I was mediocre. A bit like I am at billiards. Unlike you, Maxwell. I'm sure you're going to put us all to shame when you pick up your billiard cue,' he added with a smile.

Maxwell sat back. 'You're very confident I'm the best, even though you haven't yet seen me take a shot.'

'I don't know about William, but from what I've seen of you, Maxwell, I'm sure you're good at everything you do,' James said. 'And not only in sporting matters, but in business, too. I heard through the tortuous route of Frank and my sister, Harriet, that you've made some excellent contacts in Jaipur, and that you've helped Frank a lot. It's down to you that he's confident he'll make a success of his business.'

Maxwell nodded. 'I hope he does. He deserves to.'

James picked up his brandy and took a drink. 'I agree. From what he's said about his time in Bayana, he deserves some luck,' he went on. 'The indigo trade was in decline, so it was hardly his fault that he failed at it. The circumstances were beyond his control. But it sounds as if he's a hard worker, and being prepared to work hard, while being guided by someone who knows what they're doing, is an unbeatable combination.'

Maxwell inclined his head in acknowledgement of the compliment.

'Talking of Frank,' Maxwell said, turning towards William. 'He told me you were thinking of dabbling in the export trade, William. He said just you, but did he mean both of you?'

James shook his head. 'I'm afraid it's just William,' he said ruefully. 'My father's in export, and one exporter in the family is more than enough. Fortunately, he doesn't expect me to follow in his footsteps as I prefer working for the government. Public Works isn't riveting, but it's considered a good job, and the career prospects aren't bad. And more importantly, it allows me time to come up to the club on occasions in the day and play a game of billiards. I can certainly put up with a little boredom for such a welcome benefit.'

'Yes, it's just me who's thinking of doing a bit of exporting,' William said. 'When I met James's father at the dinner last Saturday, and seemed to get on well with him, I'd wondered about asking him for some advice, and maybe some help if I decided to go down that path, but now I'm not so sure.'

'I'm sure he'd help you,' James said. 'So why wouldn't you ask him?'

William pulled a face. 'I don't know him well, and as it would only be a sideline, there's a limit to how much I'd want to do. I'm worried he might think I was wasting his time. Frank's still in the process of getting established, so I'm now considering whether to enlist his help. I thought I could learn by watching what he did.'

James turned to Maxwell. 'I'm sure that William's reason for seeking Frank's help, rather than asking my more knowledgeable father for advice, is nothing to do with my sister, and his not wanting my father to see him as a novice in any capacity.' He looked back at William and laughed.

William shifted in his seat and fixed an impression of discomfort to his face. 'Ignore James,' he told Maxwell. 'He doesn't know what he's talking about.'

Maxwell raised his eyebrows. 'So you're interested in Harriet, are you?' he asked. 'Then I don't blame you not wanting to approach her father with a cap in hand, even if that cap was to be filled with no more than help. I wouldn't do that, either, in your position. If I were you, I'd have a word with Frank. You can always come to me for help if Frank isn't sure of the answer.'

'That's very kind of you, Maxwell. Thank you. I hope you never have cause to regret your offer.' He paused. 'But what about you and the opposite sex?' William asked. 'As I understand it, you've been visiting Jaipur for a while now. Has anyone here caught your eye?'

Laughing, Maxwell picked up his glass and remarked how much he was looking forward to Wednesday the following week, when they were having a special tea at the club to celebrate the arrival of the high season. After the tea, they could have a game or two of billiards, he added.

12

T uesday

'DO HELP YOURSELF, Beatrice, won't you?' Ivy said, indicating the tiered cake-stand in the centre of the coffee table. 'My cook has a way with small iced cakes, so you really must try them. But do have a sandwich first.'

Beatrice leaned forward and put a sandwich and two small cakes on her plate. 'Julia mentioned a book group,' she said, sitting back.

Ivy nodded. 'That's right. You might be interested in how it came about. Roughly five or six years ago, the maharaja's wife, or one of his three wives, founded what she called the Jaipur Women's Club. It had the lofty aim of improving the social, moral and physical condition of women, but that wasn't really relevant for us. One of the interesting ideas they had, though, was a bazaar inside the premises. The women were able to swap books and talk to each other about what they'd read.'

'Well, it's enterprising, I suppose,' Beatrice said.

Ivy smiled. 'From the look on your face, Beatrice, I can tell that such a club wouldn't suit you.'

'Founded by royalty? I don't think so,' Beatrice said.

'And as I indicated, we felt the same,' Julia went on. 'Also, we've got the Royal Jaipur Club, so we don't need another club. But we liked the idea of sharing books and talking about them, so we decided to set up our own book group. There were only five of us, and it's even fewer now as three of the women rarely come these days.'

'How often do you meet,' Beatrice asked, 'and where?'

'We meet in different homes. The women who now seldom come live on the other side of the town, near the Residency, and I think they found it a little far to come here. And to be honest, it's easier for us to stay this side of the old city. When we meet is determined by the length of the book. We have to have time to read the book we're discussing at the next meeting and then pass it on.'

'Where d'you get your books?' Beatrice asked. 'It isn't easy to get hold of English books and journals, and when you *do* come upon them they're expensive. I found that out in Bayana.'

'We get them from lots of places,' Ivy replied. 'From people like you, for a start, who've moved into the area. I'm sure you've got books you could share.'

Beatrice nodded. 'Yes, I have.'

'We also get some from passing visitors. You'd be amazed at how many books people bring with them when they travel,' Ivy continued. 'If we're given any books or we buy any, we pass them around. And there's the club, of course. We're able to borrow books from their library.'

'What are you all reading at the moment?' Beatrice asked.

'*Pride and Prejudice*,' Julia told her. 'Have you read it?'

'Yes, but it was years ago. I'd like to read it again.'

Ivy held up her cup of tea in a mock toast. 'Then welcome to our book group,' she said, and took a drink of tea. Julia and Beatrice followed suit. Then Ivy pressed a bell on the table next to her, and when their butler Gopal appeared, she asked him to bring more tea.

'So,' she said, turning back to face Beatrice, who was sitting on the sofa opposite her and Julia, 'Harriet tells me that you and Julia knew each other in Gujarat but lost contact?' She looked questioningly at Beatrice.

Beatrice and Julia exchanged glances. 'That's right.'

'As your daughters are similar in age, you'll both have been expecting a little bundle at about the same time, won't you? How exciting that must've been.'

'It wasn't quite that way,' Julia said, in discomfort. 'Although we lived on neighbouring plantations, they were still quite a distance apart, so while we visited each other, we didn't do so on a daily basis, or even a weekly one. When we moved away, I didn't even know that Beatrice was expecting a child.'

Ivy turned to Beatrice.

'How difficult for you, being by yourself at such a time. Or did you have other friends there?'

Beatrice shook her head. 'Not really. We were very cut off from everyone. But I've always been happy in my own company, and I enjoy reading, for which I don't need anyone else. Although it's always nice to have someone with whom you can discuss the book,' she added quickly. 'But there were preparations to make for Alice's arrival, and then a child to look after, so I didn't feel particularly alone. And of course, I had Sita, Alice's ayah. Sita and Eleanor's ayah, Meera, came from the same village.'

'I daresay it must be pleasant for Frank to be in Jaipur and have more people around,' Ivy said with a smile. 'All the exporters based in Jaipur join the club and meet there to discuss the market. It must be a new experience for Frank, having such a club.'

'Planters, too, have clubs, you know,' Beatrice said a trifle sharply. 'But you probably don't know that. There aren't that many plantations in the middle of a town, so you wouldn't expect to find any planters' clubs there either.'

She noticed a spot of pink on Ivy's cheeks, and softened her tone. 'Having said that, Frank did get involved with a group of people in Gujarat and took part in several protests against Gandhi when he returned from South Africa. And since moving here, it's true to say that he's enjoyed what he's seen of the club, and the people he's met. But generally he isn't a man who needs company all the time.'

'He sounds an interesting man, and I look forward to getting to know him,' Ivy said with a tight smile. She leaned forward and pushed the cake-stand a little closer to Beatrice. 'Do have another cake, Beatrice. You, too, Julia.'

'WHAT A NOSY WOMAN THE HOSTESS WAS,' Beatrice remarked to Frank as they sat at the table after dinner. 'I didn't say anything until Alice had gone upstairs, lest it got back to Harriet, but Ivy McKenna struck me as quite unpleasant. It was all done with a smile, of course, but I felt she was prying, trying to find out if we were the sort of people she'd want to know. I'm sure she didn't like me. If they hadn't already invited me to join their book group, I think they'd probably have kept quiet about it. Well, they needn't worry.

I've no intention of joining the coven. I certainly don't want to see any more of Julia than I need to.'

'You *will* read the books and go to the meetings, and you'll have a smile on your face when you do so,' Frank said sharply.

'Why should I?' she snapped. 'The less I have to do with them, the better.'

'But the more I have to do with their husbands, the better. As a wife you've been fairly useless, but in this you can make amends. I've heard a lot about Arthur McKenna in the past few days, and I've learnt that he's a highly respected, well-established exporter of long standing. He has a lot of contacts – far more than Maxwell, I'm sure. From the little I've seen of the man, I doubt I'm going to like him any more than you like his wife, but I'd like the advantages that being associated with him might bring me.'

'And what's that got to do with the book group?'

'I would've thought it pretty obvious, even to you. You being one of them will secure us a place in their social circle. So you'll read the damn books and you'll make sure that McKenna's wife thinks you respect her opinion. You can start building bridges tomorrow when we go for the tea at the club. Is that clear?'

Glaring at him, she threw her napkin down on the table, got up and walked out.

'I DON'T THINK Beatrice has improved with age,' Julia said as she followed Philip out on to the veranda. 'She was quite brittle this afternoon. Yes, brittle's the right word. She answered Ivy's reasonable comments in an unnecessarily sharp way. After she'd left, Ivy and I looked at each other without saying anything. We didn't have to.'

'Without saying anything? That must have been a rare and memorable occasion,' Philip said in feigned surprise.

'Without saying anything for a minute or two,' she said in amusement. 'I broke the silence by remarking that Beatrice didn't look as if she'd be slow to express her opinions of the books she reads, which will guarantee a lively discussion. Beatrice doesn't seem to sort of person to do things half-heartedly, I added.'

'And what did Ivy say?' Philip asked, sitting down at the veranda table and opening *The Times of India*.

'That she didn't like Beatrice either,' Julia said with a laugh. 'Beatrice certainly didn't come across as someone who'd fit easily into our pleasant little group. So much so, that I might give the book group a miss for a while. I don't want to spend more time with her than I need, anyway.'

He glanced up from the newspaper. 'I'd rather you didn't stop going,' he said. 'We live close to each other, and it could create some awkwardness between us and the McKennas if you withdrew from the group. Ivy would notice your absence, and could be annoyed that you'd left her to cope with Beatrice on her own. You and Ivy are the main members, not the other women, who attend erratically, I believe. If I were Arthur and I saw Ivy stranded in such a way, I'd be annoyed with you, and with me by association.'

Julia pulled a face. 'I suppose that's true. When you put it like that, I can see it wouldn't be fair on Ivy.'

'There's also the matter of the social side of things,' he continued. 'The dinners, for example, that we give here or go to in the homes of our friends. You'd create a problem for the hosts if you were seen to be avoiding Beatrice, as that's how it would appear if you suddenly shunned the group. Believe me, these things get out.'

Julia bit her lip. 'I hate to say it, but you might be right.'

'And think of the club dinners on Saturday night. If you stepped back from the group, it could create an atmosphere that spoilt things for everyone. When we last talked about the Fletchers, we agreed to make an effort to be friends with them, not because we liked them, but because we'd hate them ever to feel vindictive and tell Eleanor that Beatrice is her mother, and some unknown man her father.'

Julia nodded. 'You're right, Philip. I'll be sweetness itself to Beatrice.'

'Temper the sweetness, won't you?' he said mildly. 'You don't want to scare her.'

'Fear not. I'll practise at the club tea tomorrow. You can kick me under the table if you think my smile too wide.'

IVY SAT in front of the mirror and stared at her reflection. She could see Arthur moving around in the room behind her, and then sitting down on the bed to pull off his shoes. He pulled one off and then stopped. She saw him stare at her.

'What's wrong, Ivy?' he asked. 'You were in a strange mood throughout dinner. If it wasn't so unlike you, I'd say you felt depressed. Did anything unusual happen today?'

She turned on her covered stool to face him. 'Not unusual, as such. I'd invited Beatrice Fletcher and Julia to tea so we could talk about the book group. We'd suggested it to Beatrice when we'd been chatting with her after church on Sunday and she'd seemed keen. With them living so close, and with Harriet and Eleanor getting friendly with Alice, and Frank Fletcher an exporter, too, it seemed a good idea to include her in some of the things we do.'

'But?' he asked when she paused.

'But I didn't like her. I thought her ungracious. She had a

bluntness, a forthrightness, that isn't very easy to live with. I can see her spoiling our pleasant book group afternoons, and I'd hate that.'

'In what way was she blunt? What did you talk about?' he asked.

'Just the usual things. I asked a few friendly questions about her interests and Frank's, and their friendship with the Graingers, and how often they used to meet each other in Gujarat, but she was quite sharp in her reply. Unnecessarily so, I thought.'

'They're our neighbours so it would be better to get on with them,' he said steadily. 'And apart from your book meetings, the only time we'll see them will be when we invite them and our other friends for dinner, or meet at the club or after church, for example. It won't ever be just you and her.'

'The book group's the problem. There are only five of us, and at times not even that many. There's nowhere for anyone to hide, so to speak. I'm going to have to give the book group a miss in the future, much as it'll hurt me to do so as I really enjoy it.'

'I'd rather you continued with the group, and what's more, I'd be grateful if you did your best to see that Beatrice didn't pull out. If you make your dislike of her obvious, she might well choose not to join you.'

'I'd be delighted if that happened,' Ivy said with satisfaction.

'Well, I wouldn't,' he said firmly. 'I want you to be friends with her. You'll see her at the tea tomorrow so you can undo any damage you might have done today.'

'Why would you want me to do that?' she asked in bewilderment. 'What difference does it make to you if she leaves the group or if I do?'

'At most of the social things we do with others, we talk to each other in a superficial way. It's only when we meet people in small groups that we really get to know them. I'd like us to get to know the Fletchers. The book group gives you a chance to get close to Beatrice Fletcher in a way that you couldn't do in a large group, and I'd like you to participate in it.'

'Why, Arthur? You've never interfered with my friendships before, so why now, and why with the Fletchers?'

He gave her a wry smile. 'It's hard to say. In fact, I don't really know.' He paused. 'Have you ever wondered what James does all day?'

'Not really,' she said slowly. 'He's in the Public Works department, isn't he, but I'm not really sure what that entails? He's tried to explain, but I've given up any attempt at understanding. Do *you* know what he does?'

'Not really. He rarely mentions any building projects he's on, such as road planning, repair or construction, or bridges, or hospitals, or the system of water supply. Or supervising building repairs after the monsoon. The sort of tasks you'd expect to fill his day.'

'That's true,' she said. 'But that could be because he doesn't think we'd be interested.'

'He knows I am. I've asked him on a number of occasions what he's working on. He replies. But later, when I think about what he's said, I realise that I'm no closer to knowing what he's doing than I was before I asked. And now it's two of them. William was equally vague when I asked.'

'They're working all day, darling, and when they've finished work, they want to leave it behind them and relax.'

He raised his eyebrows. 'Do they?' he asked.

'Of course they do.' She hesitated, frowning. 'What are you trying to say, Arthur?'

He smiled at her. 'I don't quite know, my dear. But I'm looking at William's arrival and his enthusiasm to do a spot of exporting in addition to the governmental job he holds. Strangely, I'm not going to be asked to help him, despite being an exporter and the father of his friend. He's going to ask Frank Fletcher, who's effectively starting out himself and who knows only what Maxwell Anderson has taught him.'

'Perhaps he finds Frank easier to talk to than you. Asking you could be daunting for someone who's starting out. You know so much that they could be afraid you'd think their questions silly.'

'Perhaps,' he said. 'But then I also look at James. He's suddenly showing a massive enthusiasm for billiards and is becoming chums with Maxwell Anderson. Maxwell's a close friend of Frank. And I'm wondering what's going on.'

She frowned anxiously. 'You're making it sound very sinister, Arthur. This is James we're talking about.'

He got up and went up to her. Leaning slightly down, he put his arms around her and hugged her.

'I'm probably being very silly,' he said, 'but humour me. If possible, I'd like you to become a good friend of Beatrice Fletcher, and it'd be easier for you to do that if you were in the book group.'

She looked up at him. 'Prepare to be dazzled by the brilliance of the smile I give her at the tea tomorrow,' she said, and she slid her arms around his waist and hugged him back.

13

---

*L*ate, Wednesday afternoon

BY THE TIME the Graingers were walking down the drive to the club, people were standing in groups on the patio or sitting around the tables, chatting among themselves while they sipped their drinks. Large white umbrellas had been strategically arranged above the patio tables to shield the guests from the rays of the late-afternoon sun.

'There's James!' Eleanor exclaimed, pointing to one of the tables. 'He's with Uncle Arthur and Aunt Ivy, and Harriet, too. Let's go and join them.'

And she promptly ran past the stone elephants, up the terracotta steps and across to the McKennas' table.

James rose to his feet as she reached them.

Her steps slowed as she felt suddenly awkward, remembering the last time they'd met and the way she'd spoken to him. Would James think badly of her, she wondered as she went anxiously up to him, determined to get the worst over with so that she could then enjoy the rest of the day. He remained standing.

Out of the corner of her eye, she saw her parents sit down opposite him.

Instinctively, she and James moved slightly away from the table.

He definitely hadn't forgotten their exchange, she saw with a sinking feeling. The pleasure he'd initially shown at the sight of her had faded and been replaced with uncertainty.

It was the first time she'd seen him look less than confident, she realised with a sense of wonder.

She smiled nervously. 'I want to say I'm sorry, James,' she began. 'The last time we met, I was very ungracious. You were only trying to help me and I should have been more aware of that. I really do apologise. You're such a good friend that I should have known you'd never knowingly suggest any course of action you didn't truly believe was for my own good.'

She saw his face fill with relief, and she felt her spirits rise.

He smiled down at her. 'You make me sound like the human embodiment of a noxious cough medicine.'

She laughed.

'So you're not still angry with me for my rudeness?' she asked.

'I wasn't angry with you at all,' he said quickly.

'Yes, you were.'

'All right, yes, I was,' he said with a wry smile. 'You know me too well. But I shouldn't have been angry at you – I should have been angry at myself, and I was. I had lectured you about something that was nothing to do with me. I'm sorry that I butted in where I shouldn't have done. I hope it didn't spoil your day.'

'It didn't, and you're forgiven,' she said lightly. 'You've seen me as a child for so long, as Harriet's little friend, that your vision is clouded and you can't see that I've now grown up. Because of that, you still feel very protective of me, as you do with Harriet. I'm lucky to have such a good friend as you.'

His gaze travelled down her upturned face to the low-waisted scooped-neck pale blue cotton dress that skimmed her slender body, and back to a face that was liquid gold in the sunlight. At the same time, with her eyes she traced the planes of his face, his strong jawline and the strength in the arms that had always been there to catch her.

With his eyes on her face, and her eyes raised to his, neither said a word for a long moment.

'As I said,' she repeated, needing to break the mood and end the sudden strangeness she was feeling, 'you're forgiven.'

'I'm beside myself with disappointment,' a shrill voice sounded from the table behind them. 'My new cook has turned out to be completely dishonest, as so many servants are. It's so disappointing.'

Both glanced towards the woman behind them who had started to regale the people at her table with an account of her various servants' foibles. They moved closer to the table where Arthur, Ivy and Harriet were sitting with Philip and Julia.

'Heaven forbid I ever become the sort of person who goes to a lovely gathering like this and spends the evening talking about my servants or children,' Eleanor murmured to James.

'If you did, I'm sure you'd manage to make it interesting.'

She looked at James in surprise. 'Why are you being so nice to me?' she asked. 'It's unnerving me. I'm used to being bossed by you, not praised, even though your praise just now wasn't honest.' She gave a little tutting noise. 'A conversation about servants and children could never be interesting.'

'It could,' he said quietly, 'if the servants and children belonged to the other person who was party to the conversation.'

Their eyes met, and held.

'What about a game of billiards later?' they heard Maxwell ask.

Turning, they saw that Maxwell and William were heading for their table.

'Did someone say billiards?' James asked, and he moved across to them. Eleanor stared after him as the three men fell into a conversation, then she went and sat next to Harriet.

Harriet leaned towards her. 'You look flushed,' she said under her breath. 'Could it be anything to do with the handsome exporter James is talking to?'

'I don't know what you mean.' Eleanor made an attempt at archness. 'If you turn round, though, you'll see that William is coming towards us. Prepare yourself, Harriet,' she said under her breath. 'A public display would have your mother in vapours. Hello, William,' she called to him over her shoulder.

'May I join you?' he asked, coming up to the table.

He promptly sat down on the empty chair on the other side of Harriet.

Seeing her parents engaged in a conversation with Harriet's parents, Eleanor glanced at William.

'Did I hear the word billiards?' she asked. 'I hope we're

not going to lose you to the billiards table. At least, not until we've had tea. They serve the most lovely cakes on these occasions.'

'I'm sure you won't,' he told her. 'I'd rather be sitting here, and not because of the cakes,' he added, looking at Harriet, who blushed with delight.

'I'm very impressed by the help that you and Harriet are giving Alice Fletcher, Eleanor,' Arthur called from across the table. 'Alice is a lucky girl. Where are you planning to take her next?'

With Arthur McKenna claiming Eleanor's attention, William turned to Harriet. 'I believe such a tea is an annual event, isn't it, Miss McKenna?'

'Do, please, call me Harriet. We've now met on several occasions. We don't have to be so formal.'

He smiled warmly. 'I believe such a tea is an annual event, isn't it, Harriet?'

She went pink. 'Yes, it is. It's a way of celebrating the end of the very hot summer months and the ghastly monsoon rains, and the arrival of the cooler weather. With people no longer needing to stay glued to their punkahs and fans and every means they have of keeping cool, they come here more frequently to play cards, bridge, and so on. Even billiards, I believe.'

Both of them laughed.

'What's your choice of game?' William asked.

'Croquet and tennis,' she said, 'if I'm allowed two choices. I play croquet when I'm feeling lazy, and tennis when I feel energetic. Eleanor's a good tennis player,' she added. 'Are you?'

'I know the rules,' he said with a smile. 'Perhaps we could play together some time. You and I could play against Eleanor and James.'

'Or Eleanor and Maxwell,' Harriet said quickly. 'Though perhaps I shouldn't have suggested that. I imagine that Maxwell's a very good player, and that would lessen our chances of winning. Although I suspect you're probably being modest about your ability, and you're much better than you're implying. You look very athletic.'

'Do you think so?' he asked, gazing into her face.

She nodded. 'Yes,' she said with a shy smile.

They sat still, gazing at each other.

The sound of the chair next to William's being pulled out by a waiter broke their mood, and both glanced towards the chair as Maxwell sat down next to William. James moved across and sat on the other side of Maxwell.

'The empty seats between you and Arthur, James, can be for the Fletchers,' Ivy said. 'I imagine they'll soon be here.'

Just as she spoke, she saw Frank, Beatrice and Alice standing at the edge of the patio, scanning the tables.

She stood up and waved to them. She saw the relief on their faces when they saw her and that she was beckoning to them to join them.

'We saved places for you,' she told them as they approached the table.

'That's very kind of you,' Frank said, and they went towards the empty chairs.

'Before you sit down,' Arthur said, rising to his feet. 'It's not a formal dinner, it's just an afternoon tea, so there's no need to do the one man one woman seating arrangement, or worry about status. I'm sure the girls have things they'd like to talk about among themselves, and I'm certain the same is true of their mothers. Ivy was saying last night how much she looked forward to getting to know Beatrice better. Let the girls sit together, and the wives sit together. And then we men can put the world to rights.'

Philip nodded. 'That sounds sensible.'

'Right,' Arthur continued. 'The girls over there on my left, the men opposite, and the mothers to my right. Does everyone agree?'

There was a murmur of assent, and everyone changed to their new position.

'I'm glad it's ended up that we're still sitting next to each other,' William said under his breath to Harriet.

'Me, too,' she whispered back. 'Even if we're not meant to be talking together.'

With their table now full, several waiters appeared with small white bone china plates, silver cake forks and white linen napkins, and put a place setting in front of each of them. One of the waiters placed a large tiered cake-stand in the centre of the table on which there was a selection of sandwiches and cakes, while two other waiters poured tea and gave a cup to each of them.

'I'm afraid their cakes and sandwiches put my book group offerings to shame,' Ivy remarked.

'Not at all,' Beatrice said quickly. 'The tea you gave us was absolutely delicious. I only hope I'm not too far below your standard when it's my turn to host you.'

'How very kind of you, Beatrice,' Ivy said, and they smiled warmly at each other.

'Where's Charles?' Alice asked Eleanor.

Eleanor pulled a miserable face. 'He's at the factory. Papa has too many orders to be able to close the factory this afternoon, and someone in charge has to be there. As Papa wanted to come here, I'm afraid it's Charles who's had to work.'

'What a shame,' Alice said. 'He's very pleasant to talk to. I'm looking forward to visiting the factory. It should be extremely interesting.'

'Indeed, it is,' Eleanor said with amusement. 'But before that, Harriet and I thought we could all go to Jantar Mantar. Perhaps on Friday. That's the observatory I told you about. It's very close to Hawa Mahal, so you could take a photograph of the palace when we're there. We could go to Amber Fort next week, and perhaps you could tour Papa's factory the week after that. They should be less busy by then.'

Alice beamed at her. 'That sounds a lovely plan. Seeing Jantar Mantar and the fort, of course,' she added.

'Of course,' Eleanor said solemnly.

'The girls seem to be getting on very well,' Ivy told Beatrice, who'd been watching Alice and Eleanor.

'Yes, they do,' Beatrice replied, giving Ivy her full attention. 'I'd just been thinking that. The move here was a good one for Alice. She'd hardly any friends in Bayana.'

'I hope it won't just be our daughters who are friends,' Ivy said a trifle hesitantly. 'I should like us to be friends, too, and I know that, like me, Julia very much hopes that you'll be a part of our little circle. The coven, Arthur likes to call it.'

Both of them smiled.

'I feel we got off on rather a bad footing yesterday,' Ivy continued, 'though it's hard to pinpoint how it happened. It wasn't what I wanted, and I'm hoping we can start from today with a clean slate.'

'I agree,' Beatrice said. 'I feel I must take some responsibility for what happened. I might have been more terse in my responses than I should have been. I'm afraid that the many years of being effectively on my own, in an area I didn't like, has made me lose some social graces. But being surrounded now by such pleasant company,' she smiled at Ivy and then at Julia, 'I'm sure any hard edges will soon be rubbed off.'

'Nonsense,' Julia told her, leaning forward. 'Yesterday wasn't your fault, Beatrice. I was partly to blame. I was more abrupt than necessary in what I said. You're to be commended for the fact that you were gracious enough not to chastise us to our faces.'

'Both of you are being very nice about what I know was partly my fault. I think the idea of starting afresh is an excellent one.'

'Good. And you'll join our book group?' Ivy asked.

'With pleasure,' Beatrice said. 'So the next book is *Pride and Prejudice*. That will be interesting. I'll need to read it through again, though.'

'I've almost finished it,' Julia said. 'I'll pass it on to you as soon as I've done so. Ivy's already had it. It's so long ago since I first read the book that it's been a pleasure to go through it again. The first time I read it, I was at an impressionable age, and I all but drooled over Mr Darcy. But now, at the ripe old age I've reached, I'm relieved he isn't one of our circle of friends and won't ever sit next to me at the dinner table.'

'Why's that?' Ivy asked in surprise.

'He's no sense of humour, and I think he could be quite boring,' Julia said cheerfully.

'I remember thinking so, too,' Beatrice said with a smile. 'So that's something you and I agree on, Julia.'

'And I'm sure we also agree that we've looked at those cakes for far too long, and we should start eating them,' Julia said. 'I see that the men haven't held back. Which sandwich would you like, Beatrice?'

She caught the eye of one of the waiters who'd been standing near their side of the table, and he came up to their table, tongs in his hand and a white napkin over his arm.

. . .

'IF YOU'RE interested in exporting, William,' Arthur said as a waiter stepped forward and transferred to his plate the two small egg and mango chutney sandwiches he'd indicated, 'it might be helpful for you to know that the demand for carpets is steadily increasing.'

'Carpets?' William said in a tone of surprise. 'That does amaze me. You only ever hear about the gems, textiles and handmade goods that are typical of the area.'

Arthur nodded. 'They'll always form a huge part of Jaipur's export trade, but that doesn't stop new markets from growing in importance. The skill of the carpet weavers in the outlying villages that I've recently visited is eye-opening. In any of the small houses in which the villagers live, you'll quite likely find several weavers working on one or two looms, making carpets with intricate designs and vibrant colours.'

'Speak more loudly, Father, will you?' James said. 'I'm sure Maxwell and Frank would be interested in what you're saying.'

'*I* certainly am,' Frank said.

'As I was saying,' Arthur continued at a slightly higher volume, 'the work of such weavers is of a very high quality, whether it's a hand-knotted, hand-tufted or hand-woven rug. I'm becoming particularly interested in hand-knotted rugs as there's an increasing demand for them. I'm talking about the real thing, not the pale imitations. The genuine hand-knotted rug takes months to produce so commands a very high price. As the carpet weaver gets a minimal sum, there's a huge margin of profit for the exporter.'

'Do *you* export hand-knotted carpets, Maxwell?' Frank asked.

Maxwell shrugged. 'So far I haven't. I've stuck to hand-tufted and hand-woven carpets, which are made more rapidly. But I'm taking on board the points you're making, Arthur, and I shall give this some thought.' He paused. 'I can't believe we've got this far into the afternoon and haven't mentioned billiards,' he announced in a tone of surprise. 'Does anyone want to play when we've finished our tea?'

His smile swept around the men and continued around the women, too. At the sight of Beatrice's face, he imperceptibly straightened up.

She was staring at Eleanor with a degree of intensity that was far from normal.

Without it being too obvious, he glanced at Eleanor. She was talking in a lively manner to Harriet and Alice, completely unaware of the scrutiny she was under.

He looked back at Beatrice.

Her gaze was still fixed on Eleanor. There was curiosity in it, and something else, too, something indefinable.

Why such a degree of interest in Eleanor, he wondered. If he saw it again, he'd be tempted to see if he could discover the cause.

14

F *riday*

'WHERE'S SITA, MOTHER?' Alice asked as she reached the bottom of the staircase and could see only her mother. 'She and Meera are chaperoning us today.'

'No, they're not. Ivy and I will be coming with you instead.'

Alice stared at her mother with a less than pleased surprise. 'But you've never accompanied me anywhere at any time, so why now? Sita and Meera take chaperoning very seriously.'

'This isn't about their abilities. I told Ivy at the club tea that I thought I ought to make more of an effort to get to know Jaipur than I've done so far, so when I heard you say you'd be going to the observatory today, I thought there'd be no better time to begin than now. And as Ivy had said she'd be very happy to accompany me when I went into town, as that would make a change to her day's routine, I asked her yesterday if she still felt that way, and she did.'

'I'm sure she already knows all there is to know about Jantar Mantar,' Alice snapped. She glared at her mother. 'Having mothers there is going to spoil it for us.'

'Of course it isn't,' Beatrice retorted. 'Ivy and I will stay some way behind you, but where we can see you. You'll forget we're there. When Harriet and Eleanor tell you any facts about the observatory, we'll move in closer so we can hear what they say. But apart from that, we'll be talking to each other. We want to get to know each other better, just as you and the girls do. Now, if you're ready, we'll go.'

'DID YOU GET A GOOD PHOTOGRAPH?' Eleanor asked Alice as she turned away from the Hawa Mahal clutching Eleanor's Brownie camera.

'I think so. I took a couple in case one didn't come out. I tried to get the whole building as I wanted to show the shape.'

'Then let's get off to Jantar Mantar. We'll walk along the courtyard, past the maharani's gate which you'll remember is the main entrance to Hawa Mahal, and the observatory is at the far end of the buildings on the left,' Harriet said. 'You'll see that a lot of the palace buildings are yellow. Yellow is the colour of the Singh dynasty, so their buildings weren't painted pink. Saffron yellow and terracotta pink represent peace. But don't make notes while we're walking around. The two mothers will be hovering over our shoulders to hear what we say and we want to shed them as soon as we can. We'll go to Sukha Haveli afterwards and you can write down everything while we wait for our drinks.'

'I'll have a sherbet this time, I think,' Eleanor said.

Alice smiled. 'That's a good idea. And about the sherbet, too.'

'Come on, then,' Eleanor said, and they started to stroll past Hawa Mahal to the observatory, with Ivy and Beatrice keeping their distance behind them.

'It's so impressive!' Alice exclaimed as they reached the edge of a large sandy area and found themselves facing a collection of stone and marble shapes. They stood and stared at the array of geometric structures in front of them, some of which were large bowls hewn from the ground.

Ivy and Beatrice moved forward and hovered just behind them.

'You'll see that there aren't any trees, bushes, walls, or anything that would cast a shadow,' Eleanor said. 'Sawai Jai Singh II, who built Jantar Mantar, was adamant about that. He was the ruler who founded Jaipur, if you recall. We mentioned him before.'

Alice nodded. 'I remember. They look like giant sculptures, bizarre giant sculptures. Or not sculptures exactly. It's more like a collection of circles, walls and stairs. They look very dramatic.'

Eleanor nodded. 'They do, but they're actually scientific instruments. There are nineteen of them, and between them, they can forecast how hot the summer months will be, the date the monsoon will arrive, how long it will last and how intense it'll be. And they can tell if there's any risk of floods and famine. They can also tell the local time within twenty seconds. That's not bad for instruments that old.'

'How old are they?' Alice asked.

'The observatory was completed it 1734,' Harriet told her. 'Jai Singh II was a real scholar. From the age of twelve or thirteen, he showed a particular interest in astronomy and he used to join adults in discussions about the stars and the zodiac signs.'

'What does Jantar Mantar mean?' Alice asked.

'"Instruments for calculation",' Harriet said. 'That's what those structures do – they calculate. So, let's go and have a closer look at them.'

'The stone sundial is the largest in the world, I believe,' Eleanor remarked as they started walking.

'Eleanor's impressively knowledgeable,' Beatrice remarked to Ivy as they followed the girls. 'And Harriet, too,' she added quickly.

IN SUKHA HAVELI, the rays of the late-morning sun bounced off the large white umbrella above the round metal table at which the three girls sat, each with an iced sherbet in front of them. A plate of bhajis had been placed in the centre of the table.

'Did you get all of that down?' Eleanor asked when Alice finished writing and put her pen down.

Alice nodded. 'I think so. It was a good morning and I enjoyed it,' she said. 'I'm glad I've been to Jantar Mantar, but I'm not really interested in astronomy and I wouldn't particularly want to go there again. But my photographs will look striking in the book I'm making.'

Harriet leaned forward. 'I'll let you into a little secret, Alice – Eleanor and I think it's boring, too.'

All three laughed.

'But it's a place that everyone who comes to Jaipur should visit,' Eleanor said. 'Once.'

'It was very kind of you to take me somewhere you don't really like,' Alice said.

Eleanor waved her hand dismissively. 'We always enjoy

showing off our knowledge, and these trips out are very pleasant, no matter what we're visiting.'

'Eleanor's right,' Harriet said. 'But you'll genuinely like the place we thought we'd go to next week. The Amber Fort. It's near the town of Amer. If you want, you can say Amer Fort, as you don't have to pronounce the B.'

'The girls seem to be getting on well together,' Beatrice remarked to Ivy as she turned her attention away from the three girls across the courtyard and looked back at Ivy.

Ivy nodded. 'They do. But I'm not surprised. Harriet and Eleanor have been friends for years. They've one or two other friends of a similar age, but as those girls don't live in Victoria Crescent, seeing them always requires some planning. Alice seems a very sweet girl, and with you living so close to Philip and us, the girls can visit each other quite easily. Alice is a welcome addition to their little group, I'm sure.'

'I hope so. It's a real treat for her to have friends she actually likes,' Beatrice said, again glancing fleetingly at the girls. 'She's grown up as quite a lonely child.'

'Then you and Frank are to be congratulated on how well you've taught her how to behave in society,' Ivy said with a smile. 'It can't have been easy.'

'It wasn't,' Beatrice said bluntly. 'There was no real society for either her or me where we lived.'

Ivy gave her a sympathetic smile. 'That must have been very difficult.'

Beatrice glanced again towards the three girls. 'It was. It was the hardest thing I had to do. The second hardest was checking the weekly outgoings, especially the items the cook had charged us for. It's amazing how often the servants made the odd mistake or twenty. And surprisingly, it's always in their favour.'

They both laughed.

'Books were my escape, and I read whatever I could get hold of,' Beatrice went on. 'I've never been interested in sewing and embroidery, but books can transport you to different times and places, which was more than welcome during those difficult years. As we both know, it's not easy to get hold of books, so I frequently read them more than once. Being able to discuss what I've read is something I'm very much looking forward to.'

'Is Frank much of a reader?'

Beatrice snorted. 'He could read the sky and tell you when the time was ripe to plant the indigo dye seeds. Three months later he could tell you that it was time for the harvest to begin. When the plants were weighted down in the vats with logs, he could read when the fermentation in the vats was beginning, and by studying the blue and purple froth that rose to the surface of the water, and the violence of the boiling, and the obnoxious odours, he could tell you the exact moment when the fermentation had to be terminated. Don't ask me about the rank smell of the rotten weed! You could smell it for weeks throughout the plantation.'

Ivy murmured sympathetically.

'He could read exactly when the water had to be drained from the thick blue sludge left in the bottom of the tank, and the sludge then poured into a mould. He knew just how long to leave the moulds to dry in the shade before being cut into cakes that when completely dry could be ground into indigo dye powder. Frank can read the weather, the soil, the important signs at every stage of the indigo dye process, but can he read a book? No!'

'It must have been very difficult for you,' Ivy said, her

voice heavy with sympathy. 'Frank must have loved the business to have persevered so long with it. I'm surprised he wasn't tempted to abandon it when Philip did. I imagine that as good friends, he and Philip would have discussed their plans for the future together.'

'They didn't. They weren't good friends, but they were good neighbours. As Philip was the closest plantation owner, we stepped in to help each other when necessary. The people Frank was closest to were those involved in trying to influence Gandhi after he'd set up an ashram in Gujarat, in Ahmedabad. He'd have discussed anything personal with them, not with Philip.'

'He must have some interesting tales to tell,' Ivy said brightly. 'I'd love to hear about any contact he had with Gandhi. I'll ask him about it when there's a suitable occasion to do so.'

'I'm sure he'd be happy to tell you,' Beatrice said. 'But what about you, Ivy? When did you and Arthur move to Jaipur, and where did you move from?'

'So be prepared, Frank,' Beatrice said as she sat on the veranda sipping her Marsala wine. 'Ivy intends to interrogate you about the occasions you demonstrated in front of Gandhi's ashram.'

'She can ask what she bloody well likes,' he snapped, putting his brandy glass heavily on the table. 'It's none of her business and I won't be telling her anything.'

'You were the one who wanted us to be friends,' she said tersely. 'But as I thought you might say that, to get her off the subject, I asked how long she'd lived here. In answer to that simple question, she all but gave me her life history. She and Arthur met in Simla, not long after he'd arrived from

England and had started working for the British government.'

'For the government?' he exclaimed.

'That's right. Her father, too, was a government official. They married and went to Delhi, or New Delhi as we're now expected to call it, where he worked in the government offices. James was born in Delhi. Apparently, Arthur didn't like the work, and was increasingly drawn to the export business through the people he came across in Delhi, especially some exporters from Agra and Jaipur. Finally, he decided to take his chances as an exporter and moved the family to Jaipur. Harriet was born here.'

'Very different from your background,' he said with almost a sneer. 'Even though it suits me that she does, I can't think why she wants to spend her time with you.'

'That's because you've no imagination,' she snapped. 'She's not interested in me as a person. She strikes me as the sort of woman who likes to collect information from others that she can share when meeting her friends, thereby making herself sound interesting and cultured. Your recollections of Gandhi would fit the bill. She's also naturally nosy. I can tell she senses a mystery lurking in the past about what happened between you and Philip, and bored with her life, as I suspect she is, she's trying to find out what it is.'

Frank stared at her with incredulity. 'Where's the mystery in two former neighbours going in separate directions and not keeping in touch?'

'None at all. Unless they reacted in a dramatic way when they saw each other again almost twenty years later. As we all did. Your face and Philip's spoke volumes. And did you see the colour Julia went when she saw us there? She went white. Anyone at the table will have seen that, and any of them could have mentioned it to Ivy and Arthur. You know how everyone talks to everyone else.'

He thought for a moment. 'If I recall correctly, only Charles and Maxwell were there, apart from the women.'

'You can forget Charles. But Maxwell is ambitious, and Arthur is one of the top exporters in Jaipur. Maxwell is bound to think it's in his interest to get close to Arthur, and I can see him passing on a piece of information like that to James over a chotapeg at the club. From there it would get to Arthur, and thence to Ivy.'

'So what do you suggest we do?' he asked, irritated.

'There's not much we can do, except make a show of friendliness towards both the Graingers and the McKennas. You can start by working out what you're going to tell Ivy about the activities you undertook in the past. I suggest you embellish them a little so they sound a lot more interesting than they actually were. She won't know.'

'THANK HEAVENS THAT'S OVER,' Ivy said with a sigh. She leaned forward and helped herself to one of the little disc-shaped cakes on the plate between where she and Arthur sat. 'I must stop eating these ghevars or they'll have a fatal effect on my waistline, and with women having waists once again after being curve-free sack-like silhouettes for much too long, that would be disastrous.'

Arthur smiled at her. 'You don't need to worry, my dear. In all the years we've known each other, you've always had the same slender figure. You're as beautiful today as the day I met you.'

'You say the nicest things, Arthur, even if you're prone to massive exaggeration.' She held out her hand to him. Smiling, he took it, and gave it a gentle squeeze. Then, releasing her hand, he poured himself a small amount of brandy from the crystal decanter that he'd asked the *khitmutgar* to leave on the dining table.

'So what didn't you enjoy about your Jantar Mantar day?' he asked.

Ivy gave a theatrical sigh. 'I suppose it's that I'm really finding it difficult to like Beatrice, and as she's a neighbour, I want to do so. I accept that she's reserved as a person, but so are others we know, and we still warm to them. But Beatrice seems different.' She took another ghevar from the plate and leaned back. 'Perhaps reserved is the wrong word,' she said, nibbling the ghevar thoughtfully. 'Guarded might be a better word. My every instinct is screaming out that she's hiding a secret, and that it involves the Graingers. I wouldn't call myself a nosy person—'

'Of course not,' Arthur said, cutting in, his expression grave. 'Exceedingly curious, maybe, but certainly not nosy.'

They looked at each other and both burst out laughing.

'All right, I'll allow myself to be a curious person,' she said.

'And what were you curious about today, my dear?'

'I wondered why she was unusually forthcoming compared with that last ghastly tea I hosted, and I was surprised that her comments about Frank demonstrating against Gandhi were potentially interesting. We then went on to books, and I asked if Frank was a reader, too. My reward was the most tedious account of the life of a manager of an indigo plantation. When she finally drew breath, I said something about Frank and Philip being good friends in the past. I was curious, you see, as to why they'd reacted so strongly when they met again at the club, which Maxwell described to us, if you recall.'

'Of course, you were, being a curious sort of person,' he

said soothingly. They smiled at each other. 'Well, did you succeed in uncovering any dark secrets?' he prompted.

'No, I did not,' she said indignantly. 'Somehow or other, she took over the role of interrogator and I found myself recounting our life together, starting with meeting you in Simla and ending up with us being here. My sole consolation is that it must have been as boring for Beatrice as her account was for me.'

'It seems you had a wasted day. I'm sorry about that.'

She slowly shook her head. 'I'm not entirely sure it was. There was something strange about the day. It doesn't help with the mystery in the past, but I think it's worth noting, nevertheless. Beatrice kept on staring at the girls. Even when we were chatting, she would glance across at them. We ended up in Sukha Haveli and the girls were on the other side of the courtyard from us.'

'But you were there to keep an eye on them, weren't you?' he asked in surprise. 'You were their chaperones.'

'That's absolutely right, Arthur. Except that Beatrice wasn't looking at all three girls – I had the distinct impression she was looking only at Eleanor.'

'At Eleanor? Why would she do that? Was Eleanor wearing an unsuitable dress, or was her hair in a novel arrangement?'

'Neither of those, nor anything else along those lines. She looked as she always does.' She paused and took the last ghevar from the plate. 'I may be mistaken. All the same, I think I'll watch Beatrice closely when she's next in the same room as Eleanor, and see how she behaves. We're lunching with the Graingers on Sunday, and Beatrice told me they've been invited, too. Without it being obvious, you must watch her, too, and see who you think she's looking at.'

He doffed an imaginary cap to her.

15

T*he following Sunday*

'YOU'RE to be congratulated on your cook, Philip,' Maxwell said, leaning back in contentment. 'The curry was quite delicious. In fact, the whole meal was excellent. Your cook has found the ideal balance between the dishes the locals eat and what we British like.'

'That's what we asked him to do,' Julia said.

'Well, he certainly succeeded today. The mild chicken curry was perfectly spiced. It was smooth, rich, and creamy with just a hint of sweetness. It's so much more pleasant than the fiery curries found in Indian homes. And the *kheer*, which is one of the few Indian puddings I like, was rice pudding at its best.'

'Are you often invited to Indian homes, Maxwell?' James asked.

He pulled a face. 'Yes, I am. You'd be surprised how

often. It's because I like to make contact with the people who actually make the goods I buy, not only with the bosses of the production units into which some of the workers are grouped. All of them, workers and bosses alike, scramble to show their gratitude for the money they get from me, and inviting me to eat with them is a way of doing so. I can't say it's something my stomach and I enjoy, but it has to be done.'

'Then you must come to us again and allow us to prove to you that our cook's success wasn't a one-off,' Eleanor said.

'I'm sure Maxwell has better things to do than spending his free time with us,' Philip said quickly.

'Not at all, Philip,' Maxwell said. 'I can't think of a more pleasant way to pass the time.' He changed the angle of his chair to face Eleanor. 'So what have you been doing since we last met?' he asked, his smile embracing Alice and Harriet too.

'Usually it'd be easy to answer that,' Eleanor said. 'I'd list what we always do, such as calling on friends in the morning, or them calling on us, a siesta in the afternoon, then reading or drawing, both of which I enjoy. And there might be an evening stroll in the town before dinner. Maybe we'd have guests, and maybe we wouldn't. Or we might have been invited to friends, or we might have gone to the club. Normally the days in the week don't vary much, but this week was different.' She smiled at Alice. 'And it's Alice we have to thank for that.'

'What have I done that deserves such praise,' Alice asked, blushing with pleasure. She glanced quickly at Charles, who was smiling at her, and then looked away.

'Just by being here,' Eleanor exclaimed. 'And for that we have to thank Mr and Mrs Fletcher, too.' She smiled warmly across the table at Frank and Beatrice. 'By moving here, the three of you have brought new life into days that had become a little routine.' She glanced at Harriet. 'Don't you agree, Harriet?'

Harriet nodded. 'I certainly do. For example, it's years since we really looked at Hawa Mahal and Jantar Mantar. Normally we pass them by when we're in the tonga and don't even notice them. Yet we've been to both this week and actually looked at them. And as adults, we've appreciated them in a way we didn't when we were children. We went twice to Hawa Mahal, in fact. And once to Jantar Mantar.'

'Why did you go to the palace twice?' William asked in surprise. 'I rather thought there wasn't a lot to see in a building so narrow in depth, and not much of interest in the courtyard behind it, apart from some of the carved stonework, or so I hear. I've not been to either of them yet, but I hope to go very soon.'

'If I'd known that,' Harriet said, 'I would have told you we were going, and you could have come with us. I'll let you know when we're taking Alice to somewhere else of interest, and perhaps you'll be able to join us.'

'I'd like that,' he said.

They gazed at each other, and then each smiled.

'We went to Hawa Mahal for a second time because Alice decided to illustrate every place we visited with a photograph,' Eleanor told him. 'She didn't have a camera with her the first time we went there, so we went back again, and then across to Jantar Mantar. That's right, isn't it, Alice?'

'It is, and in a way, James is to be thanked, too,' Alice said. 'When he bumped into us outside the palace the first time we went there, he kindly gave me some paper so I could jot down what Harriet and Eleanor were telling me. That's when the idea of illustrating my notes came to me.'

'I thought it a very good idea. And like William, I'd be

interested in joining you on a future outing,' James volunteered.

Eleanor looked at him in surprise. 'You never fail to amaze me, James, with your breadth of interests,' she said with amusement.

'You'll have a fascinating book by the time you've been everywhere, Alice,' Charles told her. 'It's the kind of thing a travel company might be keen on. A sort of guidebook for tourists, in effect. You could sound out some publishing companies.'

'I'm not sure that's such a good idea, Alice,' Beatrice said quickly. 'If you entered into an agreement with a company, you'd have to deliver what you'd promised on the day you'd promised it. That's the way things work in business, as any of the men will tell you. But things might turn up in the coming weeks that you'd rather do than visit more ancient monuments. With a commitment, though, you'd have to give those more attractive activities a miss, and before long, you could find yourself starting to dislike something that you're enjoying at the moment.'

'Your mother's right, Alice,' Frank cut in. 'If I were you, I'd continue writing for pleasure. When you come to the end of your sightseeing, if you feel you've a possible guide-book, that's the time to approach someone. Don't you agree, Charles?'

'Of course, sir,' Charles said quickly.

'I do hope you'll do as your father suggests, Alice, and show your book to a publishing company when it's finished,' Ivy said. 'Arthur would be able to suggest some companies you could approach. You'd be able to do that, wouldn't you, Arthur?'

'Most definitely. It wouldn't be difficult to discover who'd be most likely to be receptive,' Arthur told her. 'If you decide to go ahead with this, Alice, don't hesitate to ask me for help.'

'That's very kind of you, Mr McKenna. Thank you.'

'And if it comes to any paper you need,' Charles said, grinning, 'I've a pretty good idea of a company that could help you.'

Harriet smiled around the table. 'I think the guide book's a very good idea, and not just because I like the idea of my words and Eleanor's being enshrined in print, though that's a part of it if I'm honest,' she added with a little laugh. 'But it'll be written in a non-stuffy way, and that would make it more pleasant for visitors to read it. That was a clever idea, Charles. But I think it's sensible to wait till the book is finished before contacting anyone.'

'Yes, it *was* a good idea. Thank you, Charles.' Alice smiled warmly at him. 'It's very satisfying to have a purpose for the notes I make. Now I can't wait to go on our next visit.'

'What's next on the list?' Maxwell asked.

'Amber Fort, I think,' Alice said. 'Isn't that right, Eleanor?'

Eleanor nodded. 'It is. We thought we'd go there next week.'

'And don't forget, Alice wants a tour of the paper factory,' Charles cut in. 'I hope it can be fitted in before too long, Eleanor. After all, a book is produced on paper, and the more the writer knows about the various kinds of paper, the easier it'll be for her to decide what's best for her book. Don't you think, Alice?' He gazed at her hopefully.

Alice beamed at him. 'Yes, I do. I think I ought to go there very soon, Charles.' She turned to Philip. 'Would that be all right, Mr Grainger?'

'Of course, it would,' Philip said. 'What's more, I'll be

happy to show you around myself,' he added, and threw an amused glance at Julia.

Alice's smile vanished, then swiftly reappeared. 'Thank you, Mr Grainger. It's very kind of you,' she said politely.

Philip and Julia laughed.

'He's teasing you, Alice,' Julia said. 'Charles will be tasked with showing you around.'

Alice giggled. She looked at Charles, and blushed.

'If it suits Harriet and Eleanor's plans, why don't we plan Alice's visit for Wednesday in a couple of weeks?' Philip suggested. 'The next two weeks are quite busy,'

'Will you be going on the factory visit, too, Eleanor, or have you been there so often that you feel you've seen it enough?' Maxwell asked.

'Harriet and I will certainly go, too, won't we, Harriet?' Eleanor said. 'We might not take quite as much notice of what Charles says as Alice does, though,' she added with a laugh. 'But it's not so far past the club that we couldn't stop at the club for lunch on the way back, and that would be fun.'

'The thought of lunch with good company sounds quite appealing,' Maxwell remarked. 'As I'll need to meet you before too long in order to put in an order for paper, Philip, I could make it that day, assuming you're free. Or would that be an unsuitable day, given you'll have visitors in the factory?'

Philip inclined his head. 'Not at all, Maxwell. Charles will be dealing with the visitors, so I'll be at your disposal.'

'Harriet and I would be delighted if you came with us, Maxwell,' Eleanor said, dimpling with pleasure at the thought of having an opportunity of seeing Maxwell again, which would help her to get a clearer idea of what she felt for him.

'And would you and Harriet be equally welcoming if I, too, decided to broaden my knowledge by learning about paper, and invited myself to eat with you afterwards?' William asked. 'I might have to force James along as I'd need the use of his car. Would that be all right, James?'

'Of course,' James said. 'It's shaping up to be a most unusual outing.'

'We'd be delighted if you came, William. And you, too, James,' Harriet added quickly. 'Wouldn't we, Eleanor?'

Eleanor glanced at James. 'I suppose so.'

'Then that's decided,' Philip said. 'Well, then, to come back to the present, I thought to go into the study to enjoy brandy and a cigar. Whisky may be replacing brandy in a lot of homes, but not in this one. Would anyone care to join me?'

'Count me in,' Maxwell said. He stood up, and so did Frank and Arthur. They followed Philip out of the dining room and into the entrance hall, at the end of which was the study.

'A brandy sounds good. And it'll give James and me a chance to fix up a few games of billiards at the club with Maxwell, perhaps next Wednesday,' William said, and he and James got up and went out after them.

With a reluctant glance at Alice, Charles stood up and trailed after the other men.

Eleanor put her napkin down on the table and rose to her feet. 'I think that Harriet, Alice and I will go out on to the veranda. If you don't mind, that is?' She directed her question to Beatrice, Ivy and Julia.

'The three of us are going into the sitting room, and we'll have our coffee there,' Julia said. 'If you girls would like to join us, please do.'

'Thank you, Mama,' Eleanor said, 'but I think we'd prefer to sit outside.'

They went quickly through the door that led to the veranda, and closed the door behind them.

'Joining our mothers for coffee, I don't think so,' Eleanor said with a laugh as they sat down at the wicker table. 'If it's like any other Sunday afternoon, they'll all be asleep within minutes.'

The butler came out on to the veranda and asked what they would like by way of refreshment. All three asked for a pineapple juice.

'Please, don't bring anything to eat with it, though,' Eleanor told him. 'We've had enough.'

'I'd much rather be out here with just the two of you,' Harriet said as the butler went back into the house. 'I wanted to ask you about Charles, Alice.'

'What about him?' Alice asked, colouring. 'If there's anything you want to know about Charles, shouldn't you ask Eleanor? He works for her father, after all.'

'It's not his career prospects that Harriet's interested in,' Eleanor said, leaning slightly forward, 'it's what's in his heart.' She and Harriet exchanged glances. 'And what's in your heart, too.'

Alice blushed more deeply. 'I have no idea what's in his heart. How could I know? I've hardly met him. As for me, I'm not going to say that I don't find him attractive, because I do, and if I'm truly honest, I'd like to get to know him better. But that's not going to happen, so the less said about it the better. My parents think he isn't suitable. They want me to marry someone who owns a factory, rather than works in one.'

'I don't think Mama would be happy about that,' Eleanor said lightly. 'I think she enjoys being Mrs Grainger.'

They all laughed.

'You know what I mean,' Alice said. 'But whatever my parents say, I intend to get to know Charles better. For example, when we're in the same room together, I'll find a way of us talking. And I can't wait for our visit to the factory.'

'Nor can I!' Harriet exclaimed.

'You're as bad about William as Alice is about Charles,' Eleanor told her. 'I'd better start looking for a suitor or I'll end up alone on the shelf.'

Harriet raised an eyebrow. 'And you think Maxwell would let that happen? I don't. Alice has been honest about her feelings for Charles, and I'll admit that I find William attractive, very attractive even. But what about you, Eleanor? I've seen the way you look at Maxwell and the way he looks at you.'

'To be honest, and this is the truth, I do think he's very attractive and I like talking to him, but I'm not sure that I've fallen in love with him, or am likely to do so in the future. I just don't know. And I won't get the chance to find out,' she added gloomily. 'I imagine you saw Papa's face whenever Maxwell's name came up, unless it was to do with orders for paper. It's pretty clear that for some unknown reason he doesn't want him in the family.'

'Like Mr Fletcher with Charles,' Harriet said.

'It's depressing to think that Papa might try to keep me away from Maxwell, so let's change the subject. If we go to Amber Fort on Tuesday, it'll leave us free to go to the club on Wednesday. I quite fancy a game of croquet. And before you say anything, it's nothing to do with the fact that the men mentioned they might be playing billiards on Wednesday.'

'Of course it isn't,' Harriet and Alice chorused in unison.

16

T *uesday*

ELEANOR STOOD with Alice and Harriet on top of the thick sandstone wall that surrounded the Amber Palace and Fort, and stared across the deep blue Maota Lake to the panoramic views of the town of Amer that lay in the gorge below.

A little way further along the honey-covered wall, Ivy and Beatrice were standing together, talking.

'What a place,' Alice said with an audible sigh, turning from the view to look back at the buildings that made up the fort. 'It's so dramatic, and reeks of history. You can easily see the different layers that have been added over the years by ancient dynasties, as there are slight variations in style. But I suppose you'd expect that. It was built more than three hundred years ago, didn't you say?'

Harriet nodded. 'That's right. Amber was the capital of

the area until 1727, when the capital was moved to Jaipur. They started building the fort in 1592 but it took over a hundred years to build. You saw all the marble and the details in the building, and the moulded silver doors, for example. It's really high quality, and that takes time to do.'

'I loved it. I loved all the carvings, and the elephant gate and the stunning main entrance and all the four courtyards, especially the fourth courtyard, the one for the maharani and her ladies, with no men allowed. It was all magical.'

'I agree,' Eleanor said. 'There's a reason for all the elephants.' And she told Alice that the elephant gate, and the number of elephant statues throughout Jaipur, were because Ganesha, the elephant god, was believed to remove all obstacles and everything negative. The Hindus highly revered elephants, she told her, seeing them as an incarnation of Ganesha.

'That may be, but I felt sorry for the elephants that had to carry people up to the entrance to the fort,' Alice said, and turned again to the view. 'Having the Aravali Hills as a backdrop makes it even more spectacular. The photographs I took will be fantastic,' she said enthusiastically.

'I saw you making notes as we crossed the courtyards and went into the different rooms and halls,' Eleanor said. 'What part of the fort did you like best?'

Alice thought for a moment. 'The Mirror Palace, or Sheesh Mahal to give it its Indian name.'

'Me, too!' exclaimed Harriet.

'I thought it breathtaking,' Alice said, 'with all those tiny mirrors covering the walls and ceilings. Although there was only a single candle, they sparkled like stars when the light touched them.'

'The mirrors were imported from Belgium,' Harriet told her. 'Jai Singh II bartered jewellery and textiles in exchange for glass and metals. The hall was designed to need only one candle as the maharaja didn't want light to shine in people's eyes.'

'Whatever the reason, the effect was unforgettable. I've never seen anything like that before. And I also liked the lovely courtyard garden, which was like a peaceful oasis. And I liked the stepwell next to the fort. I was surprised at how large it was.'

'That was so that a number of people could use it at the same time,' Harriet said. 'They'd know how deep it was because they'd see the number of storeys above the water. Not many of the nine storeys would be visible after the monsoon rains.'

'What's your favourite part, Eleanor?' Alice asked.

'The zenana,' she said. 'You might not remember it clearly, having seen as much as you did this morning, but it surrounds the fourth courtyard. It's where the wives and concubines lived. All the chambers are independent, but they all open out on to a common corridor. As we told you, it's very clever in that it's designed so the maharaja can visit the rooms of his wives and concubines at night without any of the others knowing who he's with.'

'And only one apartment had access to the maharaja,' Harriet cut in. 'That was the maharani's. Remember the long ramp leading to his rooms, which narrowed in height near the top so that soldiers with spears would struggle to get up there? Well that was the maharani's access to the maharaja's chambers.'

'I certainly do. Thank you, both of you, for bringing me here,' Alice said. 'I've really enjoyed the day.'

'And it's not over yet,' Harriet said brightly. 'We're stopping for lunch at the club on the way back. There might be some interesting people there.'

'I'm not going to ask who you have in mind,' Eleanor said with a laugh. 'But I've a feeling that both of you might be disappointed. I'm sure William wanted to go, but he might not have been able to get away, and the same applies to James. And I'm sorry, Alice, but I imagine that Charles will be working. Maxwell might be there, though,' she added.

'Will our mothers mind us going to the club, d'you think, Harriet?' Alice asked.

'I doubt it,' she said. 'They'd have to sit by themselves, of course, as they're our chaperones, not our companions.' She glanced towards Ivy and Beatrice. 'But we'll soon find out as they're coming over to us.'

'It's a little early to suggest lunch,' Harriet said hastily. 'Delaying tactic ahead. I should very much like to go back to the Hall of Mirrors,' she said, raising her voice so that the mothers would hear. 'Alice and I like it so much. Once we've been there again, it'll probably be time to leave.'

'I couldn't help overhearing what you were saying, Harriet,' Beatrice said, stepping in front of Ivy. 'Why don't you and Alice go with your mother, and I'll stay with Eleanor?'

Harriet and her mother exchanged surprised glances.

Beatrice smiled at the girls. 'An advantage of having two of us with you is that we don't have to stay together all of the time. I've walked more today than I'm used to, and it's getting warmer, so I'd rather like to enjoy the view from up here and the breeze for a little longer. I thought Eleanor could keep me company.'

Eleanor looked at Harriet and gave a slight shrug.

'Well then, let's go, girls,' Ivy said, failing to keep the surprise out of her voice. 'We won't be long, Beatrice.' She waited for Alice and Harriet to go ahead of her, and then followed them.

'I'M QUITE surprised you wanted to talk to me without the others present,' Eleanor said lightly. 'Not that I mind,' she added quickly. 'My parents aren't famous for asking me to speak. On the contrary, in fact.' She paused. 'Did you want to talk about Alice?'

Beatrice smiled at her. 'In a way, yes. But you're wrong in thinking I've drawn you away from the others to speak to you. I was allowing Mrs McKenna to have some time with Alice. If all three of you were together, that would be impossible. Alice is quieter than you and Harriet, and wouldn't say much. But I couldn't ask to speak alone to both you and Harriet, as that would look very odd, so I restricted my request to you.'

'I know you like reading, Mrs Fletcher, but perhaps, like Alice, you should start writing, too. I'm sure you could easily write a mystery story. What you've just said sounds most intriguing.'

Beatrice laughed. 'I'll give it some thought.' She turned to look ahead of her. 'What a glorious view,' she remarked with a sigh.

'I hope you aren't going to leave it at that,' Eleanor said with a smile. 'I want to know why Aunt Ivy wants to talk to Alice.' She hesitated. 'If I'm being impertinent, please forgive me.'

Beatrice shook her head. 'You're not,' she said. 'I suppose the way I explained what I'd done was bound to make you curious. And it wasn't entirely accurate, either. I implied that Mrs McKenna wanted to talk to Alice. It's actually more that she wants to get to know Alice, and for that to happen she and Alice need time to talk to each other.'

Eleanor stared at her in surprise.

'Why does she want to get to know Alice?' she asked bluntly. 'You're Alice's mother, so you can tell her what a nice person Alice is.'

'It's possible that Mrs McKenna might think me a trifle biased,' Beatrice said drily.

'Would that matter?'

Beatrice inclined her head. 'It would if you thought your son was interested in her.'

'James!' Eleanor exclaimed. 'Does Aunt Ivy think James is interested in Alice?'

She felt the blood drain from her face and put her hands to her cheeks.

Beatrice smiled. 'She does. She's sure she's seen signs of such an interest on his part. And Frank and I would be delighted if that were so. He's such a nice man.'

'But Alice is keen on Charles! I know he's a factory foreman and not an owner, but he's really kind. Alice obviously likes him, and he likes her.'

'We feel she can do a little better for herself,' Beatrice said stiffly. 'But since we've time to kill, tell me about yourself, Eleanor. I remember you saying that you liked reading and drawing. So that's where we'll start. You can tell me about your favourite books, and then what sort of things you like to draw.'

17

L *ater that day*

WHEN THE OTHERS HAD RETURNED, Eleanor had lied and said that she had a headache and preferred to go straight home, rather than stop for lunch.

Despite feeling very guilty at lying, she persevered in the lie, blaming the way she felt on so much walking up and down stone staircases, and through endless mazes of rooms. It was very tiring if you're not used to it, she'd told the others, and even more so when it was as hot as it had become.

They had all agreed to go straight back to their homes and to have lunch there and then a siesta.

The siesta over, Eleanor had been contemplating going to Harriet's house and apologising to her for cutting short their day. Also, she was keen to hear how the discussion between Ivy and Alice had gone.

Plus, very importantly, she needed to know if Harriet thought that James had developed feelings for Alice.

Picking up her straw cloche, she'd been about to go downstairs and go to the McKennas' house when she heard a rap on the front door. She paused, and a moment later, the butler knocked on her door to tell her that Miss McKenna was downstairs, anxious to see how Eleanor was feeling. Miss McKenna had added that if Eleanor felt well enough, they could perhaps take a short walk.

Eleanor had run down the stairs in delight.

'Don't you think it very strange, Harriet, that your mother thinks James is interested in Alice?' Eleanor asked.

Frowning, she stared across the deep blue Man Sagar Lake to the sun-hazed palace that floated on its surface, two storeys visible above the water and three storeys hidden below, and beyond that to the low red spurs of the Aravali Hills that rose up behind the lake.

Caught by the rays of the sun, peaks in the water glinted with gold.

As she gazed ahead, mesmerised by the sparks of gold bouncing off the deep blue surface, several black-and-white birds darted across her line of vision. Skimming the tips of the water, they flew low over the glittering expanse, their bright bills open to catch any unguarded fish.

'Be honest, Harriet, have you ever seen any signs of James liking Alice in the way that Mrs Fletcher said Aunt Ivy has?' Eleanor asked, turning back to look at Harriet.

'No, I haven't,' Harriet said. 'None at all. It's a ridiculous idea. I'm sure Mrs Fletcher's wrong. She's probably so keen on stopping Alice and Charles from falling in love that she's latched on to James as a possible replacement for Charles in

Alice's affections. If you're desperate to see something, you often can, even though it isn't really there.'

Eleanor nodded vigorously. 'Yes, I'm sure that's what's happened. After all, she's bound to consider James better husband material than Charles.'

'And if you think about it,' Harriet went on, 'whenever James was in the same place as Alice, so were we. If he'd shown any interest in her, we would certainly have spotted it.'

'You're right again,' Eleanor said. She leaned back against the bench and smiled at the view ahead. 'I can relax.'

Harriet looked at her in surprise. 'Why wouldn't you be relaxed if James felt something for Alice?' She paused. Then a slow smile spread across her face. 'You're not interested in James in a romantic sort of way, are you? After all, I suppose he *is* very good-looking.'

Eleanor straightened up. 'Of course not,' she said indignantly. 'He's like a brother to me, a very bossy brother. But naturally I'm curious about what my sort-of-brother is up to, just as you are. No,' she said, settling back again on the bench. 'If it's anything, I suppose I'd be worried if you were Alice's sister-in-law. You might become closer to her than you are to me.'

'That could never happen.' Harriet waved her hand dismissively.

'If James married Alice, it could. It was always just you and me till Alice arrived, and although it's the three of us now, I still feel that you and I are closer to each other than we are to Alice. It's not that I don't like her,' she added quickly, 'because I do. But you're like a sister to me. We grew up together, and I wouldn't want Alice to take my place. Yes,' she said, nodding with satisfaction. 'That's why I wasn't completely relaxed about the idea of James being keen on Alice.'

'Just to prove that both Mrs Fletcher and Mama are wrong about James liking Alice,' Harriet said, 'as soon as I can, I'll catch him before he rushes off on one of his mysterious activities and ask him what he thinks of her. He won't think it strange of me to ask such a thing as he believes that all that women think about are men and marriage. Then I'll tell you for certain what he thinks about her. But I won't be relying on what he says. I'll know from his manner if he's got feelings for her, even if he denies it.'

Eleanor smiled broadly. 'That would be wonderful, Harriet. Thank you.' She picked up the drink she'd rested on the bench. 'Just now you said that James was involved in mysterious activities. What activities?' she asked. 'Isn't his department very dull?'

Harriet shrugged. 'I don't really know. It's just that when William visits us, the two of them are always whispering together, and they break off if anyone goes near them. It's really annoying as I'd like William to be whispering to me, not to James,' she added with a giggle.

'Also,' Harriet said, her face serious again, 'd'you really think James is the sort of person who'd do a dull job day in, day out? Or William for that matter? 'Cos I don't. That would make them very dull people. I know James is my brother, so maybe I'm biased, but I don't thinks he's boring. Do you?'

'Of course he isn't. But what else could he be doing when he goes to admin or the Residency?'

They looked helplessly at each other.

'Of course, there's something we could do to make absolutely certain that James and Alice don't get too close to each other,' Harriet said suddenly.

'What's that?'

'We could do everything possible to see that Charles and Alice marry. They're keen on each other. It's just her parents who're the problem. But if we get Charles and Alice together as much as possible, I'm sure he'll soon declare himself, and Mr Fletcher will have to come round.'

'He won't. He'll refuse his consent,' Eleanor said bluntly. 'Alice is still underage, as we are. She can't marry without his permission till she's twenty-one. With both of the Fletchers hoping for a match between Alice and James, which I assume they are, he'd never agree to her marrying Charles.'

'Ah, but if they were convinced that James had no intention of pursuing Alice, they might look upon Charles more favourably,' Harriet said. 'After all, he's got a secure job and I'm sure he'll soon have a place of his own. Neither of Alice's parents seems so devoted to her that they'd want her to live with them indefinitely, and there aren't that many eligible British men in Jaipur.'

'Even if both you and James swore to them that he had no romantic feelings for Alice, I don't think they'd believe you. They'll believe what they want to believe,' Eleanor said in a weary tone of voice.

'That would be true,' Harriet said steadily, 'if they had only our words to go on. But what if they saw for themselves that he had designs on someone else?'

Eleanor's brow wrinkled. 'What d'you mean? There's no one else.'

Harriet's brow arched in surprise. 'Oh, but surely there is. There's you, Eleanor.'

They stared at each other, Harriet's expression knowing, Eleanor's incredulous.

Then Eleanor laughed derisively. 'The emotions that

pass between James and me are more often or not disappointment on his part,' she said cheerfully, 'at something I've said or done, or annoyance on my part at being chastised by him. It's brotherly and sisterly behaviour, but no more than that.'

'I believe you,' Harriet said hastily. 'But in the past, you used to pretend to be fascinated by the carvings at Amber Fort so that our governess would take us there. You were so convincing that even *I* believed you were obsessed with them! So it wouldn't be beyond your acting ability to convince the Fletchers that you and James were in love.'

Eleanor stared at her. 'I suppose I could do that,' she said slowly. 'And we could try to help Alice and Charles get together at the same time. D'you think I ought to tell James what we're planning?'

Harriet nodded vigorously. 'Yes, I do. If you suddenly looked up at him with eyes that were gooey with deep devotion, he might think you were serious, panic and run screaming in the opposite direction!'

They both laughed.

'Actually it's not a bad idea,' Eleanor said, finishing her lemonade. 'Pretending to be keen on James could be quite amusing. But it's probably better not to tell him what I'm doing. If he knew, he might give the game away by not responding properly. I'll keep the sickly gooiness to a minimum, I promise.'

Harriet sat back. 'That's decided then. We can start tomorrow. We're going to the club for a game of croquet, aren't we? I'm sure James said that he and William were meeting Maxwell there tomorrow for a game or two of billiards. And they're bound to have invited Charles as they'll know that unless the factory is unusually busy, he has Wednesday afternoons off. The more people playing the better, they'll think.'

Eleanor lay in her bed, staring through the uncovered window as the dying sun dipped behind the horizon, sending the last rays of vibrant colour across the sky – luminous green, followed by liquid gold, salmon-pink and deep rose. And then darkness.

Outside the house, she heard the evening calls of the roosting birds soar up into the sky, rising above the relentless song of the cicadas and above the occasional mournful cry of a lone peacock. How strange, she thought. Everything seemed so normal in the world outside, but everything was so far from normal within her.

Tears trickled down her cheeks.

She turned her head to look up at the mosquito net hanging above her bed. The mosquito season was over, so she must remember to ask the servants to remove the net, she thought.

She looked back at the window. She really should pull down the bamboo blind or the bright light of dawn would wake her before she was ready.

And it was still hot enough for the servants to put dried grass between the strips of bamboo, and sprinkle the grass with water so that when it was wet, the wind would catch it and cool the room. She must ask them to do that, too.

Wiping her cheeks with the back of her hands, she gave a deep sigh and forced herself to think about what she'd been trying to avoid all afternoon. Why had she felt such a sharp pain when Mrs Fletcher had told her that Aunt Ivy thought James was romantically interested in Alice?

In Alice of all people!

The very idea had been a source of great distress.

But why should that be, she wondered. She rolled over on to a cold patch of sheet. As she'd told Harriet, her feelings for James were strictly sisterly, so it shouldn't have troubled her to think of him being with Alice.

But it had done. And it still did.

So there was a question she must ask herself, a question she'd been trying to evade. Was she right in thinking her feelings for James were strictly sisterly, or had she been deceiving herself?

Without doubt, she'd felt sisterly towards him in the days gone by when he used to tease her and Harriet. But thinking about it, that was now some time ago. They'd grown up since then, and James had grown up, too.

The man James had become was tall and handsome, in fact very attractive and great fun to be with. He'd become someone she enjoyed spending time with, someone she always looked forward to seeing. And funnily, even when she was annoyed with him, she still couldn't wait for their next interaction.

So it had actually been a while since she'd thought of him in a sisterly way. That must mean that although she hadn't been conscious of her feelings for him changing, they had.

How, then, did she think of him now?

The truth was, she didn't know.

All she knew was that the thought of James with Alice had been devastating. Yes, devastating was the word that best described the way she'd felt at Amber Fort. And such a response must have been caused by something more than mere surprise.

And that must mean something significant.

But if it did, where did Maxwell fit into any of this?

If she had feelings for James, even though she hadn't realised it, how could she be finding Maxwell attractive? But she had done. So much so that she'd actually flirted with him on the occasions they'd met.

She'd never flirted with James, though.

Tears of despair sprang into her eyes. She didn't know what she felt about the two men.

She rolled on to her back again and looked up above her. The mesh of the mosquito net accurately reflected the turmoil in her mind, she thought miserably.

But perhaps the following afternoon would shed some light on her feelings.

She'd be going to the club with Harriet and Alice after they'd had a short siesta, and she knew that James and William would be going there, too. Charles would probably go home and change before he joined them, so she'd have time before he arrived to watch Alice and James together. The Fletchers wouldn't be there so she wouldn't have to feign any feelings for James. She would be able to decide whether he really was interested in Alice, and if he was, whether she minded.

She would also try to fathom out what she felt about Maxwell. She'd wondered before about her feelings for him, well now it was time to find out.

So, if all went well, by the end of the next day, she would have a much better understanding of herself. Swallowing the urge to burst into tears again, she rolled over on to her side, closed her eyes and waited for sleep.

18

T he Royal Jaipur Club,
The next day

HEAT HUNG heavy above the ground as the late-afternoon shadows lengthened across the patio where the tables had been deserted for the shade and cooler air offered by the veranda. Whirring fans had been placed along the length of the veranda and were bringing a welcome breeze to those sitting there.

'That must have been the shortest croquet game ever,' Maxwell said, glancing towards Eleanor, Harriet and Alice as they came out of the building, breathless and laughing. They went up to the table where he was sitting with William, and sat down. James followed close behind them and took the seat next to William.

'We didn't even get as far as hitting the ball through the first of the hoops,' Harriet said, fanning herself with her hand. 'It was much too hot. Who'd have expected an

October day to be as hot as this, and a bit humid, too? Normally our heat is a dry heat. We did a swift walk around the back lawn just to say we'd done some exercise, then sped back here as fast as we could.'

Eleanor leaned her head back and stretched out her arms behind the chairs on either side of her. 'The breeze from the fan is heavenly,' she said.

'I agree,' Alice said, and she copied Eleanor's action.

'It's a relief to be out of the heat. It's unbearable today,' Eleanor went on. She straightened slightly and glanced around her. 'Where're our mothers?'

'They're inside the club, where it's much cooler,' William said. 'I doubt we'll see them out here for a while, if at all. They said something about using being together today to plan what books they were going to read in the future. When I last went inside, the three of them were huddled in the lounge, deep in discussion.'

Maxwell signalled to the waiter to approach the table. He, William and James ordered a coffee. Each of the three girls asked for a lemonade.

'To be honest, I'm not too sorry that we decided against playing today,' Alice said when the waiter had left. 'I'm terrible at tennis so I'll probably be equally bad at croquet. Ball games don't like me.' She gave them an apologetic smile. 'I'm happy for you to stay in blissful ignorance of how bad I am for a little longer.'

'Did you have many opportunities to play croquet in Bayana?' James asked.

Eleanor and Harriet exchanged surreptitious glances, then watched James's expression closely.

Alice shook her head. 'Not really. There was nowhere to play it. It was never even suggested as an activity. As for tennis, I went to a small school with others from a similar background. No one had a tennis court at home, and there wasn't a club like this anywhere near us. The school had a small tennis court, and they made sure we knew the basic rules. In the cooler months, we'd play a couple of times a week, but no one was any good as we hadn't been properly taught. As Eleanor had partnered you with me, James, you've been spared a humiliating defeat at the hands of her and Harriet.'

He smiled at her. 'I'm sure you're being modest. But if you aren't, it wouldn't have really mattered. You'll get better once you've played a few games. It's an easy game to learn, and no one here takes it very seriously. Maybe tennis is taken a bit more seriously, but billiards is the worst of all. Which reminds me, my friend,' he said, turning to Maxwell, 'we were going to plan that billiards tournament we keep talking about.'

'Well remembered, James,' William said enthusiastically. He grinned at Maxwell. 'But maybe, after the game we had early this afternoon, you'd prefer to leave me off the list.'

Maxwell laughed. 'As James said to Alice about croquet, you'll get better.'

'I noticed you and Maxwell deep in conversation earlier on, William,' James remarked. 'Was Maxwell giving you instructions on how to improve your game?'

'Not exactly,' William said, with a rueful smile at Maxwell. 'I was bending the poor man's ear about the exporting business. I'm sure he's fed up to the back teeth with the subject by now.'

Maxwell smiled. 'Not at all. I never tire of showing off what I know.'

They all laughed.

'We'd better not draw up a list of games till Charles gets

here,' James said. 'I'm sure he won't be long. I wouldn't want him to feel left out.'

Alice half rose to look down the steps, past the elephant statues and along the lawn-flanked drive to the stone arch on the far left, behind which the cars and tongas were left. There was no one walking through the archway or up the drive.

'There's no sign of him yet,' she said sorrowfully, sitting back down. 'I hope he gets here before the mothers come out and join us.'

'Lucky Charles, having such a lovely lady so anxious for him to arrive,' Maxwell said, a smile in his voice.

Alice looked alarmed. 'Don't let my mother hear you say that,' she said quickly. 'She'd whip me off home at once.'

Surprise crossed Maxwell's face. 'Like that, is it? Then I promise I'll be very careful what I say.'

Raising an eyebrow, he glanced at James, who gave a slight shrug.

'To go back to billiards,' Maxwell went on. 'When I last checked the message we'd posted on the noticeboard, which was a good few days ago, no one had signed to take part in our tournament. If no else is interested, it'll be just the four of us, along with Philip, Frank and Arthur.'

William stood up. 'It might be worth making sure no one's signed the list since then. I'll go inside and check. I've got paper and pencil, so if you come with me, Harriet, you could jot down the names of anyone else who's said they're interested.'

Beaming, Harriet jumped up from her chair.

'I hope you can come up with a better reason for cosying up inside with Harriet, should Mother challenge you,' James said drily.

'I'll work on it,' William said with a smile. 'Come on, Harriet.'

'What's the betting she comes back after some time without a single name on the paper?' Maxwell said in amusement. 'Ah, look, there's Charles!'

Charles was crossing the patio at speed, making straight for their table. Alice half rose again. Charles glanced at the empty seats where Harriet and William had been sitting, and promptly sat down next to Alice, in the seat vacated by Harriet.

'Hot today, isn't it?' he said, pulling off his cream-coloured jacket. 'It was a relief to get out of the factory, I don't mind telling you. Your father will be here shortly, Eleanor. The electric fans could only do so much and we were both melting.' He glanced at Alice in admiration. 'You look as fresh as a daisy, Alice. I don't know how you do it.'

'I know you're just being kind, Charles, but I shall pretend to believe you and thus I'll feel confident that my forehead and nose aren't shining, my cheeks aren't scarlet and my dress doesn't look like a limp rag.'

Charles leaned towards her. 'You look beautiful, Alice,' he said, lowering his voice.

'I'd be careful, you two,' James remarked. 'Mrs Fletcher could materialise at any moment.'

'Where's she now?' Charles asked, swiftly straightening up.

'With the other two mothers inside the club,' Eleanor said. 'They're talking about the books they're going to be reading.'

Under the table, Charles and Alice found a hand of the other.

'It might be wise if you changed seats with me?' James suggested to Charles. Eleanor looked at James in sudden alarm. 'That way, Mrs Fletcher could have no cause for complaint if she decided to join us,' he went on. 'We'll need another chair anyway when William and Harriet return, but we don't need to worry about that now. I think I can put up with being next to Eleanor for the moment. And next to Alice, too, of course.' He smiled at Eleanor and then at Alice.

Eleanor tried not to show the relief she felt at James's implication that she was the one he wanted to sit beside.

James stood up. Charles squeezed Alice's hand tightly in his, and then he, too, got up. As he sat down on the other side of the table opposite Alice, they exchanged regretful smiles.

'Aha, the wanderers return!' Maxwell said cheerfully as William and Harriet came through the doorway that led from the lounge. Engrossed in conversation, they walked slowly up to the table. Maxwell moved his chair to be as close to Eleanor as possible.

Harriet sat down next to Charles. A waiter hurried forward with another chair.

'A thorn between two roses,' William said, sitting down between Harriet and Alice.

'My friend is nothing if not corny,' James said with a smile. 'I apologise for him.'

They all laughed.

'What's the situation then, William?' Maxwell asked. 'Did you find any other potential players?'

William shook his head. 'Not a single one, I'm afraid. But one of the stewards suggested that if we had a little tournament on Saturday, the Saturday crowd would see us and it's very likely we'd get some volunteers from among them, both to join in on Saturday and for any future games.'

'Sounds sensible,' Maxwell said.

James turned to speak to Eleanor, but Maxwell forestalled him. 'You were at Amber Fort yesterday, I believe, Eleanor,' Maxwell said. 'It's one of my favourite places.'

Suppressing her irritation at having to speak with Maxwell when she'd been keen to hear what James had been about to say, she turned to Maxwell, smiled.

'Mine, too,' she said. 'Harriet and I were fortunate as children that our governess liked the place enormously, and we were able to escape the oppression of the schoolroom and go up to the fort on a number of occasions. On hot days like this, we used to sit on one of the upper steps of the step-well, gazing down at the water. It was cooler there than anywhere else. We've actually been known to eat a picnic there.'

Eleanor turned to look at James. She opened her mouth to say something to him.

'I love picnics,' Maxwell said quickly. 'We should organise one. Even if it's a hot day, though few this side of Christmas are likely to be as hot as today, we could choose somewhere that guarantees a breeze.'

'I haven't been up to the fort yet,' William said, 'so I'd be happy to go there.'

'Were you thinking of having the picnic at Amber Fort?' Harriet asked in surprise. 'There aren't really many picnic spots up there, and setting up the tables could be a problem.'

'Where d'you suggest, then?' Maxwell asked.

'What about Kanak Vrindavan Garden?' Harriet suggested. 'It's sort of north of Man Sagar Lake. The garden is lovely, which makes it an ideal place for a picnic.'

'That's an excellent idea,' Eleanor and Charles said at the same time.

'And it has a breathtaking view over the lake,' Harriet went on. 'I know we can see the lake from our houses, but you see it from a different angle when you're in the garden. You can't see the Water Palace for a start. And there's a lovely pavilion in the centre of the garden. The servants could set up the tables under it.'

'That's a brilliant idea, Harriet,' Eleanor said eagerly. 'It wouldn't be difficult for the servants to transport the food and tables there. And it's one of the places you need to visit, Alice. Picnicking there would be a good way of doing so. You could include it in the guidebook that you may or may not do.'

'So, a picnic at the garden, three weeks on Sunday, shall we say?' Maxwell asked, looking around. 'We'll need time to plan it, and the weather should still be comfortable for sitting around. A Sunday would obviously be best for Charles and Philip, and for Arthur, too, I would think.'

There was a general buzz of assent.

'Then we'll tell the others when they get here,' Maxwell said with a smile.

'Talking of your guidebook, Alice, how's it coming along?' Charles asked.

'Very well, thank you. It was such a good idea to have a purpose behind my note-taking, even if the purpose comes to nothing, as my parents believe it will. And Harriet and Eleanor know so much that they're excellent tour guides.'

'Oh dear. I feel Eleanor's head is swelling,' James said in a doleful voice. 'I shall soon be forced to slide beneath the table in order to allow sufficient room for its growth.'

Eleanor turned to him with a smile. 'My head is grateful to you for your consideration,' she said. 'It's happy to know that its expansion won't be stifled.'

'I'm pleased to hear that.' He paused. 'It is, after all, a very lovely head,' he added quietly.

Her smile faded, and she stared at him, questioningly.

'But don't let my latest comment further increase the size of your head,' he murmured. 'There's a limit to how far beneath the table I want to go.'

Both smiled, and then looked back at the others.

As William was talking to Alice, and Maxwell was asking Harriet and Charles about the sort of things they did when they went on a picnic, which was something he hadn't often done, James turned back to Eleanor.

'I know I've apologised before,' he said, 'but I wanted to do so again. I was wrong in the way I spoke to you that day at Hawa Mahal. I was slow to open my eyes and see you as you are today, a grown woman, and no longer a child in the schoolroom, someone I could upbraid in the way I could Harriet. Those days are past, I know that now. Have you truly forgiven me?'

She smiled at him. 'Of course I have. I've always seen you as a friend, James, who's unfailingly had my interests at heart. I forgave you almost as soon as you'd finished your dire warnings.'

He raised his eyebrows in incredulity. 'You did?'

She giggled. 'Well, maybe it took a little longer than that.'

'The thing is,' he went on, 'when I asked myself why I'd spoken as I had, I realised that I was trying to quell any interest you might have in anyone other than me.'

She caught her breath and held it.

'I knew then,' he continued, 'that I would have tried to deter you from William or Charles or anyone else who might have attracted your attention. It wasn't just a Maxwell thing. And I questioned what this was telling me.'

She cleared her throat. 'And what was it telling you?' she managed to ask, a tremor in her voice.

'That while I'd spoken nothing but the truth, it was more about the way I felt towards you.'

For a long moment, neither moved.

'Who's for a game of billiards, then?' Maxwell's voice shattered the highly charged air that was growing between them. 'Are we all playing? If so, we could organise a mini tournament for four, and end up with a grand winner. Is everyone up for that?'

Both Eleanor and James turned their attention to Maxwell, and joined the general chorus of agreement.

'Then why don't you and I go first, James, and the winner plays William? Charles will play whoever wins that game. That gives you longer with Alice, Charles, assuming the mothers have no intention of leaving the cool interior for some time yet.'

'Thanks, Maxwell,' Charles said with a broad smile at Alice.

'If we don't get through the tournament today,' Maxwell continued, 'we can carry it over to when you go to the paper factory. You'll be coming to the club afterwards, if I heard correctly. I'll join you in the factory tour if I can, but if it proves impossible, I could meet you here.'

'It sounds like a plan,' William said.

Eleanor nodded in agreement, feeling shaky as she did so.

In her exchange with James, in which a warmth had unmistakeably flown between them, there'd been nothing of the pretence that she and Harriet had talked about, not on her side, and not on his, she was sure.

WHEN THE MCKENNAS' tonga reached the Fletchers' house, Beatrice got down.

'Ask Alice to come back home, would you, please?' she called up to Ivy and Julia as the tonga started moving again.

'We'll speak to you tomorrow,' Eleanor told Alice as they drew up to her house, and she heard Ivy pass on Beatrice's message to Alice.

'I hope so,' Alice said, and she climbed down and headed back to her house, waving to Ivy and Julia as she passed them.

'You'll come in for a juice, won't you, Harriet?' Eleanor asked as she and Harriet got down in front of the Graingers' house. 'If our mothers say it's all right.'

Both mothers agreed with alacrity. Julia said she was going to sit quietly and read, and Ivy told them she intended to lie down as soon as she got back to her house. Eleanor's company would make a good substitute for hers, she added.

'I'm certain I'd be Harriet's second choice, Aunt Ivy,' Eleanor said primly. 'But as you're not available, Harriet will have to make do with me.'

'You took the words out of my mouth, Eleanor,' Harriet said with feigned gravity.

The two mothers smiled at each other, then Ivy turned and went along the crescent to her house.

Eleanor, Julia and Harriet went up to the front door. As they reached it, the butler opened it and stood aside to let them enter the cool of the hall.

'It's still unseasonably hot,' Julia said, wiping her brow with her white cotton handkerchief. 'Our discussion this afternoon has given me quite a headache, enjoyable though it was. I think I'll follow Aunt Ivy's example, and rather than read, leave the two of you to gossip about your friends, male and female.'

Eleanor and Harriet feigned expressions of surprise.

'I'm sure that's what you plan to do,' Julia said, a smile in her voice. 'It may amaze you to know that I was once your age.'

A SHORT TIME LATER, Eleanor and Harriet were sitting on the veranda, each with a glass of lemonade and a plate of shortbread in the middle of their table.

'While I like Alice,' Eleanor began, 'I'm not sorry she had to go home. I wanted to hear what you thought about this afternoon, mainly how you thought James seemed with her.'

'He's completely uninterested. It was clear he has no feelings at all for her, apart from liking,' Harriet said firmly. 'If he has designs on anyone, it's on you, Eleanor.'

Eleanor went red. 'I don't know that you're right about that, but I agree about Alice. He didn't pay her any attention. And as for Alice, she's clearly madly in love with Charles, and he with her. Anyone can see that.'

'What d'you feel about Maxwell?' Harriet asked. 'He's definitely taken with you, and he didn't show any interest in Alice. You must have seen him move his chair closer to you. For a ghastly moment I thought he'd end up sitting on your lap!'

Eleanor laughed.

'I also noticed that whenever James was about to say something to you, he cut James off,' Harriet continued. 'Maxwell clearly has designs on you. So which of them do you dream about – James or Maxwell?'

Eleanor laughed. 'What a vivid imagination you have. But you won't deflect me from asking you about William. You were inside with him for so long that I began to wonder if you'd eloped! You're so lucky that Aunt Ivy and Uncle

Arthur seem to like William and think him suitable. Alice has a real fight ahead.'

Harriet nodded. 'Poor Alice. I feel very sorry for her.'

Eleanor paused and bit her lip. 'I'm not saying that I think you're correct about Maxwell wanting to court me,' she began after a few moments of thought. 'But just in case you are, d'you think it'd be sensible to stop doing what we've recently got into the habit of doing, which is going up to the club in the day, rather than going into town to Sukha Haveli like we used to do?'

'What do you suggest?'

'That we go to the *haveli* instead of the club You could let James know if we were going to be there, and he'd tell William. If Maxwell was back at the club, and James and William were with us at Sukha Haveli, James might actually be able to complete any sentences he begins.'

'So it's James you want to sit with, is it?' Harriet said slowly. 'Not Maxwell.'

Eleanor stared at Harriet, her eyes opening wider.

'No, it's definitely James,' she said slowly. 'And I've only just realised it.'

Both were quiet for a moment.

'It feels funny to think of you and James together,' Harriet said at last.

'Nice funny or nasty funny?'

'Nice funny. We've been such good friends for so long, there's no one I'd rather have as a sister.' Harriet's eyes filled with tears.

They hugged each other, and then drew back. Both of them wiped their eyes.

'Let's talk about the picnic,' Eleanor said, 'or I'll start crying again.'

'Good idea.' Harriet leaned forward and took a piece of

shortbread. 'Kanak Vrindavan Garden's the perfect location. It's gorgeous there. I don't know why it's so long since we picnicked there. Not only is the view beautiful, but it's fairly close to where we live so it's easy to get to. So that's for three weeks on Sunday, and we've got the visit to the paper factory the week after next. I know that's really only for Alice and Charles's benefit, but it'll be fun. I haven't been there for an age.'

Eleanor's heart gave a sudden leap at the thought of seeing James again.

'I can't wait,' she said.

19

F *riday*

FRANK WALKED SLOWLY along the colonnaded pavement in front of the line of open-fronted shops that flanked the wide Johari Bazaar Road. While a number were selling brightly coloured saris, ankle-length *lehengas* and embroidered *juttis* for feet of every size, the majority of shops were selling gems.

He paused in front of one of the jewellery shops and stared down at the crowded display of Jaipuri jewellery made of gold, silver, diamonds and emeralds. What on earth should he buy, he wondered.

It was Beatrice's birthday the following day, and while he'd never bothered to get her anything to mark the day when they'd lived in Bayana, a public display of generosity to Beatrice in front of his new friends might engender an upsurge of warmth towards him, which could result in orders.

He had thought that in Johari Bazaar, the oldest market in the town, which was renowned for its wide range of exquisite gems, he would instantly find what he wanted. The trouble was, he didn't know what he wanted.

Gazing at the rows of sparkling gems, he realised that he didn't know what to look for, didn't know the right price to pay for the different gems, didn't know how to tell if a gem was fake. Some of the gems on sale in the bazaar would be made of paste, he was sure. But how would he know which ones?

And there was so much to see, so much variety, so much glitter and colour. Too much, in fact, to make a decision.

He should have asked for Maxwell's advice before he'd embarked upon such a quest, he thought, irritated with himself. Even though Maxwell had told him he didn't deal in gems, he was bound to have some knowledge of jewellery and be able to advise him.

Perhaps it'd be better to go to the jewellery stalls in Bapu Bazaar, he mused, staring blankly at the array of gems on the table in front of him. He might not feel quite so out of his depth in a bazaar he knew.

Yes, he'd do that, he decided. And if he didn't find anything, he'd be seeing Maxwell later that day and he could ask him then for advice.

He continued walking.

Hearing a familiar voice, he stopped abruptly and glanced across the street.

'What the—?' he muttered to himself as Maxwell emerged from one of the jewellery shops further back.

Without thinking, he took cover behind the terracotta column next to him.

Maxwell had been followed outside by two Jaipuri men, to whom he appeared to be giving instructions. Then the three of them stopped, shook hands, made a *namaste* to each other, and the two Jaipuri men returned to their shop.

Maxwell glanced quickly in both directions of the road, then, seeming to relax, he started walking in the direction of Bapu Bazaar.

Knowing that Maxwell would have to walk by him, he instinctively inched further back and slipped into the closest shop. His heart beating fast, he waited for Maxwell to go past him.

When Maxwell had gone by, he stood up and stared down Johari Bazaar Road at Maxwell's retreating back. He must be heading for Bapu Bazaar, he thought in surprise. He would be somewhat too early for the appointment they'd made for that afternoon, so he must be going somewhere else first.

But why had he said that he didn't deal in gems, when it looked as if he did?

He waited for a few minutes and then started to walk after him, but keeping well back.

To his annoyance, an elderly Jaipuri on a bicycle was cycling directly in front of him in the same direction as Maxwell was walking. Between the scraggy cyclist, a black-and-white cow ambling down the road, several tongas and clusters of pedestrians blocking the walkway as they studied the gems on offer, he lost sight of Maxwell.

Inwardly cursing the elderly cyclist, he hung around for a few minutes, anxious that Maxwell should be well out of the area before he proceeded towards Bapu Bazaar. It would have been embarrassing if Maxwell had come upon him, and even worse if Maxwell had thought he was following him.

Finally, sorry that he hadn't been able to see where Maxwell was going, but relieved that his presence hadn't been discovered, he continued to Bapu Bazaar. Reaching the temple where the two roads met, he turned right. Looking ahead, he couldn't see any sign of Maxwell, and he felt himself relax.

Deciding not to turn down the narrow road in which he had his showroom, he crossed over it and made his way to the southern corner of the bazaar where the air was heavy with the pungent incense from the cluster of temples there.

It was where the gem shops had congregated, and he thought he'd have a look there for a piece of jewellery, and after that return to his premises.

If he hadn't found anything, he'd ask Maxwell for advice when they spoke later that afternoon.

Would he tell Maxwell that he'd seen him shaking hands with jewellers in Johari Bazaar that morning, he wondered.

He didn't think so.

Not for any particular reason. It was just an instinctive feeling that if Maxwell had wanted him to know that he did business with jewellery dealers, he would have told him. And he certainly wouldn't have explicitly told him that he didn't deal in gems.

He reached the first gem stall and stood there staring at the display, uncertain what to look for in the face of so much choice.

It was no use, he thought in despair. He hadn't a clue. He'd have to ask Maxwell's advice, being careful how he did so. Thrusting his hands into his pockets, he went back up the road and turned towards his showroom.

· · ·

'It's got a marble veranda overhung with bougainvillea and jasmine vines that extends along the front and sides of each of the two storeys,' Maxwell told him, as he sat on the other side of Frank's desk, a beer in front of him. His eyes shone with pride and delight. 'It means that the house will be cool throughout the summer.'

'It's quite a surprise to hear that you're buying a house at such a relatively young age,' Frank said jovially, trying to swallow the envy he felt at Maxwell's ability to buy what sounded a much better house than the one he'd bought. 'So you got fed up with living at the club, then?' He attempted to sound pleased.

'I only ever intended to stay there temporarily. I stayed there longer than I'd planned as it was such a pleasant environment to be in. With so many friends and acquaintances regularly up there, I was never allowed a dull moment. Very importantly, the house I'm buying isn't that far from the club. Or from Victoria Crescent, for that matter. I imagine I'll be up at the club almost as much as when I was staying there.'

Laughing, he picked up his beer and took a drink.

Frank shook his head in wonder. 'I'm in awe of you, Maxwell. I know you've been in exporting for some years, but nevertheless, it's quite an achievement to be able to buy such a grand house for yourself.'

'It's kind of you to say so,' Maxwell said. 'It's been what I've wanted for some time now. I'm now at the right age to get married, and if I want a wife, I need a home.'

'Well, I take my hat off to you. The knowledge you have of which exports currently yield the highest return must be second to none.'

'For someone who's not been in the business for long, you're doing pretty well, too,' Maxwell told him.

'I'm not complaining,' Frank said hastily. 'On the contrary. You know how grateful I am to you for everything you've done and for what you've taught me. I couldn't have got this far without you. Thanks to you, I've avoided a lot of pitfalls and mistakes, and because of your introductions, I'm building up a body of suppliers much more quickly than I would've done if I'd been on my own.'

Maxwell smiled. 'I look on you as a friend, and friends help each other. Think nothing of it.'

'I want to make as much money as I can, and as quickly as I can, and I'm not ashamed of it,' Frank said. 'I'm sick of being the poor relation to Philip Grainger. I want people to look up to me, like they do to him, and for that I need financial success. I'm not afraid of hard work. After the fruitless struggle I had in Bayana with indigo, I need to make up for those wasted years, and I intend to do so.'

'No one should be ashamed of being ambitious. You and I are both ambitious. That's probably why we're such good friends.'

Frank nodded. 'All I hope is that it won't be too long before I'm making a really good income. If that makes me sound greedy, so be it.'

Maxwell finished his beer and replaced the bottle on the table. 'You could be seeing a huge improvement to your income fairly soon,' he said steadily. 'If you wanted to.'

Frank stared at him. 'What d'you mean?'

Maxwell put his hand in his pocket and pulled out six small canvas bags. He put them in the centre of the table and sat back.

Neither spoke.

'I've been in the business long enough to have picked up rumours of what's going on around me,' Frank said slowly. He raised his gaze from the bags and stared at Maxwell. 'I'd like to pretend I've no idea what's in the bags, nor why you've shown them to me, but what would be the point? I'm guessing they've got stolen gems inside. I'm not going to hold it against you, but I'd like you to tell me the truth.'

'That's correct.'

'And that's why you're making as much as you are?' Frank said.

'Again, correct. I think we're not both just ambitious, Frank, but we're also impatient,' Maxwell said with a wry smile. 'You certainly sounded that way just now. Impatient men are often willing to step off the straight and narrow if it's in their interests to do so. At least, *I* was. I'm wondering about you. In no time at all, you, too, could have a show-room on Amer Road.'

Frank looked back at the bags.

'But if I'm reading you incorrectly,' Maxwell continued, 'and you'd be unhappy to be a part of this, just tell me and I'll put the bags back in my pocket and leave them there.' He patted his pocket. 'If so, we'd forget the whole thing and carry on being good friends. I'll continue to help you as I've been doing, and everything you do will be entirely legal.'

'But I won't make as much as if I pick up those bags.' Frank stared at them thoughtfully. 'I take it you'd like me to include their contents in my next shipment for export,' he said at last.

Maxwell gave him a dry smile. 'Not immediately, but at some point before too long. But only if you feel you'd like to. I'll repeat that you don't have to do it – it's entirely up to you. If you don't want to be party to this, nothing between us will change.' He paused. 'You'll appreciate that I'm trusting you not to say anything to anyone else about this. This must remain between us.'

'Of course,' Frank said. He stared for a moment longer at

the bags. 'I don't know, Maxwell. I'd like a few minutes to think about it.'

He stood up, went across to a wall cupboard behind his desk, reached up for a bottle of whisky and two glasses, and returned with them to the table.

'I think we'd better have something stronger than beer,' he said, sitting down. 'I know I need it.' He poured whisky into the two glasses, pushed one across to Maxwell and sat back, nursing his glass.

'So how about going through the whole process,' he said, 'from the moment the gems are dug up from the ground to the moment they end up in a rich man's safe in Europe. How did you get into it?'

'You asked for it,' Maxwell said. He took a drink of whisky and began to tell Frank how he got into exporting stolen gems among his consignments. 'I think you'd like Paul,' he finished.

'I can't see why I wouldn't.' He hesitated. 'As you and Paul are already so successful and have got everything sewn up, why d'you need me?'

'That's a good question,' Maxwell said. 'It's because more people are stealing gems, so there's a greater supply. At the same time, the demand from overseas is increasing. There's a limit to how frequently I can export shipments before I arouse suspicion. Having someone else sending shipments to the addresses I've been given would be a tremendous help. My business would expand. No one wants their business to stand still. So this would help me a lot. And you, too, of course.'

Frank nodded slowly. 'You know me well enough to know that I'm in a hurry to get where I could've been by now if I'd started exporting much sooner. But as for smuggling, I'd never for a moment considered that.' He bit his lip.

'I suppose there's a first for everything, though,' he said finally. 'But if I wanted to stop at any time, would I be able to?'

'Of course you would. Is that a yes, then?'

Frank thought for a moment. 'Could gems be concealed in consignments of paper?' he asked.

'They can be hidden in anything,' Maxwell said. 'Why d'you ask?'

Frank shrugged. 'No reason. Then it's a yes, but with some reluctance. As you say, though, I'm impatient to make real money, and that makes it hard to resist your offer. And you've helped me a lot in the past, and in the present, too, so the least I can do is help you in return. I owe you that. I'll do it.'

Maxwell smiled warmly. 'Good man,' he said. 'When I next see you, I'll give you a pile of blank address labels for customs. They'll have my name on them as the exporter, and will need only the details required by the customs authorities, and the address to which they must go. You can use those for the first few gem deliveries, until you feel comfortable about everything. Then we'll use your labels. I'll order a pile that have you down as the exporter. I doubt you've sufficient at the moment.'

'I'd appreciate it.'

Maxwell raised his whisky glass. 'Let's drink to profitable enterprises for both of us.'

They clinked their glasses together. Frank drank first. After staring hard at Frank, Maxwell, too, put his glass to his lips.

20

L *ater*

DAYLIGHT WAS FAST FADING and dusk was falling as Frank sat on a stool in front of his showroom, deep in thought, and somewhat depressed.

It had been with misgivings that he'd agreed to Maxwell's suggestion of putting a few gems in some of his shipments of goods. He hadn't liked the idea at all. He'd always seen himself as a man who worked hard and was essentially honest. He had even refused to take short cuts with his indigo plants and had been scrupulous about observing the best processes.

But he hadn't really had any choice. After all the help that Maxwell had given him, both in Bayana and in Jaipur, he could have hardly turned his back on Maxwell's request. Maxwell wouldn't have asked for his help if he hadn't needed it.

Honouring his debt to Maxwell was one of the most important reasons for agreeing to the proposal. The money he'd make was secondary. This wasn't how he wanted to grow his business, and he'd only take part in the smuggling until he felt he'd paid Maxwell back. After all, Maxwell had said he could stop whenever he wanted.

But the debt to Maxwell wasn't the only reason he'd agreed to help him. It was that as he'd stared at the bags of jewels on the table, he'd had a sudden idea for a way of making Philip Grainger suffer. That was a reason equal in importance to the debt he owed Maxwell.

His gaze being on the dusty street in front of him, he hardly registered the lights coming on in the stalls in Bapu Bazaar, and the glow rising up on both sides of the road as the stallholders readied themselves for the hordes of people who came every night, bringing with them a wild exuberance, excitement and the sheer enjoyment of living.

And he hardly heard the sound of the night birds screeching and wild dogs barking, so focused he was on an idea that had come to him as Maxwell had been waiting to hear whether he was going to join him and Paul in their illegal enterprise.

He'd realised that if he arranged for gems to be concealed in an order for paper, he could alert the customs officials to the presence of gems in the packages, and Philip would be arrested.

The exporter named on the labels would be him, Frank Fletcher, but because he'd be the one who'd reported the matter, it would be assumed that Philip had concealed the gems inside the paper during the packing, and that he had discovered them quite by chance when he'd gone in to check on his order.

This would pay Grainger back for what he'd done all

those years ago, firstly when he'd cheated on him with Beatrice, and secondly, when he'd taken him for a fool by making him hand over Eleanor, which he'd never have done if he'd known the truth.

Bile rose in his throat as he remembered how Philip had stood there and deliberately lied to him.

As soon as he'd found out that Beatrice was pregnant with someone else's child, conceived at a time when he'd been away on a longer demonstration protest than usual, he'd gone straight to Philip, thinking him an honest, upright person. Blazing with anger at being cuckolded, he'd asked Philip if he had any idea of the identity of the snake who'd done the deed.

Instead of admitting his guilt as a better man would have done, Philip had connivingly supported what Beatrice had told him, that it had been a liaison with a passing exporter. As a result, instead of the baby going to an orphanage or to the home of people completely unconnected with Beatrice's adultery, Philip had ended up having his daughter to himself for eighteen years.

He was certain that Julia didn't know the truth. But one day she would. He'd make sure of that. The happy home was going to be broken up by Philip's arrest, and Philip would no longer be able to enjoy the company of Eleanor or his wife, not for a long time, if ever again.

When that moment finally came, he'd feel totally vindicated.

Realising this after Maxwell had confirmed that gems could be hidden in handmade paper, he had agreed to do as Maxwell had asked, and they'd drunk to it. He had intended to leave it at that, but Maxwell had raised the subject again as they'd continued sitting there, drinking in a companionable way.

'I'm curious as to why anyone would choose to ship gems in paper and not in shipments of rugs, for example?' Maxwell had remarked, a question in his voice.

He'd shrugged. 'Why not paper?'

Maxwell had stared at him thoughtfully. 'Is this to do with Philip?' he'd eventually asked.

He'd paused. 'Only indirectly,' he'd replied at last.

'Concealing gems in paper is possible,' Maxwell had said, 'as you can always find a palm to grease.' He'd paused. 'But there's a value to the gems you'll be given, and they'll be expected to reach their destination.'

He'd nodded. 'Of course.'

'It's not escaped my notice that you and Philip aren't the closest of friends,' Maxwell had said drily. 'Would I be wrong in guessing that at some point you plan to frame Philip for illegal activity?'

He'd nodded again. 'I won't lie to you, Maxwell, that had occurred to me. But it wouldn't be for a while. I'd choose a time that caused maximum damage to the happy family, and I assure you it'd be with poor-quality gems that I'd bought and paid for myself. They wouldn't be gems that had come from you.'

'I'm glad that's understood. What you do with any gems you buy is up to you. But I mustn't in any way be involved, nor my suppliers. You mustn't do anything that could lead back to me or to anyone with whom I work, and that includes the officials who turn a blind eye to my shipments. And when you plant the gems in your consignment of paper, it must be when there isn't an order from me in the factory, waiting to be shipped out. Is that clear?'

'I assure you, I won't take any chances,' he'd stressed. 'I'm assuming you have a contact at the factory and you'll tell me who it is,' he'd added.

'Of course,' Maxwell said with a smile.

'As I say,' Frank assured him, 'I won't be moving against Philip for a while. And when I feel ready to start, I'll let you know before I put my plan into action.'

'That's a very good idea.' Maxwell had looked at him curiously. 'On a slightly different topic, you obviously have it in for Philip. May I ask why?'

'It goes back some years,' he'd said. 'Nothing's gained by reliving the situation. Suffice it to say, he did the dirty on me, and I haven't forgotten it. I'd like to leave it at that.'

But now, looking back at their discussion as he despondently kicked the dust at his feet, he regretted making it quite so obvious that he planned to destroy Philip, and telling Maxwell how he was going to do it. He'd made himself more vulnerable than he liked.

Despite the warmth that lingered in the night air, he felt a chill within him.

The reality was, he had exposed himself to risk.

Maxwell was obviously interested in Eleanor, and it was possible he might decide to ingratiate himself with Philip by warning him that gems were to be smuggled in batches of his paper. And if Maxwell did that, he, Frank Fletcher, who'd put in the order, would be in deep trouble.

And he couldn't comfort himself by thinking that Maxwell would feel constrained by it being widely known in the exporting community, and therefore in the customs department, that Maxwell and Frank worked closely together, and that if Frank got into trouble, Maxwell might come under suspicion, too, and his exports be subject to an intense scrutiny.

He wouldn't fear that at all.

From the moment he told Maxwell he was ready to move against Philip, every one of Maxwell's exports would be above reproach, he was sure, and could withstand any in-depth search by non-corrupt authorities.

It meant that any attempt to counter an accusation against him by accusing Maxwell of smuggling would be found to be without substance.

Not that he would ever accuse Maxwell of anything. He'd never do that. While Maxwell seemed a normal young man who'd have no truck with violence, you never truly knew of what another person was capable.

All those years ago, he'd been wrong about Grainger's character, so it was possible that he could be wrong in thinking that Maxwell would eschew violence. The smuggling trade must have brought him into proximity with dangerous people, and even if Maxwell wasn't inherently violent in himself, he'd know people who were.

So as there was no way of knowing for certain how Maxwell would respond to any threat against him, it was much safer never to make one.

He didn't like feeling that Maxwell had a hold over him, and that although he had a hold over Maxwell, it was something it'd be too dangerous to use, but that was the situation he'd got himself into.

He sighed heavily. His only comfort was that Maxwell clearly needed another exporter working with him, and if he turned him in as a way of winning favour with Philip, he would have lost the exporter he'd just gained, and would be back where he'd started.

It wasn't that much comfort, though, and he was going to have to tread very carefully in the future.

WELL, well, Maxwell thought as he sat in the club's library, a glass of whisky at his side, a cigar in his fingers. What an unexpected end to his visit with Frank.

He wasn't a betting man, but he'd have bet anything that Frank would have instantly agreed to smuggle stolen gems. After all, throughout the months he'd known Frank, he'd known that he was an impatient man, greedy for money.

But he'd seen the dislike that had spread fleetingly across Frank's face as he'd eyed the bags of gems, and that had surprised him. So, too, had Frank's obvious reluctance to join him and Paul.

And it had alarmed him, too.

The other surprise was that Frank hated Philip Grainger as much as he did. Right from the night they'd met at the club, there'd been an unmistakeable tension between the two men that no amount of fake bonhomie had been able to disguise, but for Frank to dislike Philip so much that he was prepared to see him incarcerated and his family broken up had been something he'd never have been able to predict.

What could have caused such animosity on Frank's part? And on Philip's, too, as the antagonism between them seemed mutual?

Philip seemed a thoroughly pleasant, sociable man, a good businessman who was widely liked and respected in Jaipur. Personally, he liked Frank, and found him easy company, but Frank wasn't of the same calibre as Philip. Despite an unexpected attachment to honesty, Frank had a hardness and a greed that Philip Grainger appeared to lack.

Their dissension clearly went back to their time in Gujarat. One of these days he would find out the cause of it, of that he was sure.

He shifted his position in the chair. The animosity between Philip and Frank was interesting, he told himself, and it would have been even if he hadn't been seriously thinking about marrying Eleanor Grainger.

But that was his intention.

She was extremely pretty, with an attractive liveliness. Too often good-looking women thought that with their looks they need not worry about a personality, but there was a sparkle to Eleanor, and an interest in people and things around her, that meant she'd never come across as boring or self-obsessed.

He knew himself well enough to know that Eleanor wasn't really the type of woman he'd normally pursue. But now he was buying a house, he needed a wife to run it, to be a hostess to his friends and customers, and to be a fun companion between the sheets, all roles Eleanor would satisfactorily fill, he was sure. And he hadn't met anyone else in Jaipur he'd felt would be better qualified to do so.

The advantage of an alliance with her family was that it would increase his respectability, that was the deciding point. So all in all, meeting her at the very time he'd been thinking of settling down had been a stroke of luck.

So, too, had Frank's desire to harm Philip, as that had given him an idea.

Much as he hated to admit to carelessness, he had been guilty of it that day, and he was keen to get out of the position into which he'd put himself.

He should never have described the smuggling chain to Frank. He had gone into far more detail than he should have done, the drink having loosened his tongue, and although Frank had finally agreed to join him and Paul, there was a worrying lack of enthusiasm on Frank's part.

Instinctively he'd felt that Frank's involvement was more about his obligation to him, and his desire to hurt Philip

Grainger, than it was about the advantages he'd gain by joining the ring.

Frank's question about whether he could stop at any time had borne that out. He obviously intended to frame Grainger, and then, his mission accomplished, stop smuggling and start to accrue money solely by an honest route.

And he was naïf enough to think he'd be allowed to walk away from them, knowing what he knew.

It meant that he'd have to decide what to do about Frank, while at the same time look for a replacement for him. They badly needed another exporter to add to their ranks, but it had to be someone more committed than Frank.

Paul would be furious at the position in which he'd placed them. He knew Paul well enough to know that he would insist on Maxwell taking steps to ensure that they didn't find themselves under investigation. But fortunately, he was beginning to see a way of using the situation to his advantage.

When Frank decided to give effect to his plan to hurt Philip, he would be telling him well in advance. It meant he could intervene at the eleventh hour to save Philip from disgrace. Quite simply, he'd tell Philip what Frank was planning to do.

He'd advise Philip to go to the authorities and tell them he'd found some gems in a consignment waiting for delivery from his factory. There'd be no need for Maxwell's name to be mentioned. The customs officials would go to the factory, search the shipment, which would have Frank's name as the exporter on every label, and find the gems concealed within.

Frank, of course, would accuse him, Maxwell, of giving him the gems, and of smuggling stolen jewels himself. But as all of the shipments of exports sent off in the name of Maxwell Anderson, Exporter, would be gem-free well before the day on which Frank informed against Philip, Frank's accusations would be dismissed.

It meant that the sooner the framing of Philip began, the better. He'd encourage Frank to move faster than it sounded as if he'd intended to do, as he didn't want to waste much more of his time in helping someone who was going to end up arrested.

He very much regretted that he was going to have to bring about Frank's arrest. He felt comfortable with him, liked the man, and would miss his company. But on the bright side, Philip would know that he'd saved him from possible disgrace, and thus he'd appear to both Eleanor and her parents as a knight in shining armour. Any objections there might have been to him as a suitor for Eleanor would disappear.

All it would take was a little cleverness on his part. But he had cleverness in abundance, he thought with satisfaction.

I'll miss you, Frank, but thank you, anyway, he said in his head as he summoned the waiter and ordered another whisky.

STANDING in front of the *haveli* in which he and William had rooms, James thanked the elderly cyclist for the information he'd given him, and handed him a bag containing the agreed number of rupees.

Tightly holding the paper bag, the cyclist nodded, turned away, wheeled his bicycle down the drive to the road, and cycled off.

Having closed the door behind him, James went back to the small lounge they favoured and settled again in the armchair that was opposite William's.

'You're looking pleased with yourself,' William remarked. 'I take it we've finally confirmed that Anderson's working with Johari Jewellery.'

James nodded. 'That's right. It took long enough. I was beginning to think he might never go to their shop himself. Not only did he do so, though, but he was seen through the window to the upper room, photographed there, and then again when he left, and that confirms the link.'

'To be so careless as to go to the jewellers openly, and also to be allowed on to the upper floor where they do the cutting, indicates there could have been a problem with the cutting or with the designs he'd given them,' William said. 'He's obviously nervous about taking on something new, as anyone would be, especially if it's illegal. This is the first time he's dealt with uncut gems. But having jewels cut to his request shows that he's stepped up in the smuggling world, so it's just as well that we'll soon be able to put a stop to him.'

'And about time,' James said. 'We need to stamp out these rogue exporters before Jaipur becomes known as a centre of crime. With five teams, all pursuing different smuggling chains, it's a great start, but it's only a start. But with luck, when we arrest all the links in the chain, it'll send shockwaves through the criminal community, and a few names we hadn't come across might be whispered into our ears.' He paused. 'So when are we going to move against him?'

'It'll depend on our bosses in the customs department,' William said. 'It won't be until we can tell them that we've got every link in the chain, starting with the villages outside Jaipur and ending in Bombay, and the other four teams are in a similar position with their targets.'

James nodded. 'Obviously.'

'Also, while we've got a great deal against Maxwell,' William continued, 'I'm not sure how well it would hold up in court, especially if some of the officials were bribed to lie, which they would be. I think it's worth me making a greater effort to get closer to Maxwell and Frank in the hope I pick up some details that could flesh out our case.'

'Maxwell clearly likes you, so there's every chance you'll succeed.'

William shrugged. 'I hope you're right.'

'So do I! I'd be furious if he slipped away,' James said fervently.

'Indeed,' William said with mock gravity. 'Maxwell Anderson deserves to be locked up and the key thrown away, if only for his nerve in hotly pursuing one Eleanor Grainger!'

James laughed dismissively. 'Eleanor's not interested in me,' he said. 'Instead of your fanciful ideas about Eleanor, tell me how things are going with a certain Harriet McKenna. I expect you're looking forward to the picnic.'

William nodded. 'I am, and also to the visit to the paper factory, which happens first. Harriet will be there, too. I'm afraid, though, it's going to be more about work on both occasions than it is about Harriet,' he added ruefully. 'It'll be a difficult balancing act. To get what I want, Maxwell and Frank must see me looking and sounding like a man disillusioned with his job, who's anxious to get into a position where he can marry Harriet. But Harriet must see me as the man she'd like to marry, who'd be able to support her. It's not going to be easy.'

'You could start with your clothes,' James said, nodding towards William's jacket. 'The well-cut tailored look and the polished shoes could be somewhat at variance with your tale of verging on being a pauper.'

William held up his foot and studied his shoe. 'I see what you mean,' he said woefully.

21

The paper factory,
Wednesday week

'I DIDN'T THINK you were coming today, Maxwell,' Charles said, a note of surprise in his voice. 'Don't get me wrong, it's always a pleasure to see you, but you've already heard my talk a couple of times. In fact, we've just packaged an order from you, for which we're grateful. You must be a stickler for punishment to want to hear my spiel for a third time.'

Maxwell laughed. 'Maybe I am. But I found I had a free morning and felt like some company, so instead of waiting for you all to get to the club later today, I thought I'd join you this morning, too. If listening to you again is the price I have to pay for charming company, so be it,' he said. He smiled at Eleanor and then looked back at Charles. 'Carry on as if this is my first visit.'

'Thanks, Maxwell,' Charles said, and he turned to the rest of the group, which comprised Alice, Harriet, Eleanor,

James and William. Meera and Sita had been asked to wait outside the factory.

'Let's go, then. To begin, we have a lot to thank Gandhi for,' he told them as he led them into the first large hall of the factory. 'Handmade paper was having a shaky time under the British as they encourage the import of mill-made paper from Western countries, but Gandhi came to our rescue. On his return to India, he ordered handmade paper in bulk for his ashram and for his other associates. It led to a real revival in the handmade paper industry which is still going strong. We have a workforce of forty-five people.'

'Look at all those piles of cotton rags!' Alice exclaimed.

Charles smiled at her. 'We get sent cotton scraps from all over the country. We use them to make our paper. We make the paper from a number of natural materials, but not from wood, and we use natural dyes. It means that our handmade paper is stronger, lasts longer, and has an elegant natural look to it.'

'It's never occurred to me before, but why don't you use wood?' Maxwell asked, as they walked slowly through the hall, past large piles of cotton rags that had been separated into colours. 'There are enough trees in the Aravali Hills.'

'For paper that's made by hand, like ours, you wouldn't get the high whiteness and permanence that's often required,' Charles told him. 'Cotton is our main base at the moment, but we also use rose leaves, marigolds, cornflowers, bougainvillea, grasses and so on.' He picked up a handful of cotton pieces and let them fall through his fingers. 'We make these into a pulp,' he said. 'The amount of water you use for the pulp depends on the thickness you want for the paper and the colour you want.'

'You know so much, Charles,' Alice said, gazing at Charles with open admiration.

'I've been doing this for quite a while,' he told her, beaming with pleasure. He looked back at the others. 'After that, we press the pulp to extract as much water as possible, using a tray and a layer of muslin. It reduces the bulkiness of the paper and makes the sheets more compact. As there'll still be some moisture in the sheets, when they're pulled from the muslin, they're hung upstairs to dry in open areas of sunlight. This removes the last of the moisture.'

'How long does that take?' William asked.

'It depends on the weather,' Charles said. 'Generally, two to three hours in the sunlight in summer, and four to five hours in the winter. When dry, the paper is passed through a series of metal rollers, which makes it smoother and glossier. It can be cut to any size by what you'd call a guillotine. Look here,' he said, pausing. He indicated the machine next to him where two men were working. 'You can see it in action.'

They stood for a few minutes and watched as one worker pushed a measured pile of paper into the front of the machine, and then the other man, sitting high up on the other side of the machine, slid the cutting arm across the paper.

'With so much pulp to make, I take it you need a lot of water?' James commented.

Charles nodded. 'That's why the factory's where it is. We've access here to all the water we need. Right, we'll have a look at block printing. Then, after that, we'll look at where we store our shipments for export, and then take a look at the shop. You'll see what a wide range of things we make with our paper. To name but a few, there are notebooks, gift bags, writing paper, large bags for carrying goods and albums. And you'll see how varied our designs are.'

'And I think after that you'll deserve lunch at the club,

my friend, and maybe a hefty drink,' Maxwell said cheerfully.

Charles smiled. 'I don't know about that, but an afternoon with Alice would be very pleasant.'

Alice laughed happily.

AFTER THEY'D WALKED through the packaging and export area, which was a room into which only Philip, Charles, the packaging supervisor and his assistant were permitted to go, they headed for the gift shop.

'Darn!' Maxwell suddenly exclaimed. He stood still and felt in his jacket pocket. 'I seem to have dropped my pen. I know I had it at the start of the tour. If you'll excuse me a moment,' he said, a note of apology in his voice, 'I'll retrace my steps and look for it. It's my favourite pen.'

James and William glanced quickly at each other. Surreptitiously, James moved to the back of the group.

'You were about to show the others the uses to which you put your paper, Charles. Why don't you go ahead?' Maxwell suggested. 'It won't take me long to find my pen, I'm sure, and then I'll catch you up.'

'I admire your optimism amid this mountain of discarded cotton,' Charles said, laughing as he looked around him. 'This way, then.' He indicated that the others should follow him.

COMPLETELY UNAWARE THAT he was being watched from a distance by James, Maxwell turned and hurried towards the room where the orders were packaged, labelled and stored, ready to be transported to the station.

Reaching the room, he went up to the two distinct

sections containing blocks of paper, all of them wrapped and waiting for export, each of them individually labelled. On each label was the address to which they were going, full details of the factory where the paper had been made and from which it had been dispatched, and the details of the exporter who'd paid for the order and its delivery.

In the largest of the two sections of packages, Maxwell's name was visible on every label. There was another exporter's name on the packets in the smaller section.

As he walked slowly down the line of his goods waiting for shipping, he looked closely at the packages in each of the three tiers. Then he crossed to the smaller section waiting for export and studied the packaging of those blocks of paper, too. There was nothing different about the packaging of that exporter's goods from his.

He smiled to himself with satisfaction.

James had seen all he needed to, and he turned and went quickly back to the others.

It all looked excellent, Maxwell thought, glancing around him. He'd had no doubt at all that from a workforce of that size he'd find someone who wanted to make a little extra. It was a shame that someone wasn't Charles. Recruiting Charles had been his first thought, but he'd realised soon after he'd met him that Charles wouldn't be open to anything dishonest.

Fortunately, a lot of people were, though, he thought wryly, as with a last look at his order, regretful that it was going to be the last of his shipments with gems, he turned to go back to the others.

A few minutes later, he took his place alongside James and William who were standing at the rear of the group, deep in conversation, while the others were examining little pads of writing paper and matching envelopes.

'Found it,' he called to Charles, and he brandished the pen which had been in his pocket all the time. 'So my optimism was justified, ye of little faith.'

Charles gave him a thumbs up sign.

James moved closer to Maxwell. 'William and I were saying that we're very ready for a drink,' he said quietly. 'We think we've heard as much about paper as we want for a very long time. What about it? We thought we'd make a start on our journey to the club.'

Maxwell grinned. 'Count me in,' he said.

Glancing down at their feet as he walked behind them, he saw a light film of dust on James's polished shoes. William's shoes weren't just dusty, but were scuffed, too, he noticed.

So times really are hard for some, he thought, and he smiled to himself.

THE NIGHT AIR was still warm as James and William sat in one of the small side lounges in the *haveli* where they had rooms, each with a glass of brandy on the mahogany table between them.

'Are you still certain that neither Philip nor Charles is involved?' James asked William.

'As sure as I can be. I think both are essentially honest.'

James nodded. 'Me, too.' He paused and took a sip of brandy. 'I'm rather surprised that Maxwell risked going back to the forbidden packaging area when there were so many people around,' he remarked, putting the snifter back on the table. 'To anyone seeing him, it could've seemed a strange thing to do, reprehensible even.'

'I don't know,' William said. 'When you think of it, the whole area was fairly empty. With them closing early that afternoon, everyone was looking forward to getting home and you wouldn't expect the same degree of vigilance as you would on other days.'

'Nevertheless, he could have been caught,' James said, shaking his head.

William shrugged. 'He'd claim he was looking for his pen. He probably weighed up what was more important: avoiding having to come up with an excuse to explain his presence in a room he shouldn't have been in, or his need to check the appearance of his order, which I imagine was what he was doing.'

'I suppose you're right,' James said. 'If I'd been him, I'd have probably wanted to see that it all looked good, especially as we think it's the first batch of paper in which there are gems.'

William nodded. 'Maxwell's bound to be on edge. His details are on the label, even though the goods have been packed in Philip's factory and sent from there. If customs picked anything up, suspicion would fall on both Philip and Maxwell. Maxwell might be able to bribe himself out of trouble, but his concern would be that if the jewels were discovered, they'd be confiscated. He'd have lost a lot of money and might even be unable to pay what he owed the diamond cutters. In that case, he'd fear their wrath. Checking there was nothing suspicious about the packages would easily outweigh the risk of being caught.'

'What's the decision from our bosses?' James asked. 'Are we to seize the cargo here or let it head for its destination?'

'Both,' William said with a smile. 'We don't want to let a consignment with stolen gems go through, so we'll remove the stones before it sets off.'

James made a low whistling noise.

'We'll follow the load very closely at every stage of its

journey,' William continued, 'and confirm that we've got all the corrupt officials in our sights. The packages will be allowed to reach their destination, and then we'll see what happens when they're found to be free of gems. With luck, the names we'll get as a result of the recriminations among the thieves will help us close down this particular line.'

James thought for a moment. 'It means you'll have to tell Philip what you're doing, doesn't it? If you stopped the goods en route and removed the gems, it would send a warning signal to the smugglers. They must be removed before the cargo leaves the factory.'

'And that's what will happen. But there's no need to involve Philip. We've copies of the keys, and our people will be going into the factory when it's officially closed. They're going in this coming Sunday, in fact, while we're all at church.'

22

*K anak Vrindavan Garden,
Sunday, a week later*

FROM HER PICNIC table under the pavilion in the centre of Kanak Vrindavan Garden, Eleanor glanced back up at the trees and bushes that lined the steep hill behind them. Her gaze reached the top of the hill, and for as long as it was visible, she followed a wall that she knew ran for miles, separating the green part of the region from the large semi-desert area.

Turning back, she looked around at the other tables set up by the stewards and cooks assistants.

The servants had gone ahead of the picnickers to the pavilion and arranged the tables and food. They knew their employers liked to have a view of the Man Sagar Lake on one side as they sat at their tables, and the sweep of the hills on the other. Apart from the tables at which the families and friends were sitting, there were three other tables inside the pavilion.

On one there were pans of small grilled kebabs, a large bowl of vegetable curry, and a dish containing bite-sized portions of chicken cooked with fenugreek leaves and cream, plus a basket of naan bread and one of chapatis. On another, there were plates of scones filled with jam, small iced cakes and little squares of chocolate cake with walnuts.

On the third table stood a selection of fresh fruit juices and a large jug of the beer cocktail that the men had taken to making by adding a glass of palm wine to a fifth of a bottle of imported beer, some sugar and ginger, and perhaps dried peel of limes and oranges. They said it went better with curry than anything else.

Her gaze moved to the steps that led down from the pavilion. On the grass at the foot of the steps there was a pile of coloured mallets, balls and croquet hoops. She looked up from the items on the grass and stared ahead of her at Man Sagar Lake, a shining ribbon of blue that lay beyond the end of the garden.

She glanced at Alice, who was sitting on the other side of the table, and saw that she was throwing surreptitious glances in the direction of Charles, who was engrossed in a conversation with Eleanor's parents. Alice's and Harriet's parents were at the next table talking to each other.

It had been a perfect day, she thought as she sat comfortably back in her chair. The only thing that could have improved it would have been if she and James had found a few moments to talk to each other.

But the day was far from over, she told herself. James had been sitting with William and Maxwell, but William was sure to want to talk soon with Harriet, and then, assuming they could evade Maxwell, she'd have a moment or two alone with James.

She looked back at Alice. She hadn't moved. She was still staring at Charles. She'd never once looked at James. The mothers had been so wrong, Eleanor thought.

As if sensing Eleanor's eyes on her profile, Alice turned towards her and smiled happily at Eleanor and Harriet. 'I've really enjoyed today,' she said.

'That's exactly what I was thinking,' Eleanor said, and she looked around for James.

Feeling the need to account for why she'd been studying the other tables, she quickly continued, 'It was an inspired idea to build a garden here, with the lake on one side and the Aravali Hills all around. It was the same maharaja, Sawai Jai Singh II, who founded Jaipur and built the observatory and lots of other places, who designed the garden. He wanted it for entertainment and recreation.'

'Why's he always called Sawai when his name is Jai?' Alice asked. 'Is that a religious title?'

'Not exactly,' Eleanor said. 'He was given the title by a Mughal emperor. His great-grandfather had been the wisest of ministers, and the young Jai Singh II, when he was eleven, answered a question the emperor put to him so wisely that the emperor said that Jai Singh was of the same intelligence as his great-grandfather, plus a quarter more. Sawai means one and a quarter. It was added to his name, and to the name of all the maharajas of Jaipur since then.'

'Is this another lesson?' Maxwell asked cheerfully, appearing at the side of their table, his chair in his hand. 'If it is, may I, too, be a pupil?'

'I'm afraid we've just finished today's short historical offering, Maxwell,' she said lightly.

'Don't worry. I can read Alice's notes. If that's all right with you, Alice?'

Alice pulled an apologetic face. 'I'm sorry, Maxwell. It would have been if I had any, but I haven't. I should've bought my writing paper and pen, but I didn't think there'd be any need. Not for a picnic in a place with a view we're used to seeing. Tomorrow I'll probably be begging Eleanor and Harriet to tell me again what Sawai means so I can write it down, but the most I can do today is take a few photographs. I've got the camera with me.' She picked up the Brownie camera and waved it at him.

'Then I'll have to be patient and wait till the book is finished,' he said.

He smiled at her.

At the sound of a chair scraping against the marble floor, he glanced back to the table where he'd been sitting with William and James. 'I think James is heading for the croquet mallets. He said he wanted a game. William's wandering aimlessly on the grass and he doesn't look as cheerful as he normally does. I think I'll go across to him and see if there's anything I can do to buck him up.'

He stood up and stretched himself. Then, thrusting his hands into the pockets of his lightweight trousers, he ran lightly down the pavilion steps and walked quickly over to the section of lawn where William was standing.

'That's so annoying,' Harriet said, watching Maxwell reach William. She turned to Alice and Eleanor. 'I was about to suggest that the three of us leave our game of croquet till later and go for a walk that ends up where William is. Now I can't. If we'd been able to do so, I'm sure Charles would have joined us, Alice. I hate to say it, Eleanor, but Charles seems less than thrilled to be talking to your father. I bet Uncle Philip is going on and on about the factory.'

Eleanor glanced at her father and Charles. 'Knowing Papa, you're right. Well I'll soon put an end to that.' She caught her father's eye and gave him a stern look. Then she looked back at Harriet and Alice and laughed.

'I'm sure he'll have got the message,' she said. 'Shall we start a game of croquet? We could play till Maxwell and William have finished speaking. They can't have much to say to each other so they'll probably stop talking very soon.'

'I hope you're right,' Harriet muttered.

'I TAKE it you've had enough of the jollity and aren't in the mood for croquet?' Maxwell said as he reached William.

William gave him a dry smile. 'You can put it that way if you like.'

'Which means?'

'That I'm not really in the mood for this at all today. Don't get me wrong,' William said hastily, 'I think the picnic's been really well organised, the arrangements for the tables and so on, and the food. It's just that I've got a lot on my mind. I came over here to leave the others to get on with having fun. I'd hate the sight of my depressed face to ruin the rest of the day for them. That would be very unfair of me. The cooks in all three households would have done a superb job in vain.'

He hesitated a moment. 'If the rumour's correct, Maxwell, you've bought a house. Is it safe to assume, there-fore, that for the next picnic there'll be four cooks contributing?'

Maxwell laughed. 'So that's what you and Frank were talking about at the table, was it, or at least one of your topics of conversation? He's the only other person I've told about the house. But yes, I decided I've been at the club for long enough, and as I intend Jaipur to be my base for the foreseeable future, getting a house seemed the sensible thing to do.'

'I hope you aren't annoyed with Frank for telling me,' William said, injecting a note of concern into his voice. 'I think he was just trying to cheer me up. I'd been feeling somewhat downcast, and I'd again brought up the subject of doing a bit of exporting. To demonstrate how successful an exporter could be, he cited you and Arthur.'

'How flattering to be mentioned in the same sentence as Arthur,' Maxwell said drily. 'I don't know if I deserve such a place, at least not yet, but I hope to do so before too long.' He cleared his throat. 'I'm sorry to hear that you've been feeling low, my friend,' he said sympathetically. 'If it would help, you can ask me anything to do with exporting. Or buying a house,' he added with a little laugh.

William gave a loud sigh. 'Well, it won't be about buying a house. I won't be in a position to do so for a long time, not the way I'm going,' he said, his voice despairing. 'To be honest, I'm getting very disillusioned about working for the government. I don't quite know what's gone wrong, but something has. I seemed to get off to a brilliant start. I rose fast in Madras and appeared to have a promising career, and then I was sent here.'

Maxwell nodded. 'When you came to Jaipur, James sang your praises and said how highly you were rated as a government officer.'

'Much good that did me,' William said bitterly. 'I knew when I came here that, being a princely state, it's the maharaja's team which is responsible for most of the administrative departments in Jaipur, not the British government, and that's not going to change. Or not until India becomes independent from us, which I'm sure will happen one day.

So I'm stuck in Public Works, and the only alternative, Revenue, wouldn't have been any better. James seems quite happy with his lot, but I'm not James.'

'So it's just that the work's boring, is it?'

'The pay's not great, either. When Frank told me about your house, I was so jealous. It's not just about having a house of my own, it's what it could lead to.'

Maxwell frowned. 'I must confess you've lost me there.'

'I'm talking about marriage. You must know that I find Harriet very attractive, more than that, she's quite wonderful. I'd love to marry her but I doubt very much that Arthur would think my income good enough to do so or my career prospects satisfactory. That's why I thought about dabbling in the export business. I saw it as a way of adding interest to my day, and making some money at the same time. But I'm now wondering whether I shouldn't leave the government service and make exporting my career.'

'You could be doing Arthur a disservice. Money isn't everything. Harriet's happiness will matter more to him.'

'I'd like to think so, but I live in the real world. And so does he. He'd never agree to me marrying her in my present situation, and he shouldn't. He'd want to be sure that she'll be supported in the manner to which she's become accustomed, and I'm not able to do that. Also, as Arthur's an exporter, he might have more time for me if I was an exporter, too, provided, of course, that I was successful.'

'I can see what you mean,' Maxwell said slowly. He thought for a moment. 'Why don't we meet at the club on Friday evening and talk about getting you started? At a later stage, there may be things you can learn from Frank, but for the first few weeks it'd be better if I was the one who introduced you to the various facets of the job.'

'That's very kind of you, Maxwell,' William said fulsomely. 'But only if you've got the time.'

'I can always find time for a friend,' Maxwell said with a smile. 'And to be honest, Frank hinted that he'd reached a point where he'd rather not have anyone watching over him, trying to learn from him. He's ready to stand on his own two feet, but he doesn't want to be observed while he does so. He'll make mistakes, as we all did, and it's better that you don't see them.'

'That makes sense,' William said. 'I'm very grateful to you, Maxwell. Not everyone would be so generous with their time.'

'Not at all. It's a pleasure to help a fellow exporter,' he said with a smile. 'I'd hang on to the job you've got for the moment, though, if I were you.'

'If you think I should. I'm just worried that having to go to the office might hamper my chances of meeting the people who make the goods I want to export.'

Maxwell looked thoughtful. 'That's certainly a consideration, but one for further down the line, I think. You need to walk before you can run, if you'll excuse the cliché. In a couple of weeks I'll take you to meet some of the village co-operatives. You'll find your first suppliers from among them.'

'That's very kind of you,' William said, his voice heavy with gratitude. 'And you say that Frank won't mind me not following him? I originally asked him to help me, you know?'

'He won't, William, I assure you. In fact, I'll tell him today that I've suggested you follow me, not him.' He turned to go. 'I see that my timing's perfect,' he said, grinning back at William over his shoulder. 'A certain young lady is heading straight for you, determination on her face. I'll get off to Frank without further ado.'

THE TIMING certainly couldn't have been better, Maxwell told himself as he started to walk back to the pavilion, where Frank and Beatrice were talking to the Graingers and the McKennas.

He'd explain to Frank that it was better that William didn't get too close to him while he was finding his way with the gems. But the real reason was that William had to be kept well away from Frank until Frank was completely out of the picture. None of them, William included, must be tainted by Frank's exposure as a smuggler.

That was going to happen even sooner than Frank had anticipated.

Keen to get things going, he'd already ordered a few gems of poor quality that Frank could arrange to have concealed in what would be his first shipment of paper, and he'd have them in less than a week.

Before the afternoon was over, he'd tell Frank that he'd soon be able to give him the gems, but that he need not pay for them until he'd made a bit more money from his exports.

He'd also give Frank the name of his contact at Philip's factory, and tell him where he'd find him. And he'd give him a number of labels addressed to the destination he could use for his consignment, which was actually the address of a disused warehouse.

If anyone followed it through, they'd think that Frank had mistaken the date that the warehouse, known to have been a destination for stolen goods, had been taken out of use. The labels would have the details of Frank's company as well as the address of the recipient and the information required by customs.

Then, on the day that Frank told him the gems had been concealed in the consignment of paper, and that he intended to report Philip the following morning before the goods could be shipped out, he, Maxwell, would get in there first with a tip-off to customs about Frank.

So Frank would soon be out of the way, and William was now his focus.

But that was for the future.

For the present, it was imperative that everything appeared to continue as normal, lest Frank take fright. The village workers in each of the three co-operative groups that he'd helped Frank set up in different villages, who were making the small rugs and doormats to be shipped by Frank to Europe via Bombay, must continue with the orders they were working on. He would take them over after Frank had been discredited.

However, unknown to Frank, whose payment for the orders included an extra for each supervisor overseeing the concealing of gems, the supervisors were receiving an additional sum, paid by him, to make absolutely sure that no gems were hidden in any of Frank's orders.

They were to exchange the address labels given to them by Frank for labels that would deliver the gem-free shipments to legitimate buyers. To do otherwise, when anything associated with Frank was likely to be checked en route, would risk the gems being impounded, and a lot of money being lost.

This would continue until it was safe to start concealing gems again.

By which time, William might be on board.

So all in all, things had gone very well that afternoon, he

thought with satisfaction as he started walking towards the table where Frank and Beatrice were sitting with the Graingers.

Struck by the expression on Frank's face as he glanced in Philip's direction, his steps slowed, and he frowned.

Every time he saw the two men together, it was clear how much Frank disliked Philip.

He wondered if Philip's attitude to Frank was as hostile, and he looked at him. He definitely showed a degree of discomfort at being with Frank. Despite making an attempt to look relaxed and interested in the conversation, to anyone watching him closely, he wasn't succeeding.

Instinct told him that the cause of their dissension could be something that might be to his benefit. Not that it really mattered in the way he'd once thought it might. Frank would soon be off the scene, and he, Maxwell, would be with Eleanor, who would be grateful that he'd saved her father from possible ruin.

Nevertheless, it would be interesting to know what had happened in the past to cause their mutual dislike, and it could be useful information to have if Philip and Eleanor didn't react to his heroic intervention in the way he anticipated.

What's more, if it was something that painted Philip in a bad light, it could be useful leverage to have over him if ever he wanted Philip to take a more active role in what would be happening in his factory before too long.

Yes, he'd be wise to see if he was able to find out anything, he decided.

'Can I join you?' he asked as he reached the table where the two families were sitting. Without waiting for a reply, he sat down.

23

'Hello, Harriet,' William said with a broad smile as she approached him.

'Hello, William,' she said shyly. She glanced over her shoulder at Eleanor, James, Alice and Charles. 'You go ahead and start the game,' she called to them. 'I'll join you in a few minutes.' She turned back to William. 'Did you enjoy the picnic?'

'I did indeed,' he said. 'And I'm about to enjoy it even more, now that you've come across to say hello.'

She blushed. 'I would've come sooner, but you were talking with Maxwell and I didn't want to disturb you.'

'Feel free to disturb me any time you want,' he said, his voice warm.

She looked up at him, her eyes hopeful.

'I hope you mean that,' she said awkwardly. 'I like the idea of disturbing you very often.' She laughed with embarrassment. 'I'm afraid that sounded very forward,' she added. 'I'm glad Mama didn't hear me.'

He took a step towards her and stared down into her face.

'I'm glad *I* did, though. You put into words what was in my head. I hope you'll soon be able to disturb me whenever you want. I love you, Harriet,' he said, 'and as soon as I'm in the position I need to be in, I'll be asking your father for your hand in marriage. If you'd like me to, that is. Would you?'

Her face broke out into a broad smile. 'Oh, yes, please.'

'Even though I'm quite shabbily dressed?' he said teasingly.

'I don't mind what you wear. I love you, William.'

'And I love you very much.' He cleared his throat. 'This is going to sound a little strange,' he said, lowering his voice, 'and I must ask you to trust me. But for several reasons, I'd rather we kept our feelings to ourselves until I'm in a position to propose to you.' He took a step closer to her. 'Believe me, I feel so very happy and I can't wait to shout my happiness to the world. It's important we wait, though,' he said with a sense of urgency. 'But it won't be for long, dearest Harriet.'

'Do you mind if I interrupt you?' At the sound of her father's voice, Harriet gasped. She spun round and faced him, her face pale.

'Your mother has something she wants to ask you, Harriet,' Arthur said gently. 'You'd better go back to her now. I suggest you join in the game of croquet afterwards. I'll keep William company for a bit.'

With a nervous glance at her father, Harriet turned from William and went back to the pavilion.

'So... William,' Arthur said, when Harriet was out of earshot. 'That looked intense. And did I hear the words "dearest Harriet"?'

'You did, sir. I love your daughter and I was telling her that.' He paused, and his voice took on a serious note. 'I was also asking Harriet not to tell anyone that I've declared my feelings to her. For various reasons, we must keep this to ourselves. I must ask the same of you, sir. I intend to ask you for Harriet's hand in the not-too-distant future, but I prefer that not to be known at this time.'

'I see,' Arthur said. 'Even though you've not yet formally asked for my blessing, I imagine that at this point I should ask about your prospects.'

William cleared his throat.

Arthur put up his hand to stop him. 'As I say,' he continued, 'I *should* ask you that at this juncture, but I'm not going to. When we first met you, my wife and I thought you seemed a steady, personable young man, and it was easy to see, so did Harriet. So we asked James to tell us what he knew of you as a person. It's obvious that he thinks very highly of you, and that's good enough for us.'

'Thank you very much, sir.'

'I've no idea exactly what James does all day, and nor you. But knowing James to be thoroughly upright and moral as a person, and being aware of his high regard for you, I'm happy to remain in ignorance about the activities of you both.'

'Thank you, sir.'

'Whenever you decide you're in a position to ask for Harriet's hand in marriage, be sure you'll have a warm reception. But until then, I won't be saying anything to anyone about your intentions, not even to Harriet.' He paused. 'For once there's nothing planned for after church next Sunday. As I imagine you would like to spend some time with Harriet, and she with you, why don't you join us for a late brunch? James will be there, so anyone who knew you were coming to lunch would think it was as James's friend.'

'Thank you, sir. I should like that very much.'

'And as for your career as an exporter,' Arthur added with a wry smile, 'I think we'll take it as said that you'll be discussing anything you need to know about exporting with someone other than me. I shall nevertheless tell anyone who asks that you approached me for help, but I told you I was too busy to oblige. Therefore, we can eliminate exporting as a topic of conversation now or at any time in the future.'

William opened his mouth.

'There's no need to thank me again, William,' Arthur said with a wry smile, 'if that's what you were about to do. I already consider myself thanked for anything I've done that deserves your gratitude, both today and in the next few months.'

'Then thank you, sir, for the final time,' William said.

Arthur nodded. 'I'll tell Ivy that you'll be joining us for brunch on Sunday, and leave it at that. We'll look forward to seeing you at church beforehand.'

He turned to go back to his table.

For the sake of appearances, William suppressed the desire to smile, but forced a look of misery to his face.

Seeing her father coming up the pavilion steps and towards her, Harriet stood up, took a few steps towards him, and then stopped. Arthur smiled as he reached her.

'We had a pleasant chat about nothing in particular,' he told her. 'Oh, and he'll be coming to brunch next Sunday. James mentioned that there were some things he wanted to discuss with him.' He gave her a smile, went past her and sat down next to Ivy.

Harriet went across to William, her face anxious.

. . .

'I WONDER WHAT THAT WAS ABOUT,' Frank said quietly to Beatrice, as he looked over his shoulder at William and Harriet who were standing close to each other, talking. 'He doesn't look the happiest of men.' Turning round, he said loudly, 'Come on, Beatrice. Up you get. Let's go and have a stroll. We'll get Alice and she can join us. If you'll excuse us,' he said to Maxwell, Philip and Julia.

They nodded and watched Beatrice follow Frank from the pavilion.

Julia stood up. 'I thought Frank was surprisingly slow in realising that Charles and Alice have been together for almost all the afternoon. I think I'll go and see if the girls need me to take Alice's place in the game,' she said. 'Try not to talk about business, though,' she added with a laugh.

The stewards, who had been busying themselves organising gin gimlets and whisky for those who wished, and fresh pineapple, orange juice and lemonade for those who preferred a soft drink, came round with a tray of drinks.

Maxwell took a whisky and settled comfortably in a position from which he could see who was talking to whom. He smiled across the table at Philip.

'I take it all is well with my order,' he said. 'If there're any problems, let me know. And Frank has some orders for you, too, I believe. But Julia's right, we shouldn't talk about business on such a lovely day. We'll talk about the picnic instead. It's a much better idea. Have you enjoyed it?'

Philip shrugged. 'About as much as I usually enjoy a picnic. I think it's something for the women, rather than the men. If a person's been working all week, there's nothing more pleasant than having a quiet Sunday, and today has been anything but quiet. However, the servants did us proud. The organisation was excellent and you couldn't fault the food. And I suppose it would be rather curmudgeonly of me if I didn't admit to enjoying the company of my child. I don't seem to see Eleanor very often these days, and it's been very pleasant to spend a little time with her today.'

'I can well believe that,' Maxwell said. He cleared his throat and again shifted his position on the chair. 'Eleanor is quite charming, Philip. You must be extremely proud of her.'

Philip nodded. 'I am.'

'Of course, it's not quite the same as having a child,' Maxwell said in a conversational tone, 'but I'm very proud of my house. It's the first house I've bought. Also, in addition to the house, I'm making some improvements to my show-room. I'm extending its frontage on Amer Road. Both things have given me a real sense of achievement.'

'As they should!' Philip exclaimed. 'Congratulations, Maxwell. Your showroom was already impressive, and it sounds as if it'll soon be even more so. To have such a show-room, and on Amer Road, no less, is a real achievement. So, too, is to buy a house at such a young age. You've every right to be proud. When do you move into the house?'

'That's yet to be decided,' Maxwell said. 'I've asked for some tiling to be done, and some changes to the flooring, and both will take time. But as I'm very comfortable at the club, it's no punishment to stay there a little longer. I don't want to move into the house until everything's been done to my satisfaction.'

'Quite right, too.'

'There is one other thing, however, that could improve my life,' Maxwell said. 'It's something you could help me with.'

'Me, dear boy?' Philip asked in surprise. 'In what way can I help?'

'It's about your beautiful daughter,' Maxwell began, a

trifle hesitantly. 'Over the weeks that I've come to know Eleanor, I've realised how wonderful she is. Just as I was ready to buy a house, I'm now ready to take a wife and I've fallen in love with Eleanor. I hope I'm not deluding myself in thinking that she'd look favourably on me. I should like your permission to call on you and to take Eleanor out. Duly chaperoned, of course,' he added quickly.

He waited.

Philip coughed. 'I don't really know what to say. You tell me that you sense Eleanor's interest in you, but I'd rather assumed that her interest would one day lie in a different direction. Perhaps I've been wrong in my assumption.' He paused.

'I've certainly felt a warmth towards me,' Maxwell said quietly. 'Of an entirely suitable nature, I hasten to add. It's given me reason to hope.'

'I see.' Philip thought for a moment. 'Look, I'll be honest with you, dear boy. I'm wondering if perhaps you're a little old for Eleanor. You must be at least nine or ten years older than she is, and you're very much a man of the world. A successful man, I can see. But it's not just age. Eleanor had a governess for all of her school years, which means she's led a somewhat sheltered upbringing.'

'I appreciate that, sir.'

'She's only just starting to go out into the world and meeting a wider range of people,' Philip continued, looking anxiously at Maxwell. 'Not a very wide range of people, but more than she will have known in her schoolroom days. And I must admit that I'd prefer it if she wasn't attached, if that's the right word, quite so soon. Put bluntly, I should like her to get to know more people before she enters into any formal arrangement. It's only by doing so that she'll be sure of choosing someone with whom she'll be happy for the rest of her life.'

'I understand, sir,' Maxwell said quietly.

'That doesn't rule you out, Maxwell,' Philip added hastily. 'Not at all. You and Eleanor will continue to meet as you've been doing recently, and if it becomes clear over the passage of time that it's you she'd like to be with, I'll certainly give you my blessing. But let's not move too fast, lad.'

'What you say makes sense, sir.' He attempted to smile. 'I shall do my best to be patient.'

'Good man.' Philip stood up. 'Now, I'm going to see what my wife is doing, and then see how the croquet is going. Perhaps Julia will want to join me in playing the winning pair. And William might want to play. It could take him out of himself. He looks as if he's got the cares of the world on his shoulders.'

Maxwell watched Philip walk across the lawn to Harriet and William, whose conversation with Frank, Beatrice and Julia had just been interrupted by Ivy and Arthur, go up to William and clap him encouragingly on the shoulder, and then say something to Julia.

He saw Frank scowl and casually move to the other side of Beatrice.

He glared at them all.

I'LL FIND out what that's about, he promised himself. And if it's bad, I'll certainly use it against Grainger when there's an occasion to do so.

Philip wouldn't have hesitated to give his approval if William had asked to be allowed to court Eleanor, he thought with rancour. He wouldn't be bothered about

William's age, nor that Eleanor had been given a sheltered upbringing, nor that she'd been exposed to only a limited number of people.

If it had been William who'd asked, he wouldn't be bothered about William's income. Even if he'd thought that William's pay left a lot to be desired, he would have seen William as an employee of the British government, with a secure job, and with the right sort of background, and he'd have willingly sanctioned their engagement.

Clearly Philip Grainger didn't think that he, Maxwell, despite the visible success that should have made his background irrelevant, was good enough to marry his daughter, and was hoping that any attraction towards him that Eleanor might feel would disappear if he left it for long enough.

And suppose it had been James who had asked to be a suitor for Eleanor, what would Philip have said?

Would he have turned James down, too?

He didn't think so, he thought bitterly. Like William, James, with his nice little government job, and his demonstrably solid background, would be just the sort of man that Grainger would want for his daughter.

Well, Philip Grainger would be sorry he'd rejected him, for rejected was how he felt.

He'd stop wasting time wondering what the secret was and make a real determined effort to find out. He'd start the following Sunday. He'd surprise them all by turning up at All Saints' Church, something he rarely did, and by joining in with the general conversation that took place in front of the church after the service. It was just the sort of environment where he might pick up something useful.

He'd have a few words with Frank, too, after the church, and tell Frank that he'd call at his premises the following morning as he had something to give him. Frank would realise that he was about to be given the cheap gems and labels he needed.

He'd already arranged to see William on the Friday evening before that, so the process of absorbing William would have started. He very much hoped that he'd succeed in recruiting William. He would be an excellent man to have in his ring. Working as he did in the administration building, William was in a superb position to pick up useful titbits of information.

He'd suggest to William that the week after that they go to a village he'd had his eye on for a while, and in which he'd been instrumental in forming a co-operative group of the villagers with skills in making carpets and rugs.

Frank had never been to that village, and he was hoping it might be the first of William's list of contacts.

WHY HAD he rejected Maxwell's suit, Philip asked himself as he took his leave from William and Harriet and started to take a solitary stroll up the hill, pausing occasionally to admire the large bushes of crimson bougainvillea that proliferated on either side of the dusty track.

But he couldn't find in himself a good reason why he had discouraged Maxwell from pursuing Eleanor. He sat heavily down on a clump of stone. He just knew, however, that the idea of Eleanor with Maxwell made him uneasy.

Yet, if he were being truly honest, he would admit to himself that he, too, had noticed a partiality on Eleanor's side for Maxwell's company, so it wasn't just a fanciful wish on Maxwell's part. But as she also seemed to enjoy being with James, he hadn't given it any thought. But maybe he should have done. Maxwell had obviously taken it seriously.

He fervently hoped that Maxwell was mistaken, because if he hadn't been, the subject of him courting Eleanor was certain to come up again in the future. And while he'd be as reluctant to agree in the future as he was in the present, without any good reason on which to base his refusal, in the face of any protest by Eleanor, he might feel compelled to give them his blessing.

He must talk to Julia about this, and ask her what her instincts were telling her about Maxwell.

Yes, the problem was his instinct.

He hadn't anything to go on against Maxwell, but instinctively, he sensed that Maxwell wouldn't be above a little dishonesty.

It wouldn't stop him from doing business with him, however, as their business dealings were conducted with the utmost probity. But there was something he didn't really trust about Maxwell, though he couldn't put his finger on why he should feel that way.

After all, Maxwell was a hard worker and had made a success of his company, as evidenced by his stylish showroom. And buying a house at his age further testified to his business acumen. Perhaps, however, it was that he'd made rather too much money too quickly, and that was suspicious in itself.

He couldn't escape a niggly feeling at the back of his mind that, with some of the Jaipur exporters known to have found an irregular way of making money, Maxwell might well have been drawn towards them.

Not that he'd seen any evidence of that, he quickly told himself.

And he had no qualms about the cleanness of Maxwell's paper orders for export. As Maxwell was a new customer, he'd been scrupulous in overseeing the packaging of his orders. And on the few occasions that he or the packaging supervisor had been forced to leave the packaging area, he'd always charged the assistant foreman with continuing the close supervision.

Nevertheless, his niggly feeling wouldn't be quelled, and if ever there was to be found any substance to it, he wouldn't want Eleanor to be inside Maxwell's orbit.

Fortunately, Maxwell hadn't attempted to argue his case.

But that in itself could be seen as a worry, he thought frowning.

While Maxwell's restraint was to his credit, of course, it was also a matter of some concern. The passive way in which he'd accepted his rejection was so unlike the way that Maxwell generally came across that it raised doubts as to its sincerity.

He'd always seemed a supremely confident young man, who knew what he wanted and would pursue his goal with great determination, not someone who would give up at the first hurdle. If the determined Maxwell was the true Maxwell, he wouldn't put it past him to pursue Eleanor in a clandestine sort of way. And knowing his strong-willed daughter, he couldn't dismiss the possibility that she might enthusiastically go along with it.

He stood up and dusted down his trousers.

He'd have a word with Julia. Between them, they must keep a closer eye on Eleanor. For a start, Julia must be Eleanor's chaperone in the future, not Meera. Eleanor could wrap Meera around her little finger. But with Julia as her chaperone, Eleanor would know there were limits on what she could do. Yes, speaking to Julia was a matter of urgency, and he started walking briskly back to the garden area, gathering pace as he went.

ll Saints' Church,
The following Sunday

HAVING LEFT the church ahead of their parents, Eleanor and Alice stood just outside the stone porch, waiting for Harriet to emerge. As soon as she did, they dragged her away from Ivy and Arthur and led her over to the edge of the stone courtyard.

Philip and Julia followed Ivy and Arthur out of the church and the four of them stood talking together. As Arthur was saying what a lovely picnic they'd had the Sunday before, but how much more peaceful it was that morning, Frank went quickly past them, heading for William, who was standing with James and Charles.

Beatrice wandered across to Ivy, remarked on the pleasantness of the weather and they started talking about the picnic.

· · ·

'YOU SEEMED in a hurry to get to us,' William said when Frank reached them. 'I bet you realised we were talking about meeting up at the club on Wednesday for a game of billiards and you were anxious to get your name down. Am I correct?'

'Not exactly,' Frank said with a smile. 'I'd have to be confident that you'd play so badly that even I, with my lousy skill, would win.'

'We can't promise to let you win, I'm afraid,' James said. 'But you never know, luck could be with you and you might win no matter how well we played.'

Frank laughed. 'Isn't there a saying to the effect that pigs might fly?' He paused. 'But maybe I will join you,' he added.

'That's great,' William said enthusiastically. 'And I'm sure Maxwell, too, will be up for a game. Speak of the devil, there he is! I thought I saw him sitting behind a pillar.' He beckoned to Maxwell to come over to them. 'We're talking about billiards,' he told him.

'You don't say!' Maxwell said in mock surprise.

'Yes, indeed,' said William. 'As it's some time now since we posted the list in the club for interested parties to sign, we were wondering if any of the members have approached you?'

'Not one of them. But I've been out so much recently they might not have seen me. But even if it's only the four of us,' he added, 'we can have a mini tournament.'

'Aha,' said Charles. 'You missed the latest. Frank's playing, too. So it'll be at least five of us. You *are* playing, aren't you, Frank?'

Frank shrugged. 'I suppose so.'

'What about Philip? He might want to play,' Charles said. 'I know he's never volunteered, but some people prefer to be asked. I imagine he'd be quite good.'

'He wouldn't be interested,' Frank said bluntly. 'I've known him for a long time and I know he doesn't like billiards. Let's keep it to those who are keen to play.'

'I'm getting the distinct feeling that you've been hiding your light under a bushel, Frank,' William pronounced solemnly. 'In the space of a ten seconds you've gone from needing to be cajoled to participate to being one of those who are keen to play. I'm nervous now at the skill you might be about to reveal to us.'

Frank grinned. 'Call it a mad fever that seems to have spread from you to the likes of me. Skill doesn't come into it. I wouldn't advise anyone to bet on me lest they wanted to shrink their worldly wealth.'

'You don't think we should find out if the same contagion has spread to Philip, too?' Maxwell asked, a laugh on his lips.

'No, I don't,' Frank snapped.

'HONESTLY, the pair of you. I've nothing to tell you so we might as well talk about something else,' Harriet said, affecting an air of innocence.

'It's just that you and William seemed so intense last week, as if you were talking about something really serious,' Eleanor remarked. 'At one point, we'd actually wondered if William was going to stand in the centre of the pavilion, call for silence, and then make an announcement. He'd have been holding your hand, of course. We were quite disappointed when he didn't. And that you didn't say anything when we met in the week.'

'Yes, we were,' Alice echoed.

Out of the corner of her eye, Eleanor saw Frank leave

Beatrice, and Beatrice start to head towards them. Quickly, she moved so her back was to Beatrice.

'Your mother's planning to come over and talk to us, I think,' she told Alice. 'We don't want her here as it'll stop Harriet from telling us all the juicy details. Can you stop her?'

Alice glanced over Eleanor's shoulder. 'It's all right. She's changed direction and is talking to Mr and Mrs McKenna. I knew she wanted to talk to your mother, Harriet, about getting hold of the next book they've decided to read.'

'That's all right, then. Well, Harriet,' Eleanor said, 'what's the position with you and William? Alice wants to know, too, don't you, Alice? It's not just me being nosy. In fact, it's not nosiness, it's just friendly interest.'

'Of course, it is,' Harriet said, exaggerating a soothing tone.

Alice nodded. 'Eleanor's right. We're just curious.'

'I'm sorry to disappoint you, but we weren't saying anything in particular. I know, though, that William likes me, and I'm sure he knows I like him. But we knew that before the picnic. Nevertheless, he sort of made it clear at the picnic. And that's all there is to say. Oh, and he's having brunch with us today. But that's because he's got things to talk about with James.'

'This is serious, Harriet,' Eleanor said, staring at Harriet in alarm. 'It's suddenly hit me. I'm going to lose you.'

'No, you're not. We'll always be friends,' Harriet said.

'D'you think he'll soon be asking your father if he can marry you?' Alice asked. 'If he does, I bet your father will say yes, unlike mine, who'd certainly say no.'

'D'you think Harriet's mistaken, Alice, and that it's you William really wants to marry?' Eleanor asked with feigned amazement.

Alice giggled. 'I got the words all wrong, but you know what I mean.'

Eleanor stared at Harriet, her brow creasing. 'If you both love each other, and you do, what's stopping William from proposing?'

Harriet shrugged. 'All I know is, he wants to be in a position to support me, and that also means he has to be confident about his career prospects. He was sent to Jaipur on a sort of loan, if you recall. When he's helped them catch up with everything here, they might send him back to Madras. Much as I'd hate that to happen, I'd follow William anywhere. But also, he's shown some interest in exporting. If he became an exporter, he wouldn't have to leave Jaipur.'

Alice nodded. 'He's been talking to my father about it. And to Maxwell.'

'So it's all a bit up in the air at the moment,' Harriet said. 'I'm sure Papa would expect him to be clearer about the future than he is, and wouldn't agree to anything until he was. But when everything's decided, he'll ask Papa if he can marry me.'

'I'd forgotten he came from Madras,' Eleanor said slowly. 'It must be unsettling for William. He and James get on so well that I thought William would always be here. I'm sure James will. But if William was sent back to Madras, and you were married to him, you, too, would go to Madras.' She stared at Harriet, stricken. 'I'd hate you to go away. We always planned to live close to each other and for our children to be like brothers and sisters. I do hope William gets into exporting and tells the people in Madras that he wants to stay here.'

'Me, too, for what it's worth,' Harriet said, and she held up a hand, her fingers crossed. 'I've nothing more to tell you. So, now let's stop talking about the men.' She glanced around at the different groups. Her gaze settled on William. 'I wonder what the men are discussing,' she said.

'Well done on completely changing the topic, Harriet,' Eleanor remarked, and she and Alice laughed. As she turned to look at the men, her gaze passed over Beatrice and the McKennas.

Beatrice instantly jerked her head away, so her focus appeared to be Alice.

That's funny, Eleanor thought. Frowning slightly, she turned back to Alice and Harriet.

She was sure Beatrice had been staring at her.

First the strange behaviour at Amber Fort, and then the feeling that Beatrice had been watching her at the picnic, both when they were under the pavilion and later when they'd been playing croquet. Yet whenever she'd looked at Beatrice, Beatrice had seemed to be looking in a different direction.

She'd thought she must be mistaken, and that Beatrice had indeed been watching Alice.

She tried to think of any time when they'd all been together when Beatrice had shown even the slightest interest in what Alice had to say, or when Frank had done for that matter, but she couldn't. So why would Beatrice be watching Alice in such an intent way?

She wouldn't.

She was sure she hadn't been mistaken about Beatrice watching her. Would anyone have been mistaken about sensing on such a number of occasions that they were being watched? She bit her lip. She didn't think so.

Beatrice must be watching her. But why?

'And talking of people who love each other, here comes Charles, Alice.' Harriet's voice made Eleanor jump out of her reverie, and she turned quickly to Alice. Some way behind Alice, Frank was talking earnestly with James, and he wouldn't have seen Charles going across to Alice.

Realising that, Harriet caught Eleanor's eye and gave her a quick smile.

'Hello, Alice,' Charles said as he came up to her, his eyes on Alice alone.

'Hello, Charles,' Eleanor and Harriet chorused in unison.

Charles laughed. 'And hello, Eleanor and Harriet, too.'

'Your timing couldn't have been better,' Eleanor told Charles. 'Mr Fletcher's not noticed you've come over here.'

'In that case,' he said, and he lifted Alice's right hand to his lips and lightly kissed the back of her hand, and then each finger in turn.

'Oh, Charles,' Alice whispered, blushing.

'The picnic last week was excellent, wasn't it, Charles?' Harriet said. 'Everything was perfect.'

Charles dragged his eyes away from Alice. 'It was indeed. Alice and I were actually able to spend some time together. Usually, her ever watchful father makes that impossible. And it looks as if we're in luck today, too,' he added warmly.

'We'll see if we can help,' Harriet said, and she and Eleanor moved closer to each other, blocking Alice and Charles from her father's view.

'One of these days we'll have a picnic together, just the two of us, Charles,' Alice said shyly. 'If you want to, that is. Chaperoned obviously,' she added quickly. She pulled a face. 'I must sound very wanton.'

'No, you don't,' he said. 'You took the words out of my head. I want that, too. But I want more than that. I very much want to marry you. If only I had a house of my own, or better career prospects, then I could ask your father. I've been saving for ages for a house, and even more so since I met you, but buying a house is still a year or two away. And until I've a suitable home to offer you, I can't see your father agreeing to us marrying. And he'd be right not to do so. But I can't expect you to wait till I'm in a position to support you in the way you deserve.'

'Of course I'll wait. I love you, Charles,' she said tremulously. 'I'll wait for as long as it takes. And I won't stop thinking, either, of ways I might get my father to agree to at least an engagement. If he did, that would give us a little more freedom. Engaged couples are allowed to sit and talk by themselves. It's just a matter of finding the right way to get his attention. But there's bound to be something.'

'We'll both of us think very hard,' he said, a note of desperation in his voice.

'Think about all the different aspects of exporting,' Alice suggested. 'Making money is all he cares about. He's only at church today because he's already made some promising contacts by coming here, and he hopes to make more. If you can think of anything that would benefit his business, that could be our answer.'

'I'll certainly try to come up with something.'

'Get away from my daughter!' Frank barked from behind them.

Gasping aloud, they jumped apart. Charles took one look at Frank's face and went across to William and James.

'So, ELEANOR,' James said, taking Eleanor to one side when Charles joined them and started talking to William. 'How are you today? Have you got over being beaten last week?'

She put her nose in the air. 'A true gentleman would never have mentioned that,' she said with a sniff. 'He would have opened the conversation by remarking upon the beauty of the weather, or on how inspiring the sermon had been that morning, or on what a pleasing crowd there was at the church that day.'

'*Was* the sermon inspiring?' he asked in amusement.

'I haven't a clue,' she said lightly. 'I didn't listen to a word of it.'

They both laughed.

'I was far too busy wondering how to persuade Papa to take us up to the club on Wednesday,' she went on. 'It sounds as if it'll be a most enjoyable evening. I know about the planned billiards tournament, you see.'

'Let me guess. You're keen on entering in the hope of achieving success in at least one game within two weeks? Is that it?'

'On the contrary, I'm trying my hardest to refrain from volunteering to play against any of you. It wouldn't be kind to show you up,' she said sweetly.

They smiled at each other.

'I've missed you,' he said suddenly.

She frowned questioningly. 'But we saw each other at the picnic last week, and again in the week. And we're meeting now. And will do on Wednesday.'

'I don't mean that,' he said. 'I mean, just having the chance to sit and talk to each other, not sparring, though that's fun, but just relaxing together.' He hesitated. 'That's partly what I mean, but not all,' he added, a note of awkwardness creeping into his voice.

She stared at him. 'What are you trying to say, James?'

He shook his head. 'I almost don't know,' he said. 'All I know is that these days, when I close my eyes and see you, I'm no longer seeing the mischievous child I used to tease, or seeing you as my sister's friend.'

'You mean you think of me when we aren't together? And when you close your eyes, you see me in your head?' she asked in growing wonder.

'Yes, I do,' he said, gazing at her. Her heart seemed to stand still.

'But I don't think of you as sisterly,' he said quietly. 'I see you as you are today, a beautiful woman with a lively personality, with glorious hair, with the most wonderful eyes in the world, and a smile that would light up any room. You're absolutely lovely, Eleanor, and that's the only way I see you now.' He paused. 'Do you still think of me in a sisterly way?' he asked, and held his breath.

She slowly shook her head. 'No, I don't,' she said. 'It's a long time since I thought of you as like a brother.' She looked up into his face, and her eyes filled with tears. 'A brother doesn't cause a woman's stomach to do strange things when she looks at him, or make her want to feel his arms around her. Or make her want to put her arms around him and hug him tightly to her.' She coloured. 'It probably makes me sound much too forward, James,' she said with a smile of embarrassment, 'but I, too, miss you. And I know exactly what you mean, though I can't explain what I mean any more you than can.'

'The word neither of us has said is love,' he said gently. 'I've come to realise that I love you very much, and I'm very much hoping you feel the same about me.'

Tears started to trickle down her cheeks. 'I do, James, I most definitely do. But I didn't know it till recently. I've long assumed that you'll always be part of my life, but I'd never stopped to consider how that could come about. It was only when someone mentioned the other day that they thought you were interested in someone else that I felt an instant panic at the thought. Real panic. In that moment, I realised I loved you, and I didn't want a single day to pass without seeing you, not a single morning, not a single night. I wanted to be the person you were with for the rest of your life.'

Each took a step towards the other, and they stood staring into each other's eyes, their arms at their sides, their fingertips touching, oblivious to the conversation around them.

'I know what I'd like the next stage of this to be,' he said, his breathing ragged. 'I'd like to speak to your father. But this isn't the right time. There's an outside chance I'll be transferred elsewhere, and I need to know that first. It could influence both you and your father. But I want to stay here, and I'm pretty sure I'll be able to do so.' He hesitated. 'But would you mind if we had to live somewhere else?'

She shook her head. 'I want to live where you are, wherever that is. Provided it isn't Bayana!' she added, and she laughed.

'But seriously,' she went on, 'if we had a choice, I'd rather stay here. Mama and Papa don't have any other children, and if Harriet were to move, and you, too, your parents would be on their own, as would mine. So staying in Jaipur would be my preference.'

'Mine, too. I love the city, and I'd like to stay where our families are.'

'It would be funny if William was sent back to Madras and you were sent there, too, and Harriet and I ended up living in the same road again. But I do hope that doesn't happen.'

From across the courtyard, obscured by the people

between him and them, Maxwell stood on his own and watched Eleanor with James. He turned away in disgust.

'We'll be joining you at the club on Wednesday, Frank,' he heard Philip tell Frank.

Maxwell took a step back, making sure that none of the others could see him.

'Is that so?' Frank remarked. 'Does that mean you're planning to follow my example and make a fool of yourself at the billiards table?'

'Why don't you, Philip?' Julia said teasingly.

Philip gave a laugh that sounded forced to Maxwell's ears. 'No way! But Eleanor's been on and on about going to watch the tournament, and at a certain point it's easier to give in than continue the fight. With Frank playing, you and Alice will also be going, won't you, Beatrice?'

'I hadn't really thought about it,' Beatrice said, 'but if everyone else is going, we will, too.'

'I'll be keeping an eye on your foreman, though,' Frank said. 'He's got his eye on Alice, much good it'll do him.' Looking round, he glimpsed Charles standing again with Alice. His face went red, and he grabbed Beatrice by the arm. 'Davis and Alice are together again. Let's get over there and break it up. Come on.'

He hurried across the forecourt, dragging Beatrice behind him.

Maxwell saw Julia move closer to Philip.

'What a ghastly man,' he heard her say, her voice low. 'Charles is worth so much more than he is. But while I feel extremely sorry for Alice, I don't think we should be encouraging Eleanor and Beatrice to come into regular contact with each other. We must find a way of stepping back from the Fletchers,' she told him. 'It's too painful, and it can't be easy for Beatrice, either.'

'I feel exactly the same,' Philip said, 'but what can I do? They live near us. They're bound to mix with the British, which includes us, and that's that. We'll just have to hope that Harriet always stays friendly with Eleanor. Eleanor's got more in common with her than she has with Alice. And if Alice manages to persuade Frank to let her marry Charles, and she goes to live with him, better still.'

Then the two of them moved away and were soon out of earshot.

Maxwell stood still, bemused. So the cause for the mutual dislike was related to the two girls and Beatrice, was it? Interesting, he thought, and he headed across to say hello to Arthur and Ivy.

ALICE SANK BACK on her pillow in excitement. She knew exactly what to do!

She was mad not to have realised sooner what she could do! Of course there was a way of making it possible for her to marry Charles! The answer had been staring at her in the face for some time, she just hadn't been able to see it.

But now she could.

Her heart beat fast.

With a tremendous feeling of relief and overwhelming joy, she looked up at the ceiling and laughed happily.

25

T *he following day*

IGNORING the curious glances that Sita had been giving her
ever since they'd set off for the morning in a hired tonga,
Alice stepped down in front of the paper-making factory,
confident there was no risk of her bumping into Charles.
He'd told her the day before that he was going to be at the
railway station that morning, overseeing the consignments
of paper for export.

Indicating that Sita should remain outside the factory,
she brushed away her anxious protest, took a deep breath,
and went up to the open entrance and into the building.

She was greeted by a hubbub of noise and a bustle of
movement, and she stopped short and looked around. The
working day was just getting going and she could see people
moving around the machines. But for the moment the
cutting machines were silent and there was no one tending

to the numerous piles of cotton fragments heaped in colours on the floor.

She turned to her left and walked up to the half-glazed door that led into Philip's office. Standing in front of the door, she took another deep breath, and then firmly knocked before her resolution could weaken.

'Come in,' she heard Philip call.

She opened the door. Philip looked up as she went inside. He glanced over her shoulder and then looked back at her. With astonishment etched on his face, he quickly rose to his feet.

'Why, Alice, this is a pleasant surprise,' he said, again glancing over her shoulder. 'Are you with your parents?' he asked.

She shook her head. 'I came with my ayah. She's waiting for me outside.'

He frowned slightly. 'I feel a little uncomfortable at you being in here alone with me,' he said awkwardly. 'It's how it would look to someone else. If Eleanor were in the same position with your father, I would expect her to be chaperoned for appearances sake.'

'The trouble is, I don't want anyone to hear what I have to say to you.'

'I don't understand,' he said, bewildered. 'Look, why don't we sit down and you can tell me what this is all about?'

Coming round from his desk, he indicated an arrangement of four upholstered chairs around a wooden table in the corner of the room. Alice went and perched on the seat of the nearest chair.

'Would you like some refreshment?' he asked, hovering behind the chair furthest from her.

She shook her head. 'No, thank you.'

'Well, tell me if you change your mind,' he said, and he sat down opposite her.

'This is difficult,' she said, blushing.

'Why don't you start at the beginning?' he suggested, looking at her with growing wariness.

'It's difficult to do that because, to be strictly accurate, the beginning was back in Gujarat, but I was too young to remember it.'

The colour started to drain from Philip's face.

He gestured helplessness. 'You've lost me, I'm afraid,' he said, a tremor shaking his words.

'So I'd like to jump eighteen years,' she went on. 'Not long after we moved here, I overheard my parents talking. I hadn't intended to,' she added hastily, 'but it was a hot evening and I'd gone on to the veranda outside my bedroom and Mother and Father were talking below. And I heard them.'

The last of the colour left his face.

'What did you hear?' he asked, his voice a croak.

She took yet another deep breath and her words tumbled out in a rush. 'That Eleanor was your daughter. Your real daughter, I mean. That her mother was my mother, not Mrs Grainger.'

She fell silent.

Neither said a word.

'Do you deny it?' she asked at last.

'No,' he said quietly. 'What you heard was correct.'

'I don't understand,' Alice said, her voice trembling, her eyes filling with tears.

'I had a brief affair with your mother while your father was away, and Eleanor was the result. Your father didn't realise that I was Eleanor's father, and knowing how much Julia and I wanted a child, he gave Eleanor to us. Julia had

had several miscarriages, you see, and to our great disappointment, it didn't look as if we were going to be able to become parents. It was a gift more wonderful than I can put into words, and we've loved Eleanor for every minute of her life.'

Alice's tears fell, unchecked.

'I can't tell you how often I've regretted the strain I must have put on your parents' marriage,' he added. 'I'm so sorry, Alice. I did an appalling thing in betraying both your father and also Julia, whom I love very much, and I'm truly ashamed of myself for my weakness.' He paused, his eyes watering. 'But I can't regret it entirely as it's given us Eleanor. I love her so much.' His words trailed off and he stared helplessly at Alice. 'And so does Julia. We became parents at last.'

He took a handkerchief from the breast pocket in his jacket and blew his nose.

'What do you intend to do with the information?' he asked after several minutes in which the only sound had been Alice quietly sobbing.

She pulled her handkerchief from her sleeve, wiped her eyes and looked across at him.

'You owe me,' she said, her lip quivering. 'After my father had given you the baby, he went home and forced himself on my mother. He was so angry with her, you see. To use your words, I was the result.'

He looked at her with horror. 'I'm so sorry, Alice. I had no idea.'

She swallowed a loud sob and wiped her eyes again. 'Neither of them wanted me, neither loved me, and I've had a miserable life. I've always known they didn't love me, but not why. Not until I heard them talking. My father was angry because of what you and Mother did and because of

Eleanor being born, and my mother remembered Father's attack on her every time she looked at me.'

'That must have been so awful for you,' he said gently.

'If Eleanor hadn't been born, it would've been different. Father wouldn't have found out what Mother had done. So it's Eleanor's fault in a way. But she hasn't had to suffer like I have. She's had a lovely life, wanting for nothing, adored by you and Mrs Grainger. Very different from my life. But I want to be happy, too. It's only fair.'

He nodded. 'Of course, it is.'

She dissolved into tears again. 'And I can see a way of me being happy,' she said through her tears. 'But it involves you.'

'Are you planning to blackmail me?' he asked. 'Doing something wrong can never result in anything good.'

She vigorously shook her head. 'It's not blackmail. I'm asking you to do me a favour. I'm entitled to be happy, too, not just Eleanor. You just agreed.'

'What's that favour, then?'

Tears trickled down her cheeks again, and she looked at him with tear-filled eyes. 'I love Charles and I want to marry him, and he wants to marry me. He's the first person who's ever loved me. But Father won't allow him near me as he doesn't have what Father calls "good career prospects", and he doesn't have a house of his own. He's saving for one, but he's a long way from having sufficient money. Father sees him as a failure, but he isn't. He's a really kind person and a very good foreman. You said so yourself. He loves the work and he'd never let you down.'

'All that's true. He's an excellent person to have at my side.'

She nodded vigorously. 'That's right, he is.'

'So what would you like me to do?'

'Give him a house,' she said bluntly. 'You could say it's a wedding present as he's always worked hard for the company. No one would think it odd.' She paused. 'I'm not blackmailing you, I'm just asking. I would never tell anyone what I know about Eleanor, whatever your answer is. I'm not like that.'

'I know you're not, Alice.' He smiled at her. 'I'd be happy to give Charles a house, not because you're holding something over me, but because I, too, think he deserves it. It was a very happy day when Charles knocked on my door and asked for a job.'

Alice released the breath she hadn't realised she'd been holding and sat back in her chair with a huge sigh of relief.

'You're not angry with me, are you?' she asked anxiously, wiping her cheeks with the back of her hands.

'Not at all,' he said with a smile. 'And I'll prove it to you. When Charles speaks to Frank, he can tell him that his career prospects are very good. I want to see the factory that I worked so hard to build up, go from strength to strength in the years to come. I've no son, and it's unlikely that Eleanor will marry someone who wants to take over the factory in the future, so when I'm ready to retire, I intend to ask Charles if he'd like to buy it from me at a very low price, something he'd easily be able to pay. That's what happened to me. I bought the factory from my friend for well below the price he could've got. I've always intended to do the same for Charles. If he wants it, that is.'

She stared at him, her eyes shining.

Philip smiled at her. 'So I think you can safely say that you and Charles will be marrying, Alice.'

'Thank you,' she said tremulously. 'Thank you so much.'

'I know you'll want to discuss this with Charles, so I'll tell him about the house and factory when he returns this afternoon. But I shall ask him not to say anything to your father until I say he can. I'd like you, too, to keep the information to yourself.'

She stared at him in alarm. 'Why's that?' she asked, with obvious suspicion.

'Because now that you know what happened all those years ago, it's safe to assume that others will find out, too, and I'm going to tell Eleanor and Julia the truth. But I think it's better not to say anything before we go to the club on Wednesday, and not till after Saturday evening, when you're all coming to us for dinner. I'll speak to Julia the following day. I think it would be easier for her if she was ignorant of the truth until after the dinner.'

'You'll really tell her then?'

'Yes, on the Sunday, and with her agreement, I'll also tell Eleanor. I'm sure Julia will think that Eleanor should learn about her birth from us, and not from anyone else. Can you wait till after next weekend before you talk to anyone other than Charles, do you think?'

She nodded. 'Yes, I can.'

She stood up, and he got up, too.

'And you're really not angry with me?' she asked again.

He shook his head. 'No, Alice, I'm not. I understand the way you feel.'

'Then, thank you again,' she said. She gave a loud sob. 'I didn't want to sound as nasty as I must have done. I'm sorry.'

He took a step forward and put his arms around her. 'Be happy, dear Alice,' he said, and he hugged her. 'By the sound of it, you deserve it. It's a pity that Frank and Beatrice have been so blind to what a lovely daughter they have.'

Then he lowered his arms, stepped back and gave her a warm smile.

She stared up at him. 'I wish you'd been my father, not

Eleanor's, Mr Grainger,' she blurted out. Her voice caught and she spun round and ran to the door.

WHAT ON EARTH was going on, Maxwell thought, perplexed.

He'd gone to the factory that morning, ostensibly to discuss another order if Philip had caught sight of him, but in reality to make sure that his latest order had left the premises without a hitch. From his position under an aged ashoka tree on the opposite side of the road, he'd seen his cargo leave, accompanied by Charles.

Reassured, he'd been about to go back to his showroom when a tonga had pulled up in front of the entrance. Instantly recognising Sita and Alice, he'd hastily stepped back into the shade of the tree, and had stood and watched them.

To his surprise, Alice had indicated that Sita stay outside, and she'd gone into the building on her own. It wouldn't be to see Charles, he realised, as she'd know that Charles would be at the station that morning, so it must be to see Philip.

As he stared at Sita, he mentally kicked himself.

He should have realised that no one was closer to the girls than their ayahs, and that whenever he'd seen the ayahs with the girls, Meera and Sita had seemed to get on very well.

It was possible, he realised, that they'd known each other in Gujarat. If so, there was a strong chance that they'd know the reason why Philip Grainger and Frank Fletcher hated each other so much.

He'd been letting his plans relating to Eleanor and Frank prevent him from making a determined effort to discover something that might have given him a hold over both Frank and Philip. Well, he must now get everything back on track.

Frank must instantly arrange for the cheap gems to be put into the consignment designed to bring down Philip. He had given Frank the gems a couple of weeks earlier and Frank had just put in his first order for paper. Frank must put the gems in that shipment of paper. Sending gem-free consignments was costing him a lot of money. He needed to start shipping stolen gems again, and to stop wasting time on Frank.

So, in a week, he'd be reporting the unsuspecting Frank to customs, making sure to do so before Frank could make any allegations about Philip.

But that didn't mean that it wouldn't still be useful to know the cause of their mutual antipathy, and he'd start making an effort to be friendly with the ayahs in case there was anything to be gleaned from them.

As for Alice's visit to the factory that morning, Sita had clearly been surprised at having to stay outside. It suggested that she didn't know what Alice was up to. As she was certain to be disapproving of Alice being in the building on her own, there was no point in approaching Sita that morning on some pretext or other.

Nor was there any question of him going into the factory that morning, much as he'd like to know what Alice was doing there, as to do so would put an end to Alice's conversation with Philip, and that would be self-defeating. The best he could do was wait until Alice came out and see if he could gather anything from her expression.

He leaned back against the tree, preparing to wait for as long as it took.

Fortunately for him, it wasn't long before Alice ran out to the tonga, a bright smile on her face. To Sita's evident astonishment, she hugged her and then climbed up on to the tonga. Giggling, Sita climbed up after her. The driver pulled the reins of the horse, and the tonga set off.

Whatever Alice's mission had been, it had obviously succeeded, he thought drily as he stepped forward and hailed a tonga to take him to Johari Bazaar. He'd pick up the quality gems he'd ordered for himself, he decided, and then call in on Frank.

It wouldn't hurt to prompt Frank to arrange for the gems to be put in the packages on the following Saturday when the factory was closed. Anyone seen in the building on the Saturday would be less conspicuous than on the Sunday. He'd tell him to report Philip first thing on the Monday morning, before the cargo could be moved.

He, of course, would have contacted customs earlier on the Monday, when Frank would still be in bed, with an anonymous tip-off about Frank's consignment.

His chin on his chest, the elderly Jaipuri sitting in the dust on the opposite side of the road from the factory, a little way along from Maxwell, his bicycle lying on its side next to him, appeared to be half asleep.

Unnoticed by the man he'd been following, whom he had followed on a number of previous occasions, he had arrived there minutes after him, and had continued to cycle a little way further down the road.

Under the pretext of adjusting the chain on his bicycle, he had watched the man wait for a van to drive away from the factory, and then start to leave. But at the sight of a tonga drawing up in front of the factory, and a girl getting down from it and going into the building on her own, leaving her

Indian servant outside, the man had hastily hidden beneath the nearest tree.

Expecting that he might be there for a while, the Jaipuri cyclist had found a place to crouch down where he'd be hidden from the man by the cluster of large metal cans containing the milk brought daily into the town from the outlying villages, and by the people coming for the milk.

The man didn't move until the girl had come out of the factory, got into the tonga and left with her servant.

The British man had clearly changed his mind about going into the factory. Instead, he had hailed a tonga and set off in the direction of the old city.

The elderly cyclist had pulled up his bicycle, mounted it and followed the tonga to Johari Jewellers, where the man went inside. A short time afterwards, the man left the jeweller's and walked down Johari Bazaar towards Bapu Bazaar. Turning right into Bapu Bazaar, he walked past the first few shops until he reached one of the side roads. He turned down the road and went into a showroom headed "Frank Fletcher, Exporter".

Knowing he need go no further, the cyclist wheeled the bicycle to the end of the side road, turned it around so that it faced Bapu Bazaar, and began to cycle towards the bazaar, and thence in the direction of the *haveli* he'd frequently visited in the past few weeks.

26

The Grainger residence,
The following Saturday evening

'IT'S A BEAUTIFUL EVENING,' Eleanor said as the night breeze blew along the veranda, carrying on its back a heavenly fragrance. She inhaled deeply. 'The wind smells of flowers,' she added. Feeling James's gaze on her profile, she turned from a sky that was studded with glittering stars and glanced at him over her shoulder. 'Look at the view, not at me,' she scolded. 'It's much more lovely.'

'Not to me, it isn't,' James said quietly.

She turned to face him, leaning back against the balustrade. 'I wonder how long it'll be before someone appears, anxious to ensure that I'm no longer alone with you.'

'If they could read my mind right now, it'd be in no time at all. If I didn't think your mother and father would throw me out at once, I'd take you in my arms and kiss you.' He took a step towards her. 'It's what I desperately want to do. You must be able to hear my heart beating furiously just being near you.'

'Oh, James. You don't know how much I want that, too.' She moved away from the balustrade, went closer to him, stopped and gazed up at him.

Each took another step forward, their faces inches apart from each other.

Philip appeared at the doorway. 'The men are going to have a brandy. I take it you'd like one, too, James?'

Both jumped hastily apart.

'I would, sir, thank you,' James said with a total lack of enthusiasm.

'Come on, then,' Philip said, going back into the house.

'I don't particularly want a brandy,' James told Eleanor. 'I'd rather stay here with you.'

She laughed. 'I picked that up. But I rather think Papa was giving you an order.'

'Me, too,' he said ruefully. 'It's why I agreed.'

'Since you've got to go inside, I want you to do something for me,' she whispered, her face suddenly serious. 'You know how people can sense things, well I can sense that something's not quite right, but I don't know what it is. I want you to find out.'

James frowned. 'I don't understand. Tell me quickly what you mean.'

'Well, Papa seems unusually nervous for a start. He's spent a lot of the week in his study, which isn't like him. Also, when he's not aware of being watched, he seems quite anxious about something. And I keep catching him looking at Mama, and also at me, which is strange.'

'That does sound unlike Philip,' James said.

'And there are some things about William, too, which are a source of concern. Just recently, his clothes haven't looked as nice as they used to. I haven't mentioned it to Harriet, but I know she's noticed he's wearing old shoes, for example, and I can tell she's worried.'

'I noticed that, too,' he remarked. 'Was anyone else acting strangely?'

'Mr Fletcher was,' she said. 'He's always a bit on edge, but I'd say he looked quite jittery all evening. He's always staring at Papa, and I can tell he doesn't like him, but this evening there was almost a triumphant look about him. I may have been imagining it, but I don't think so.'

'What about Maxwell?' James asked.

She thought for a moment.

'It hadn't occurred to me, but now you've asked, I'd say that his joviality was a little forced. But it could just be that his business isn't doing as well at the moment, and he's putting on an act to hide it. Uncle Arthur and Aunt Ivy are exactly what they're always like, except that Uncle Arthur seems to be quite amused by William. I thought William might've brought up the subject of exporting, but he didn't. The only other people are Alice and Charles, and they're both glowing. And they were on Wednesday. I'm guessing he's got enough money for a house and will be asking for Alice's hand in marriage, and she knows it.'

'I'll see what I can find. I think a lot of it might be your imagination, though.'

She nodded. 'I expect it is. But I hope I'm right about Alice and Charles. I like Alice and I'd like to think she can get away from her ghastly father soon.'

．　．　．

'I TAKE it business is good at the moment?' James said with a smile.

Philip nodded. 'It is, dear boy. And I have to thank Maxwell here for a number of the orders I've been given. I know he recommended us to Frank, for a start. I'm grateful, Maxwell.' He held up his glass to Maxwell, and took a drink. As he put his glass down on the table, he glanced at Frank. 'And I'm grateful to you, too, Frank, for your order.'

Frank nodded. 'We people from Gujarat have to stick together.'

'That's right, you were friendly with each other during your time in Gujarat, weren't you?' Maxwell remarked with studied casualness.

Philip and Frank glanced quickly at each other.

'Not exactly,' Philip said. 'Our plantations were what was considered neighbouring in Bayana, but not in the way most people understand the word "neighbouring". Our plantations were a distance from each other, and quite isolated, in fact.'

'That's right,' Frank said. 'There was no British community like there is in Jaipur, and no club like the Royal Jaipur, so we didn't socialise with each other in the same way. We knew each other, of course, but we couldn't have been described as great friends.'

'I see,' Maxwell said. He pulled a face. 'It doesn't sound a very pleasant way to live.'

'It wasn't,' Frank said bluntly.

'I wouldn't want to live anywhere other than in Jaipur,' Charles said, smiling round at the rest of the men.

'I can certainly see why you feel that way,' William said. 'The town seems to have everything to offer, both in the number of things to do and in its attractiveness.'

'That's right,' Charles said. 'And as I not only live here, but I've got a job I love, I consider myself very lucky.'

Arthur smiled warmly at Charles. 'You're a great advertisement for the town,' he said. 'Philip's lucky to have such an enthusiastic employee.'

Philip and Charles smiled at each other.

'More brandy?' Philip asked, leaning forward and picking up the crystal decanter.

There was a general murmur to the effect that everyone had had sufficient, and that it was time to think about moving, so he placed the decanter back on the table, and as everyone else started to stand up, he did, too.

ELEANOR BEGAN to go upstairs as soon as all the guests had left. Philip told her and Julia that he'd sit a little longer over another brandy as he had things on his mind.

'Is it anything I can help with?' Julia asked, lingering at the entrance to the study and looking at Philip with concern. 'You haven't seemed your usual self these last few days. I'm sure Eleanor's noticed that, too. I've seen her staring quite anxiously at you more than once.'

Eleanor paused at the top of the stairs and waited for her father's reply.

Philip shook his head. 'No, it's just some awkward things I have to do,' he said with an attempt at sounding reassuring. 'I'll tell you about it tomorrow. You go on up. Sleep well.' He bent down and kissed Julia on the cheek. 'It was the luckiest day of my life when you agreed to marry me, Julia,' he told her. 'Now up you go. Sweet dreams.'

He went back into his study and sat down. As he reached for the brandy decanter, he heard a knock on the front door.

He stood up sharply, surprised at someone coming to his house at so late an hour, and waited where he was while the butler opened the door.

A moment later, he heard a knock on his study door.

'Come in,' he called. His butler, Gopal, opened the door, and he saw his packaging supervisor, Rishi, hover behind Gopal for a moment, and then come diffidently into the room.

Philip looked at Rishi in surprise. 'You can go to bed now, Gopal,' he said. 'I won't need you any more tonight.'

When Gopal had left the room, he turned to the packaging supervisor. 'What's the problem, Rishi?' he asked.

'I've worrying news,' Rishi said, visibly agitated. 'I wait till guests have left to come and tell you.'

He explained that several of the workers had been in the factory during the afternoon because they'd had an urgent request for paper to which rose petals had to be added. In order to supervise the workers, and as there was only one order to pack, he'd left his assistant to package the paper that had been ordered by Frank Fletcher. It had to be sent to the railway station on the Monday morning, so it couldn't be left for the following week.

Their work finished, they'd closed the factory, and he and the men had taken themselves to a nearby corner stall where he'd treated them to drinks as they'd had to work throughout the afternoon. As they'd stood around laughing and talking, his assistant, he'd noticed, had drunk rather too much and was becoming quite loud.

Feeling that the assistant's behaviour was beginning to reflect badly on him as his supervisor, he'd put his arm around the man's shoulder and walked with him to the end of the road, which wasn't far from where the assistant lived. He should go back home, he'd told the man as they walked.

He'd had enough to drink. His wife would be very unhappy if he got home in an even worse state than he was already in.

The man had shrugged off his arm.

His wife would soon be silenced, he said boastfully, when she saw what he'd earned that day. As he was speaking, he'd pulled a handful of rupees from his pocket. At a glance the supervisor had been able to see that it was far more than the man could have earned in even a month. Instantly alarmed and suspicious, he'd asked where the assistant had got the money, and what he'd had to do for it.

'That Mr Fletcher is good man,' the assistant had said. And laughing appreciatively, he'd stuffed the money back into his pocket and wandered down the road towards his house.

He could make some guesses as to what the assistant had done, Rishi said miserably. If he was right that gems had been concealed in Mr Fletcher's order for paper, it could rebound on Philip as the paper came from Philip's factory, and he wanted to know whether Philip agreed with him going into the factory the following day, opening the packages, and removing any gems they found.

'You did well to tell me, Rishi,' Philip told him, 'and there'll be a reward for you in the coming week. But you can get off home now and leave this to me. Don't tell anyone else what you've told me. I need to decide how best to deal with it. Expect to hear from me, though. I'll be in touch with you when I've worked out what to do.' And he walked the supervisor to the front door and saw him out.

Coming back into the empty hall, he stood for a moment, fear spreading through him at the situation he was in, and at his uncertainty as to what Frank, who hated him, might be planning to do.

Then he spun round and almost ran out of the house.

Turning left, he hurried as fast as he could to the McKennas' home.

Arthur's got a good head on him, he thought. He'll know what to do.

27

The McKenna residence

AT THE SOUND of Philip's frantic knocking, Arthur and Ivy's butler opened their front door.

'I'd like to speak with Mr McKenna, Luis,' Philip said. 'It's urgent.'

'I thought I heard your voice,' Arthur said, coming into the entrance hall. 'That's all, Luis. I'll take over from here. Come on into the library, Philip, and tell me the problem. At least, I assume it *is* a problem.'

A few minutes later, a glass of brandy in front of him, Philip had recounted what his supervisor, Rishi, had told him. 'I don't mind telling you,' he said, 'I'm quite frightened at how this could affect the company. Frank and I aren't friends, you see, and the fact that he's chosen my factory, and the product we make, for his smuggling, is alarming. I can't help thinking that Frank might be out to hurt me.'

Arthur stood up. 'You stay here, Philip. I'll go up and get James. I've a feeling he might be able to help.'

'James!' Philip exclaimed in surprise. 'How can *he* help?'

Arthur gave him a wry smile. 'I know my son,' he said. 'I've never been able to believe that adding a metalled road to the four hundred and ninety-three metalled roads there already are in Jaipur was the sum of his worldly ambition. Give me a moment.'

He went out into the hall, and Philip heard him hurrying up the staircase. Soon after, he returned to the library with James at his side.

'Fortunately, we're not being treated to the sight of James in pyjamas,' Arthur said as he and James sat down. 'He hadn't yet started to get ready for bed. Right, Philip, would you tell James exactly what you told me?'

When Philip had finished going through the account given to him by Rishi, James thought for a moment.

'I imagine your instinct, Philip,' he said, 'would have been to agree that Rishi should remove the gems tomorrow, and for you to contact the police for the packaging assistant to be arrested. I think you were right not to do that.'

Philip heaved a sigh of relief. 'I did wonder if that's what I should have done. But I came to Arthur first as I trust his judgement.'

'That instinctive action wouldn't have achieved very much, as I'm sure a lot of the police are on the smugglers' payroll. The assistant would have been sacked, but he's at the bottom of the chain, and he'd soon be replaced. The people responsible would have got away and would continue with their illegal activities. I'm talking about those at the top of the ring.'

'What would happen to Frank?' Philip asked.

'Probably nothing. You wouldn't have been able to

prove he was guilty. Someone else could have paid the assistant to conceal the gems. Frank would argue that only a fool would do something that could so easily lead back to him.'

'That didn't occur to me, but that's true,' Philip said slowly. 'So why did he do it? Or was it someone other than Frank?'

'It was definitely Frank, and I'm hazarding a guess that the intended victim was you, Philip. I imagine that Frank plans to contact the customs officials on Monday morning. He'll say something to the effect that when he popped into the factory that morning to check that his order went out on time, he noticed that someone had tampered with the consignment. The officials would find the gems, see that there'd been no break-in, and suspicion would fall on you. Your factory, your paper, your workers.'

'My God! So that's what he plans to do!' Philip exclaimed. 'He must really hate me.'

'It might be what he plans to do, but it need not get that far. Frank could be arrested on the basis of what we now know, and could be imprisoned while waiting for trial. Cases take a while to appear in an Indian court, and he could be in prison for quite some time before the charges against him are heard.'

'That would be difficult for Beatrice and Alice,' Philip said slowly. 'How would they live? And how would they cope, knowing that Frank had been disgraced in such a way?'

'And as with arresting the assistant at this stage, it'd leave the people responsible for the smuggling ring at large,' James said. 'Frank's only a tiny link in a long chain. Again, we'd be catching the small fry, but not the important players. Frank certainly didn't happen upon the gems by himself, for a start, and nor did he get into smuggling them without help from someone else.'

'We?' Philip echoed, staring at James in bewilderment.

'A slip of the tongue,' James said with a wry smile.

'What would you advise, James?' Arthur asked.

'Before James says anything more,' Philip said suddenly, 'there's something I'd like to say.'

'Of course,' James said.

'I think you're right that I'm probably the intended victim, and everything I said about the effect of Frank's incarceration on his family would have applied to mine if I'd been arrested. I very much want the guilty people caught, but I want Frank to have a chance to speak for himself first. If it's at all possible, I would like him to be kept out of this. I owe him that. In fact, I owe him much more than that.'

Arthur and James glanced at each other in surprise.

'If that's what you want,' James said, turning back to Philip. 'Then I suggest that I go and get Frank. I'll tell him we're having a very late drink and ask if he wants to join us. If he needs to change from his night clothes, I'll wait for him.'

'Thank you, James,' Philip said quietly, and he put his head in his hands.

NEITHER ARTHUR nor Philip said a word in the time it took James to return with Frank and bring him into the library. Both sat quietly nursing their brandy.

As soon as Frank entered the room, and saw Arthur and Philip staring at him, their faces deadly serious, he went white.

'Philip has something he wants to say to you, Frank.

Why don't you sit down?' James said. He indicated a leather chair between his chair and Arthur's, and Frank sat down.

Glancing at the expression on the faces of the three men, Frank ran his tongue round his lips. 'It doesn't feel very convivial in here,' he said, visibly nervous. 'Tense more like.'

'Why don't you start by telling Frank about your visitor this evening?' James prompted Philip.

Philip nodded, and in a rush he recounted everything that Rishi had said, and the conclusion that the three of them had drawn, which was that he was the intended victim.

There was a long moment of silence when he'd finished.

Frank seemed to crumple.

'I didn't want to do it,' he said, looking with watering eyes from one man to the other. 'I never cut corners in Gujarat, and when I started as an exporter I never intended to do anything dishonest. Yes, I wanted to make money, a lot of it, but only by hard work. You know how hard I used to work in Gujarat, Philip. Well, that's me. Essentially honest and hard-working. But I didn't have any choice.' His voice caught.

'Take your time,' James said gently.

'That's true, Frank,' Philip said. 'I know you worked hard in Gujarat, and I know you had principles you believed in and were ready to stand up for.'

Frank nodded eagerly at him. 'That's right. And when I moved here, that was still me. I didn't change. But like I said, I didn't have any choice. Maxwell's done so much for me that when he asked for my help I felt obliged to give it. But I made it clear to him that I was reluctant. He knows that.'

'It was Maxwell who gave you the gems?' Arthur asked.

'That's right. But not the ones in this week's order of paper. I'm going to pay for those, of course, as they'll be confiscated by the customs people. But he said I didn't have to pay him for them for a bit. I thought that when I'd paid for them, and had shipped a few consignments with gems he'd given me, I'd have done enough to show my gratitude, and I'd stop the smuggling. Maxwell said I could stop whenever I wanted to.'

'You know you could now be arrested?' James said.

Frank bowed his head.

'I don't want Frank to be arrested,' Philip said.

Frank raised his head, and stared at him with a mixture of hope, surprise and wonder.

'I want him to be given a chance to make this right,' Philip said. He turned to face Frank squarely. 'I did a terrible thing to you years ago, Frank, and I owe you for that. I also owe you a huge debt for the really happy years I've enjoyed since leaving Gujarat,' he added, his voice gaining strength. 'It's such a great debt that I'll never be able to repay it. But if I can do anything at all to stop you from getting arrested, it might go some way towards proving to you how very sorry I am, and how truly grateful to you I am.'

There was a moment of palpable silence in the room.

'I, too, don't think arresting Frank would be a good idea, but for different reasons,' James remarked.

Frank turned from Philip and stared hopefully at James.

'Maxwell is the one I want to arrest, and his partner, Paul,' James said. 'They're big players, and their arrests, along with every link in the chain of the smuggling line they've set up... now that would be a real achievement.'

'Have you any idea how you'd be able to manage that?' Arthur asked.

'We're very close already, and Frank might be able to help us with the last few pieces of the puzzle,' James said. He leaned slightly towards Frank. 'I'd like you to go through everything that happened since you got involved in this. It means telling us everything Maxwell suggested you do, all the people to whom he introduced you, both inside Jaipur and in the outlying villages, and every item he gave you. Can you do that?'

Frank nodded. 'I'll try my best.'

And he began to tell them all he could remember. When he came to the end, he stopped and looked anxiously at James. 'Is there anything there that's helpful?' he asked.

James smiled broadly. 'Yes, there is, Frank, and it means that we can keep you out of this, as Philip has requested. Before church tomorrow, I'd like you to go to your show-room and get me the pile of labels that Maxwell gave you to use before you had your own labels. They'll have *his* details on them, and no reference to you. As for you, Philip, perhaps you'd contact Rishi and ask him to meet you at the factory at one in the afternoon. Then phone Charles and tell him to go to church, but to keep the rest of the day free after that.'

'Willingly,' Philip said.

'We'll all go to church tomorrow and act normally. Perhaps you'd invite Maxwell to come back to us for lunch, Father, and William, too. Also Philip and his family. By keeping Maxwell with us, it'll ensure he doesn't go near the factory. Charles will be at the church, keen to see Alice, but you won't invite Charles to join us. You'll sound regretful, but explain to Charles, making sure that Maxwell hears you, that you know what Frank thinks about him.'

'Poor Charles,' Philip said. 'He's a good lad, Frank. It's a shame you can't see it.'

'I shall at some point in the conversation after church fill Charles in, and give him the labels with Maxwell's details on them,' James continued. 'After everyone's left for our house,

Charles should go straight to the factory and he and Rishi must change the label on every package. Each of Frank's labels must be replaced with one of Maxwell's. All traces of Frank will have gone. Rishi must stay there all afternoon, and make absolutely certain no one enters the packaging room. He can leave at six in the evening. We'll have someone watching the building after that until morning.'

'Thanks, James,' Philip said. 'I'm so glad you've found a way of keeping Frank out of the picture.'

'Yes, thank you, James,' Frank said. 'I'm very grateful to you. And you, too, Arthur. You can be certain that I'll never again get involved in any form of wrongdoing. I'll make a success of my business, I'm sure, but only by honest means.'

Arthur nodded. 'I think we all believe you,' he said. 'And what are we going to do about Maxwell, James?'

'We'll let Maxwell go ahead and tell the customs department his suspicions about Frank. I imagine he'll do that extremely early on Monday morning. I'm pretty sure he'll find a reason to go to the factory on Monday morning, hoping to see it swarming with officials, so we'll oblige. The only thing is, they'll suddenly change direction and turn their focus on him.'

'It serves him right,' Arthur said angrily. 'Men like Maxwell give exporters a bad name. We all get tarred by the same brush.'

'But it won't just be Maxwell who gets arrested,' James said. 'Every corrupt element in that chain between here and Europe will be arrested at exactly the same time by our men. We'll make sure that there's no time for anyone to warn anyone else. Furthermore, when we search Maxwell's showroom and his room at the club, I'm sure we'll find copies of all the consignments he's sent out, most of which will have housed stolen gems. It means we'll be able to put away some of the bigger names in the business. With luck, demand will suddenly drop. Of course, it'll climb again, but we'll be ready when it does.'

He turned to Frank. 'You might as well go home now, Frank,' he said.

Frank stood up, followed by Philip.

Hesitantly, Frank took a step closer to Philip.

'I've thanked James and Arthur, but I haven't yet thanked you, Philip. Thank you more than I can say,' he said, his voice shaking with emotion. 'You could have seen me locked up, but you chose to let me walk free. Consider any debt that you felt you owed me as more than fully paid.' He held out his hand to Philip.

Philip glanced down at Frank's hand, then he took it in both of his, and shook it firmly.

28

T he Grainger residence,
     Early Monday evening

THE GRAINGERS, Fletchers, McKennas and Charles sat around three cane tables grouped together on Philip's veranda.

As if by instinct, they'd all converged on Philip and Julia's house as the news about the find at the factory, and that Maxwell had been arrested, had travelled from family to family.

Mid-morning, Philip had telephoned Julia from the factory to say that Maxwell and the assistant packaging supervisor had been arrested and that the factory would be closed for the rest of the day and all the following day. The police and customs officials had removed a number of his files for inspection, he'd told her, so he should be home early that day. But he'd been asked to go to the customs section in the administration building the following morning, and he expected to be there for all of the day.

When the authorities had finished questioning Rishi and Charles, both had been allowed to go home, but they had been given instructions that they, too, should go to the administration building the following day.

With Philip's permission, Charles had gone straight to the Fletcher residence to bring them up to date. Frank, who'd chosen to work from home that day, had listened to Charles's account of the day's events, and along with Alice and Beatrice, had exclaimed at times in surprise.

Charles had then sat with Alice in the garden, telling her how much Philip's generosity to them meant for him, and talking about his hopes for their future. He wouldn't wait long to ask her father for her hand in marriage, he told a beaming Alice.

Standing watching them from inside the house, a cup of tea in her hand, Beatrice had commented on her amazement at Frank being able to see Charles sitting with Alice without tearing them apart, and also that Frank wasn't gloating at Philip's misfortune at being at the heart of wrongdoing, albeit that Philip, himself, was obviously not suspected of being involved in any criminal activity.

Frank had muttered that he, personally, was so relieved not to have been caught up in what Maxwell had been doing that he hadn't given any thought to Philip, and that he'd resolved to stop fretting about Charles.

Charles had then returned to the sitting room and suggested they call in on Philip and ask if there was anything they could do to help, and that's what they'd done.

Arthur and Ivy had arrived at the Grainger's at about the same time as the Fetchers and Charles. They, too, had been keen to help. Arthur had explained his knowledge of what had happened by saying that nothing was secret in the admin building, and James, having heard about the morning's events, had telephoned home to tell his parents.

Like William, James was still at the office and might not be home for dinner that evening. Ivy had suggested, though, that if he managed to get back in time for dinner, he should bring William with him.

As they all settled on Julia and Philip's veranda, a drink in front of each of them, Ivy asked if everyone would like to go back to their house after their drink and have dinner with them that evening. It will have been a tremendous shock for them all, she said, and they'd be very welcome. She'd alerted her cook to the fact that there might be a larger number of people at the table than usual.

They'd all thanked her for her offer, and had accepted the invitation.

'What will happen to Maxwell?' Eleanor asked.

Julia shook her head. 'We don't know exactly what he was doing, beyond the fact that he was concealing gems, presumably stolen gems, in orders he'd placed with Philip. We don't know if this was the first time he'd done that, or if he'd been making a habit of it. And perhaps he'd done the same thing with his other shipments, too.'

'I bet he's been doing it for some time,' Harriet said. 'I'd wondered how he had so much money. Papa makes a lot of money, but I'm sure he didn't make as much money as quickly as Maxwell. I remember us not having that much when I was very little.'

'You're right, Harriet,' Ivy said. 'Your father built up his business by hard work and honesty. Success like his isn't achieved overnight.'

Frank nodded. 'I'm doing it the honest way, too.' He glanced at Arthur and Ivy. 'I appreciate the offer of dinner this evening, but the events of the day have been a shock. Thinking about it, perhaps we'll go back to our place when we've finished our drinks, and have a quiet evening.' He paused. 'You can come, too, Charles, if you want.'

Alice and Charles exchanged glances of amazement.

'I'd like that, sir,' Charles hastily said.

'You know,' Philip said, 'Frank might have the right idea. I think we, too, will stay at home tonight. It's been a difficult day and we've got a lot to digest. Also, I've a long, possibly gruelling, day tomorrow. It might be sensible for us to have a quiet family evening, too.'

'I understand,' Arthur said. 'I, too, would be thrown off balance by discovering illegal activity taking place in my business. And I understand your shock, too, Frank. You worked closely with Maxwell. Although you've not been involved in any of his wrongful activities, it must be frightening to know that one day you could have been compromised.'

Frank gave him a grateful glance. 'It is, Arthur,' he said quietly.

Arthur nodded. 'As you'll no longer have Maxwell to help you, Frank, I hope you know you can always come to me for help or advice.'

'That's very kind of you, Arthur. I'm very grateful to you, and to all of you,' he added, looking around the group. 'Having something like this happen so close to home, so to speak, has shaken me to the core.'

'We've finished our drinks so perhaps we should head for home now,' Beatrice suggested.

Philip pressed the bell to summon his butler. Beatrice stood up, and Alice and Frank did likewise, followed by Charles. Ivy and Arthur, too. They all said goodnight to Philip and Julia, and were shown to the door.

·   ·   ·

Having covered the short distance to their house, Frank glanced round as he approached his front door. He saw that Charles and Alice were holding hands as they walked behind him and Beatrice. Raising an eyebrow at them, he turned back, went up to the door and opened it.

Beatrice handed her shawl to the butler who hurried up to them and then turned to go into the sitting room. Frank went straight towards his office. With a slight smile at Charles, Alice went after her mother, while Charles hastened after Frank.

'May I have a word with you in private, sir?' he called to Frank.

Beatrice stopped walking and raised her eyebrows at Alice.

'No need for anything private,' Frank said. 'The answer's yes.'

Charles stood still and stared at Frank. 'But I haven't told you about the house I'll have, or about one day owning the factory,' he said in puzzlement.

'I didn't know about that. I'm pleased for you, and you've still got my blessing to marry her,' Frank said drily.

'I don't understand, Father,' Alice said rushing up to Charles, who put his arm around her shoulders. 'You've always been so against Charles.'

'The events of today have shown me what a bad judge of character I can be, and that I can make mistakes. I was wrong about Maxwell, and perhaps I was wrong to place too much emphasis on a person's job and what they've got, and not enough on their character. Philip's always sung your praises, Charles, and so, too, has everyone who knows you. After today's revelations, I'm happy that someone like you will be marrying Alice, and I wish you both the very best.'

'Thank you enormously, sir,' Charles said. He lowered his arm, rushed up to Frank and vigorously shook his hand.

'Oh, yes, thank you, Father,' she said, clapping her hands in delight. 'You've made me so happy.'

Charles turned back to her, and at the same moment, each threw themselves forward, and Alice fell gleefully into Charles's arms.

'I love you, Alice,' he said, hugging her tightly.

'I've not gone as soft as all that,' Frank said gruffly. 'Your arms would be better employed reaching out for a drink. There's nothing in my office that can't wait, so let's all go into the sitting room and toast your engagement. Then you can tell me about this house you're going to have.'

THE McKENNAS WERE SITTING at their dinner table, waiting while the *khitmutgar* finished giving each of them a bowl of *kheer*, the Indian creamy rice pudding they'd come to like so much, when they heard a car stop outside their house. Their iron gates opened and closed, and moments later, they heard their front door open, and then James's voice.

'I see we're in time for dinner, or almost,' James said with a smile as he came into the room with William. 'We got away as soon as we could.'

'I'm sure we can find you something to eat,' Ivy said. She smiled at the *khitmutgar*, who promptly went through the back door to the small pantry at the back of the house. 'Are you staying the night, James, and obviously William, too?'

'We aren't, I'm afraid,' James said. 'It's why we came by car. We've an early start tomorrow, and it'd be easier to get going if we were in the *haveli*. But we wanted to see you this evening, to see how you were. The events of the day must have been a shock.'

'It's so hard to believe,' Harriet said. 'Maxwell didn't look like a crook.'

'I imagine most successful crooks don't,' Arthur said with a wry smile.

'You know what I mean,' Harriet said. 'And although I don't like him, I feel quite sorry for Mr Fletcher. He obviously thought very highly of Maxwell, and listened to what he said. He must feel extremely let down. But I like Alice so I'm very glad that Mr Fletcher was in no way involved.'

'Indeed,' Arthur muttered.

'What was funny this evening,' Harriet went on, frowning slightly, 'was that Mr Fletcher seemed quite pleasant towards Uncle Philip. He usually snarls at him. And he must have seen that Charles and Alice were holding hands, but he didn't say anything.'

The *khitmutgar* placed a dish of chicken korma and rice in front of James and William, and then left the room.

James picked up his fork. 'Like you said, Harriet, Mr Fletcher's world will have turned upside down today. If that were me, I'd now be re-evaluating everything I used to think. I imagine Mr Fletcher's been doing just that.'

Harriet nodded. 'I hope he has. From the way that Charles and Alice kept looking at each other this evening, I'm pretty sure that Charles will soon be asking Mr Fletcher if he can marry Alice. Given that Mr Fletcher seemed to be in a good mood, I'd ask him today if I were Charles.'

'Let's hope that's what he's done, then,' William said. 'On a difficult day like today, it's good to have some pleasant news with which to end the day. And what better news could there be than that there's to be a marriage.' He stared across the table at Harriet, who blushed.

James glanced from William to Harriet in amusement.

At the end of the meal, Arthur stood up. 'I suggest that James, William and I retire to the library and have a brandy. There are some things I'd like to ask, as would any exporter given what's happened today, and I'm afraid they'd be boring for you and Harriet, Ivy.'

William stood up. 'May I have a word in your library before James joins us, sir?' he asked.

Harriet gave a loud intake of breath. Her hand flew to her mouth, and she went a deep shade of red.

Ivy glanced at her with amusement.

'It's a lovely evening,' Ivy said, getting up. 'I think Harriet and I will sit for a few minutes on the veranda. Perhaps you'd ask for me to be sent a glass of Madeira, Arthur, and perhaps Harriet could have a very small glass, too. And you, James?'

'I'll hold off for a moment. But I shall guide you to the veranda, lest you get lost.'

Both Harriet and Ivy laughed.

Arthur and William went out into the hall. 'May I congratulate you on your well-tailored lightweight suit,' Arthur said as they reached the library and went inside, 'and on your smart, non-scuffed shoes.'

William laughed. 'The owner of our *haveli* found the slightly worn clothes I'd needed for our plan,' he said. 'I was worried that the others might comment at some point, but fortunately, even if they noticed my down-at-heel look, they were too polite to say anything.'

He cleared his throat.

'But the reason I asked to speak to you, sir, wasn't about my wardrobe,' he said. 'It's about Harriet. I love her deeply, and I very much want to marry her. I've loved her from the first day I met her. The reason I've hesitated to ask for her hand before now is that I wasn't certain whether I'd be sent back to Madras, and I felt both of you should know the full situation before making any decisions. But James and I were told before we left this evening that everyone's extremely pleased with our work, and there's no question of either of us being moved from Jaipur. That's a real relief, I don't mind telling you.' He cleared his throat again. 'So, sir—'

Arthur smiled at him. 'You need no go further, son. Harriet's a lovely young woman, and it would have been hard to give her to someone I didn't respect as much as I respect you. So, I couldn't be more delighted than I am to welcome you into the family.'

He held out his hand. With a smile from one side of his face to the other, William shook it.

'If you'll excuse me, sir,' William said, and he turned and dashed from the room. He stopped abruptly at the sight of Harriet standing in the hall in front of him. Then, at the same moment, they ran to each other, arms outstretched, and hugged each other tightly.

Beaming with pleasure, Ivy hurried across to William. Ivy put out her arms to embrace him, and he released Harriet.

'I couldn't be happier, dear William,' she told him, her voice breaking. She reached out to Harriet and the three of them hugged each other.

'When you've a free arm, William,' James said, holding out his hand.

William disentangled himself from Harriet and Ivy and shook James's hand. 'Welcome to the clan, brother,' James said with a broad smile. 'I couldn't have had anyone I wanted more for my brother than you.'

29

L*ater, Monday evening*

'WHAT'S THIS ABOUT, PHILIP?' Julia asked. 'Why are we in your study, and not on the veranda with Eleanor?' She frowned suddenly, and stared at him anxiously. 'Is this about the smuggling?'

Philip shook his head. 'Not at all,' he said hastily. 'It was my premises and my paper, but that's where my connection to Maxwell's nefarious dealings ends.'

'I thought so. Is it to do with how you and Frank were with each other this evening? I must admit to being surprised, but rather pleased, that you were both quite pleasant on the few occasions you spoke to each other. It was as if both of you were recent changelings.'

'I'm afraid there are no fairies involved, but you're not as far from the explanation as you might think,' Philip said

with a short laugh. 'This *is* about Frank in a way. And Beatrice, too. There's something I need to tell you, and if you
agree, I'd then like to tell Eleanor. If today has shown me
anything, it's that secrets can all too easily end up causing
trouble. In future, I want everything to be out in the open.'

'So it involves Eleanor in some way, does it?' she asked,
her brow wrinkling.

'That's right.'

'Then I think I know what you're going to say,' she said
quietly.

'I don't think you do,' he said.

'You want to tell me that Eleanor's not the daughter of
Beatrice and some unknown stranger, but is your actual
daughter, don't you?'

He stared at her, stunned. 'How did you find out?' he
asked, his voice shaking.

'I've known for most of her life, Philip. A growing suspicion became a certainty the older she got. Look into the
mirror, and then look at Eleanor. She's the image of you, in
her looks, in the way she phrases her words, in her mannerisms. No one else could have been her father.'

'I don't know what to say,' he said quietly. 'How I can
apologise? I'm so sorry, so very sorry. I'd do anything in the
world to turn the clock back.'

'Well, *I* wouldn't,' Julia said. She put her arms around
him. 'You don't have to apologise, dearest Philip. All those
years ago, we went through a terrible time, losing so many
babies. Naturally I was not at my best. I was so very grateful
to Frank and Beatrice to be given Eleanor, so grateful that
we could be the parents we'd so wanted to be, that who
fathered our lovely daughter was completely unimportant.
And as she got older, I was actually glad she was yours as

she felt even more my child. I loved seeing the characteristics she shared with you, which were the characteristics that had made me fall in love with you.'

'Oh, Julia,' he said softly. 'I don't deserve to have such a wonderful wife as you.'

'I love Eleanor with all my heart,' she added, 'and I wouldn't turn the clock back. If I did, we wouldn't have Eleanor. She has enriched every day of our lives, and that's all that matters. And yes, I think we should tell her. It's only fair to Beatrice to do that. I haven't dared think what it must have been like for Beatrice, seeing Eleanor with us. It can't have been easy. Eleanor must have a chance to get to know the woman who gave birth to her.'

'What're you talking about? That woman was you, Mama, wasn't it?' They spun round at the sound of Eleanor's voice.

Both Julia and Philip stared at her, without speaking.

Then Julia stepped forward. 'No, darling, it wasn't. Beatrice Fletcher is the woman who gave birth to you.'

Eleanor seemed to recoil.

'Beatrice Fletcher!' she exclaimed, stepping back. Her hands flew to her face. Hunching her shoulders, she breathed heavily. 'Beatrice Fletcher! Are you sure?' Then she paused, and stared at the floor, her brow creasing into a frown. 'It would make sense of some of the recent things that have seemed quite strange, I suppose.' She looked back up at them, her eyes brimming with tears. 'Who's my father, then?' she asked shakily.

'It's Papa,' Julia said.

Philip explained briefly that at a time when Julia was having one miscarriage after another, he'd had a short affair with Beatrice, and Beatrice had given birth to Eleanor. He had obviously never stopped loving Julia. Frank Fletcher, not knowing who the father was, and not wanting to keep the baby, had given her to Julia and him so they could be parents.

'We couldn't have loved you more if Julia had given birth to you,' Philip concluded.

Biting her thumbnail, Eleanor thought for a moment. 'So Alice is my half-sister,' she said slowly. 'Does she know?'

Julia assured her quickly that she didn't.

'Yes, she does,' Philip said awkwardly. 'I didn't know that till a week ago. Apparently, she overheard Frank and Beatrice speaking about it not long after they'd moved here. She thought I should know that she knew, but that she'd no intention of telling anyone else. It's all credit to her that she could have told you, but didn't.'

'Don't be angry with us, darling,' Julia begged, tears rolling down her cheeks. 'We so wanted to have a child, and it looked as if we weren't going to have one. And then we had you, Eleanor. We've loved you so much from the moment we got you, a tiny little baby in a basket. I've always felt as if I was your real mama.'

Eleanor rushed up to Julia and flung her arms around her. 'But you *are* my real mama! I'll always love you, both of you. And I'm not angry with you. How could I be? I couldn't have had more wonderful parents. There's never been a moment when I haven't felt deeply loved. I'm so lucky. Of course you're my mama, and you always will be. Just you and no one else.'

They hugged each other tightly.

Then Julia held her at arm's length. 'But the fact is, my darling Eleanor, you'll never forget what you now know, and I think you need to talk to Mrs Fletcher, if not now, at some point in the future. She'll never be your mama, but she can be a special friend. We all need friends.'

Eleanor nodded. 'I will do,' she said. 'I wondered why she used to stare at me. I thought it very strange. And then at Amber Fort, she separated me from the others, saying Aunt Ivy wanted some time with Alice to get to know Alice. She and Aunt Ivy thought James was interested in her. At least, that's what she said. It must have been because she wanted us to talk to each other, though. But what she'd said about James really shook me, and I asked myself why it did. So in a way I owe Mrs Fletcher a debt of gratitude.'

She paused, and thought for a moment.

'I want to go and see her now,' she said at last. 'And then I want to talk to Alice.'

'It's not too late to go,' Julia said. 'Would you like me to come with you?'

'Just as far as their house,' Eleanor replied. 'But I'd like to speak to them on my own.'

WHEN ELEANOR WAS SHOWN by the butler into the sitting room, Beatrice rose to her feet, surprise written across her face.

'Frank is in the office, and Alice is upstairs,' Beatrice told her. 'You can go up to her if you want.'

'I'll do that, but I'd like to speak to you before I go up to Alice.'

She stared hard at Beatrice, as if she was seeing her for the first time.

A red haze spread across Beatrice's face. She put her hands to her cheeks to cool them. 'You know, don't you?' she whispered.

Eleanor nodded. 'Papa told me just now. And Mama

knows, too. She guessed a long time ago, as I look like Papa.'
She paused. 'It must have felt very strange to see me, eighteen years after you last saw me.'

'It was, and it still is. We never thought our families
would meet again, that we'd be put in the situation we've
been in since moving to Jaipur. But your parents were
desperate for a child, and Frank didn't want you.' Her voice
trailed away.

'Did *you* want to keep me?'

Beatrice hesitated. 'I won't lie to you, no, I didn't. I didn't
love your father, and I'd never wanted a child. Nor had
Frank.'

Eleanor frowned. 'But you had Alice.'

Beatrice shrugged. 'These things happen in marriage.'

'Why didn't you give Alice away?'

'I don't really know. We just seemed to accept the situation.' She paused. 'Although I hadn't wanted to keep you,
when I moved here and saw you, I found myself very interested in you. That surprised me,' she said with a wry smile.
'I think you've grown up into a lovely girl, Eleanor. A part of
me is now rather sorry that I didn't keep you.'

'If you had, I'd be a very different person. I've heard
enough about Alice's childhood to know that. I'm what I am
because of Mama and Papa. I couldn't have had better
parents. I, too, will be honest. You'll never feel like a mother
to me, Mrs Fletcher.'

Beatrice nodded slowly. 'I understand. I'd like to think
we can be friends, though.' She paused. 'Alice doesn't know,'
she added.

For a moment, Eleanor wondered whether to tell her
that Alice *did* know, but the moment passed.

'I think we can be friends,' Eleanor said slowly. 'Funnily
enough, although you don't feel like my mother, I'm curious

about you. After all, there must be some of you in me. It means that I wouldn't mind knowing you a little better, Mrs Fletcher. Only as a person, though, not as a mother.'

Beatrice smiled. 'Thank you. It's more than I could have hoped for.' She hesitated. 'Calling me Mrs Fletcher seems very formal, given the circumstances. Perhaps you'd like to start to calling me Aunt Beatrice? You call Mrs McKenna Aunt Ivy, don't you?'

'I can't see myself ever calling Mr Fletcher Uncle Frank!' Eleanor exclaimed. They stared at each other, and then both burst out laughing.

'I'll think about it,' Eleanor said. 'May I go up and see Alice now, please?'

'I'll take you to her and then leave the two of you together.'

THE DOOR CLOSED behind Eleanor and she went further into Alice's room.

'What's happened?' Alice asked, staring at Eleanor in surprise and alarm. 'It's a bit late for a social visit. Is it Charles?' Her hand flew to her throat.

Eleanor shook her head. 'He's absolutely fine. It's nothing to do with him.' She glanced around Alice's room. The top of Alice's wooden table was almost hidden by sheets of writing paper.

Alice followed her gaze. 'I'm getting my notes together,' she said. 'Charles is going to help me to make the guide book, and then we're going to see if we can find a publisher. I'm going to ask your father if he'll send the film away for development.'

'Won't Mr Fletcher be furious that you're working so closely with Charles?' Eleanor asked.

'Weirdly, he seems to have changed. The Maxwell thing has shocked him so much that it's made him nicer. He's actually given his permission for Charles and me to marry. Oh, Eleanor, I'm so excited,' she said beaming. 'Father said we shouldn't tell anyone till Saturday, and then announce it at the club. So don't tell anyone, will you?'

Eleanor flung her arms around Alice. 'I'm so happy for you,' she said. 'I know how much you love Charles. He's really nice. You're going to be so happy.' She held her for a moment longer, and then stepped back and stared at her face.

Alice caught her breath. 'You know, don't you?' she whispered, her voice shaking.

'If you mean what I think you do, yes. But your mother thinks you don't know. Papa told me you'd overheard your parents talking about what had happened.'

'I did.'

'That must have been truly awful, Alice. You must have felt terrible.'

Alice nodded. 'It made sense of a lot of things, though. But my first feeling was fury. I was furious that they'd given you away, not me.' She gave a nervous giggle.

Eleanor smiled. 'I would have been angry about that, too. So we're half-sisters,' she said. 'Until today, I thought that Harriet was the closest thing I had to a sister.'

'But you would. You grew up with her.'

'That's right. She's the person I feel closest to, or felt closest to. But knowing that the same person gave birth to both you and me makes me feel differently towards you. Closer in a way, I suppose,' Eleanor added.

'What d'you think Harriet will say?' Alice asked.

Eleanor thought for a moment. 'She won't like it,' she said at last. 'She'll feel left out. She'll think I'll turn to you not her, which I would've done in the past. She may even become jealous of you. It alters the balance between the three of us, you see.'

'Then don't tell her,' Alice said bluntly.

'Not tell her?' Eleanor exclaimed.

Alice shrugged. 'Things are going to change anyway. I'm marrying Charles, and Harriet's bound to marry William. You'll marry, too. We'll all live in Jaipur, hopefully near each other. We'll stay friends, I'm sure, but the friendship's bound to alter a bit as we'll be someone's wife. Why cause Harriet unhappiness for no reason? You'd risk spoiling your friendship when there's really no need to do so.'

'You're very kind, Alice. And you're very sensible. That's a good solution. You and I will know, but Harriet won't.'

'And really, the fewer people who know about this the better,' Alice went on. 'It would be embarrassing for our parents if it was widely known. Horrible though mine have been, I wouldn't want them to be gossiped about everywhere they went. Or people to think badly of your father, who's really nice. Or people to stare at you and my mother when you were at the same table.' She shuddered.

Eleanor hugged Alice again. 'You're right. That would be too awful for words. I'm so glad I've such a lovely sister.'

Alice blushed. 'This will be funny for my mother, too,' she said. 'You knowing the truth must slightly alter things in her head.'

Eleanor pulled a face. 'She's asked me to call her Aunt Beatrice.'

Alice giggled. 'Are you going to?'

'I don't know. I'm a little old to start addressing someone who isn't my aunt as Aunt. But it could be a bit unkind to keep calling her Mrs Fletcher. And I certainly can't call her Beatrice.' They both laughed.

'I suppose I'll give it a try,' Eleanor said. 'But I'd balk at Uncle Frank.' They burst out laughing again. 'Anyway, I must get off home now. I just wanted to see you. And I don't think I've said it yet, but congratulations on your engagement. I'm so looking forward to celebrating with you on Saturday, sister.'

30

M *inutes later*

STANDING in the shadows further along the road, James watched Eleanor return to her house and go inside.

He'd been on the way to speak to her father when he'd seen her leave the house and go with her mother towards the Fletchers' home. He doubted she'd be with the Fletchers for long, given what a stressful day it had been for everyone, so he'd decided to stay where he was and wait for her return.

Her mother had come back almost at once, but Eleanor not quite so soon. But she was home now, and the glow of light that had remained in the downstairs rooms told him that her parents hadn't yet gone upstairs. If he called on them now, it wouldn't be too late to speak to Philip, and then to Eleanor.

That's what he had to do. He didn't have any choice, the way he was feeling.

The general euphoria back at his house at the engagement of William and Harriet, which had spread among their servants, and about which he couldn't be happier, had made him think about his own future.

From the moment he'd shaken William's hand, and had been wrapped in the warm embrace of William and Harriet's happiness, he'd known that he had to try to secure his own happiness, too, and do so that very evening. There could be no better way of ending a difficult, but satisfying, day than by getting Philip's permission to propose to Eleanor.

He'd promptly suggested to William that they stay over till the following day, which would give William more time with Harriet, and enable him to have a word with Philip. William had readily agreed, and leaving him sitting with Harriet and his parents, he had slipped out of the house to go to Philip.

His happiness lay in a future with Eleanor, and he desperately hoped she felt the same.

He thought she did.

She had said she did.

The very thought of being loved by her dragged the breath from his body.

But suppose she didn't love him enough to marry him?

He stared at her house, his nervousness growing.

He mentally shook himself. He must make a move now. If he stood there much longer, they'd have gone to bed and he'd definitely be too late. He could hardly knock on the door of a house that had been plunged into darkness.

With butterflies in his stomach, he went up to the iron

gates, pushed them slightly open, walked up the drive to the front door, took a deep breath, knocked and stood back.

It was Philip who opened the door.

'Hello, James,' Philip said, failing to hide his surprise. 'I've sent the servants to bed, hence the fact that I've undertaken the demanding task of opening the front door myself.' He smiled. 'I take it you'd like to come in?'

'Thank you, sir. '

'Is this about what happened today?' Philip asked, closing the door behind James. 'I understand it all went very well.'

'It did,' James said. 'It couldn't have gone better. We arrested all the people we'd been watching over the past few months. No, I'm here about something else. Or rather someone. It's about Eleanor.'

'Eleanor!' Philip said in surprise. He gave a dramatic sigh and pretended to mop his brow. 'What's she done now?'

'Nothing,' James said with a smile. 'It's about what I hope she'll do, and what I hope you'll do, too, sir.'

Philip stared quizzically at him. 'For a man who's recently shown an impressive ability to think clearly, that skill seems to have momentarily deserted you,' he said. 'Suppose we go into the study and have a brandy? Then you can tell me what's on your mind.'

He turned and started to walk towards the study.

James took a few steps after him, and stopped.

'I want to marry Eleanor, sir,' he blurted out. 'I love her. I think I've always loved her. I'll be getting a house of my own and I've a good job so I'll be able to support her. I love her so much. She deserves nothing but the best, and I'll strive to give her that. I hadn't meant to stand in your front hall and ask you this, sir, but I couldn't wait one minute longer. Will you give me your permission to ask Eleanor to marry me?'

LIZ HARRIS

Smiling broadly, Philip came back to James, grabbed his hand in obvious delight, and shook it firmly. 'Of course I will, James. Nothing would give me greater pleasure. In fact, Eleanor hasn't yet gone upstairs so you can ask her now if you wish. I'm sure Julia would agree with me.'

'She would,' Julia said, coming into the hall. 'I'm afraid it was difficult not to hear what you were saying, James, as I was just inside the sitting room.' She glanced over her shoulder. 'So what do you say, Eleanor?' she called, and then turned back to James. 'She was with me so I'm afraid she heard you, too,' she said ruefully.

Eleanor came slowly into the hall, her hand in front of her mouth, her eyes shining with unshed tears. She went straight across to Philip.

'Thank you, dear Papa,' she said tremulously, and she hugged him. Then she went across to Julia. 'Thank you, too, my dearest, dearest mama.' And she leaned forward and kissed her.

'My darling daughter,' Julia whispered.

'Come, Julia,' Philip called to her. 'I believe there's something James wants to ask Eleanor. I think we can leave the two of them to talk together, don't you? Let's go up.'

He went across to Julia and put his arm around her shoulder. Smiling up at him, she slid her hand round his waist, and together, their arms around each other, they climbed the stairs to their room.

Eleanor watched them go and then turned and went up to James, a smile hovering on her lips.

'What a strange day this has been,' she said, a couple of tears trickling down her cheeks. 'Things I thought were one way turned out to be something different. It was very unsettling, but everything's clearer now, and it's going to be all right. Everything's changed, but nothing really has. But one thing I know, that I seem to have known for ever, even if I didn't realise it, something that's never changed, and never will, is that I love you very much.'

He moved closer to her. 'Dear, dear Eleanor. I don't have the words to tell you how much I love you. But I know that you know how much I do, how much I've always done, and how much I always will. Please, will you marry me?'

She threw her arms around his neck. 'Yes, yes, yes! There's nothing in the world I want more than I want to be your wife. So a million yesses.'

'Oh, Eleanor!' he exclaimed. He flung his arms around her and held her tightly to him. 'You'll never regret it, not for one minute. I'm going to do all I can to make you the happiest woman alive.'

'Just by proposing, you've made a very good start,' she said. Stepping back from him, she wiped her eyes with the back of her hands and stared lovingly up into his face.

'I think I can improve on it,' he said, his voice thickening with emotion.

For a long moment, neither moved as each gazed into the face of the other.

'I love you very much, Eleanor,' he said.

Gently he cupped her face in his hands, and lowering his head, his lips met hers. With a deep and heartfelt kiss, they bound together the love they'd shared in the past with the love and passion that would travel alongside them into the future.

AUTHORIAL NOTE

In the 1930s, the area on the other side of Amer Road from Man Sagar Lake was completely undeveloped – it was open fields. There had been a deliberate intention to leave an expanse of undeveloped ground between the wooded hills, where wild animals lived, and the road, along which people travelled.

However, unlike on my previous trip to India and the trip the following year to Vietnam, there were no houses for me to see on my visit to Jaipur, which were likely to have been lived in by members of Jaipur's small British community early in the twentieth century. All had either been developed or demolished. I had to decide, therefore, what sort of house they would have lived in.

I felt that the British would have chosen to live in a house more like the one they'd have had if they'd been in Shimla or New Delhi, for example, so I decided to give them a similar house to those.

As I felt that they would have lived in a compact community of British businessmen and their families, I decided to locate the fictional Victoria Crescent in the area that had been open fields in the 1930s.

The administration building is fictional. The few British people who carried out the work of the British government in the 1930s would have worked out of the Residency, the home of the Resident.

There were several buildings in the Residency gardens, each of which was linked to the main building by an underground tunnel. But the distance between the Residency, now a beautiful hotel, was too far from the centre of Jaipur and the bazaars than I thought desirable for the story. Therefore, I gave James and William an administrative base closer to the centre of the town, although they paid occasional visits to the Residency.

Sukha Haveli is also fictional. In my earlier novels set in India, I knew the name of coffee shops in existence during the 1930s in which my characters would have stopped for a morning coffee. But I was unable to find any reference to cafés in Jaipur that would have been frequented by the small British community in the 1930s, hence I created a fictional café in a lovely *haveli*.

IF YOU ENJOYED JAIPUR MOON...

...it would be very kind of you to take a few minutes to leave a review of the book.

Reviews give welcome feedback to the author, and they help to make the novel visible to other readers.

In addition, it's easier for books to be promoted, given that several promotional platforms today require a minimum number of reviews.

Your words, therefore, really do matter.

Thank you!

LIZ'S NEWSLETTER

On the last Friday of every month, Liz sends out a newsletter with updates on her writing, what she's been doing, where she's been travelling, and an interesting fact she's learnt. You will also hear of promotions and special offers.

Rest assured - Liz would never pass on your email address to anyone else, and if you write to Liz, which you can do through her website, you will always get a reply.

As a thank you for signing up for Liz's newsletter, you'll receive a free full-length novel. To sign up and get a free book, go to:

https://lizharrisauthor.com

ACKNOWLEDGEMENTS

Once again, I'm beginning by thanking the superb cover designer, Jane Dixon-Smith, for a really lovely, eye-catching cover, and my excellent editor, Richard Sheehan, who doesn't miss an error.

I would like to thank, also, my friend in the north, Stella, who is always the first to read my completed manuscripts. Stella always tells me exactly what she thinks about the characterisation, structure and pacing of the novel. Her constructive criticism at that early stage is invaluable.

As usual, I've spent much of the year in the company of fellow writers, in writing retreats, in writing groups or simply over the lunch table. A huge thank you to my many friends—far too many to mention—for your friendship, support, and for all the fun we've had, sharing with each other some of the details of the fictional worlds we were creating.

In order to write *Jaipur Moon,* I returned to India, and this time I stayed in Jaipur, a place I hadn't visited on my magical trip to India a few years ago. I loved Jaipur. Thanks to my excellent guide, Akshay Singh, and my driver, Arun, who were with me for the whole of my stay in Jaipur, I learnt so much more than I'd been able to find in the pages of the books I'd bought. But any mistakes I may have made will be down to me, and not to anyone else.

I'd like to mention a few of the books that were particularly useful in coming to understand life for British people in Jaipur in 1934. They are *The Sun in the Morning*, by M. M. Kaye, *Women of the Raj,* by Margaret MacMillan, *A Princess Remembers*, by Gayatri Devi and *The Royal House of Jaipur*, by John Zubryzycki.

I should like to give a heartfelt thank you to my husband, Richard, for keeping the real world at bay while I sit in front of my computer, immersed in the fictional world I'm creating, and walking alongside the characters who live within it. Thank you, Richard.

And lastly, thank you, readers, for reading my books, and for your feedback, support and friendship. It means a lot to me.

INTRODUCING: HANOI SPRING

If you enjoyed reading *Jaipur Moon* – and I hope you did – and you haven't yet read *Hanoi Spring*, set in Vietnam 1932, you might be interested in doing so.

To give you a taste of the novel, in the next few pages you'll read the first chapter of *Hanoi Spring*.

Although part of a series, each of the novels set in Asia is a standalone novel, complete in itself.

HANOI SPRING: CHAPTER ONE

The French Territory of Hanoi,
  March 1932

'Would you stop here for a moment before turning into the drive?' Lucette Delon called from her seat behind the chauffeur.

The chauffeur nodded. 'Of course, Madame.'

As the sleek Peugeot 301 drew gently to a halt at the kerb, Lucette leaned forward and stared in delight through the car window at the three storey house with fern-green wooden shutters, which was visible in the gap between the tamarind trees that lined Boulevard Henri Rivière.

Wrought-iron railings surrounded the house and the front garden, which was filled with bougainvillea, hydrangea bushes and an abundance of lush tropical flowers whose names she had yet to learn.

Her gaze travelled up the honey-coloured walls of the house to the intricate metal grillwork that fronted the upper balconies, and thence to the sloping tiled roof that glowed rich red in the sunlight, and she found herself smiling with pleasure at the welcome thrown out by her new home.

'We can go now,' she said happily, and she sat back in her seat.

The chauffeur put his hand on the gearstick.

Thud!

Behind her, metal met metal with a loud, resounding clang.

The Peugeot shuddered, and she was thrown forward.

Wide-eyed with shock and surprise, she grasped the seat in front of her, and clung to it tightly as the car settled.

The chauffeur started to open the driver's door.

But before he could complete the action, the door next to her opened and a current of air rushed in.

A hand, light beneath her elbow, encouraged her to get out, and trembling, she allowed herself to be guided on to the pavement.

'I'm so sorry,' she heard a man say, his voice full of apology. She was vaguely aware of a tall man in a lightweight white suit standing beside her. 'It was my fault, Madame. Entirely my fault. My concentration lapsed for a moment and I let my car slide into yours.'

'It was a shock, Monsieur,' she said, trying to steady her voice. 'But no more than that. I'm not hurt, as you can see. And nor is my chauffeur. Or are you hurt, Tuan?' she asked the chauffeur in anxiety.

'No, Madame.'

Her hand flew to her mouth. 'What about the car! Is it damaged?' she asked in sudden alarm. 'My husband would be so upset. The car's new, you see,' she told the stranger.

'I'm confident that no one will blame you for what was my fault,' he said.

'But we stopped so that I could look at my house. We've

been stopping in the same place every day for the past two weeks, not thinking how dangerous it must be. If we'd driven straight on to the drive—'

'No one will blame you for an accident I caused,' he repeated firmly. 'I should have been paying attention to what was happening on the road, and I wasn't.'

The chauffeur moved to the back of the car, and bent down to look at the bumper.

'There are a few scratches on the back bumper, but nothing serious, Madame,' he told Lucette, straightening up. He glanced at the bumper that was touching hers.

'Your front bumper is scratched, Monsieur,' he said. 'But neither car has any dents in the bodywork.'

'You must allow me to have your bumper replaced,' the man told Lucette, his hand still lightly under her elbow. 'If you'll permit me to see you into your house, I can explain to your husband what happened, and we can talk about how best to arrange for the work to be done. I know a place not far from here that'll do it.'

Feeling a little steadier, she looked properly at the stranger for the first time.

He was a handsome man, well built, with dark brown hair. She guessed he was about ten years older than she was—about thirty or thirty-one, so a couple of years older than Philippe. The eyes that were looking at her with genuine concern were a piercing grey in his lightly tanned face.

She shook her head. 'He won't be home, I'm afraid. He's one of the administrative staff of the Résident Supérieur so he'll be at the Résidence.'

'Then perhaps you'll allow me to see you into the house, Madame? You're somewhat pale, and I wouldn't feel comfortable leaving you to go in alone, especially as all this was my fault.' With his free hand, he indicated the two cars standing bumper to bumper.

He turned back to her. 'I'd better introduce myself. My name is Gaston Laroche, and I'm one of the many diplomatic attachés you'll find in Hanoi. What I suggest I do is take you inside, and leave my card with you. Your husband will then know how to contact me about the bumper.'

She gave him a wan smile. 'I do feel a little shaken, I must admit, and I wouldn't mind something reviving. Perhaps you would care to join me for some refreshment? This is bound to have been a shock for you, too.'

He gave a slight bow. 'It's very kind of you, Madame. You're right, it was. And, yes, a short break before I continue on my way would be the sensible thing to do.'

And angling himself towards the gate in the iron railings, he started gently propelling her towards the short drive that led up to her house.

'So, Gaston?'

The police chief supervising Gaston leaned back in his chair in the small, undistinguished building on the southern edge of the Old Quarter that housed a branch of the French Sûreté Générale, and folded his hands across his ample stomach. 'From the expression on your face when you came in, I imagine this morning went according to plan.'

Gaston laughed. 'It's that obvious, is it, Emile? Yes, I can truly say it did. Watching her routine over the past week certainly paid off. A tap that was just sufficient for her to feel a little shaky and in need of support, and a few scratches on the bumper, but not enough to bankrupt the Sûreté.'

'I take it you were invited into the house?'

'Indeed, I was. We had brandy for our nerves, followed by sweetened tea.'

'What's the wife like?'

'It's too soon to be able to answer that. But Lucette, as she asked me to call her, seems like any young woman of about twenty-one or twenty-two, who's had a somewhat sheltered upbringing. She's looking forward to getting to know Hanoi's range of restaurants, and the many cafés with live music. From the short amount of time I spent with her, I'd say she's a typical newlywed, who clearly adores her husband, and who doesn't have a single political bone in her body.'

'I assume you didn't get to meet the husband?'

Gaston shook his head. 'No, I didn't. I watched him leave this morning to make sure he'd be at work. I wouldn't have wanted him taking over before I'd achieved my goal. As it is, I've made her acquaintance, and got her trust, if that's the right word.'

'That's a start, anyway.'

Gaston grinned at him. 'Oh, I went somewhat further than that. The brandy settled Lucette sufficiently for us to talk a little about Hanoi, and for her to mention that her husband was one of those supervising the smooth-running of the Hoa Lo Prison. I was naturally greatly impressed to learn that her husband held so important a post.'

The police chief chuckled. 'I'm sure you were.'

'I insisted that she and her husband permit me to show my regret for the accident by taking them to dinner at the Hôtel Métropole on Saturday.'

'Now that could bankrupt the Sûreté,' Emile said with a smile.

Gaston laughed. 'They'd be delighted to go, she told me. They weren't doing anything—they hadn't been there long enough to have built up a circle of friends—and she'd seen the advertisements for the hotel on the trams, and had heard it was excellent from Monsieur Bouvier, the man her husband assists. And she knew her husband was keen to go, too. It means that I'll be meeting Philippe Delon in a couple of days.'

'You *have* done well,' the chief said in satisfaction.

'And there's one more thing,' Gaston added with a smile. 'The Bouviers will be joining us on Saturday.'

The chief sat up sharply and stared at Gaston in amazement. 'I don't believe it! Just how did you arrange that?'

'By assuring Lucette before I left that she was still very pale—fortunately, she didn't have a mirror to hand or she would have seen that her colour was fully restored and that she was looking remarkably pretty, in fact—and by saying that she should have someone with her other than the servants. I asked if she'd a friend nearby. She said that the Bouviers lived in the house next to theirs, and I suggested that her maid go across for Madame Bouvier.'

The chief burst out laughing, and shook his head.

'Minutes later, Simonne Bouvier was rushing into the house, the picture of concern. As I got up, I made a great thing of saying that I'd be in touch before Saturday about our dinner at the Métropole. Madame Bouvier visibly pricked up her ears, expressed great envy of Lucette, and before you could say successful ploy, I'd invited her and her husband to join us. It was my way of thanking her, I explained, for coming to the support of Madame Delon in her hour of need, a need for which I'd been responsible.'

The chief laughed again. 'Well done, Gaston. To get all that out of a scratch on the bumper was, indeed, a triumph! I don't know how you did it.'

Gaston gave him a dry smile. 'You can do anything when

you've mastered the inanity of the small talk favoured by your peers.'

'All I can say is, France did well to send you to us. Via Africa, of course,' Emile added, and laughed again. He paused. 'You're sound on the Côte d'Ivoire, I take it?'

Gaston smiled. 'I've done my homework so well that I'm actually beginning to believe I've been there.'

'Good. This could work. If you can worm your way into Marc Bouvier's circle of friends, you'll have a strong chance of finding out whether or not he's smuggling papers out of the prison and generally supporting terrorist activity. And if he *is* guilty, you'll be well placed to discover the person helping him inside the prison, and also the person to whom he passes the information. We need to find out the delivery chain.'

'That's the idea. First of all, I intend to get an invitation to take a look at the prison from the inside.'

'From what I've seen of you, I'm sure you'll succeed. If you come here tomorrow morning, you'll meet the operatives you can call on for help. You'll be told how to get hold of them. I know you prefer working alone, but there're bound to be occasions when you need more people on the case.'

'If that's what you want, fine.'

Emile nodded. 'It is. Whoever's responsible must be stopped. Take the time you need, but get it right. The prison's become a school for terrorists, thanks to the newspapers circulating among the inmates. And the papers being smuggled out of the prison are encouraging anti-French feeling among the local population.'

Gaston nodded.

'We've uncovered one or two arms' dumps,' Emile continued, 'and rumour has it that the garrison troops have been infiltrated. It's clear they're planning an uprising, but all our intelligence can tell us is that the terrorists are organised in cells of fifteen to twenty people. It's just not good enough.'

Gaston leaned forward. 'Believe me. I'll find out for certain if Bouvier *is* responsible, and if he isn't, I'll discover who is. Whoever it is, they're going to learn that France won't tolerate any betrayal of the colonial administration. If Bouvier's guilty, he'll pay the highest price. And so will anyone else involved.'

ABOUT THE AUTHOR

Born in London, Liz Harris graduated from university with a Law degree, and then moved to California, where she led a varied life, from waitressing on Sunset Strip to working as secretary to the CEO of a large Japanese trading company.

Six years later, she returned to London and completed a degree in English, after which she taught secondary school pupils, first in Berkshire, and then in Cheshire.

In addition to her twenty published novels, she's had several short stories in anthologies and magazines.

Liz now lives in Berkshire. An active member of the Romantic Novelists' Association and the Historical Novel Society, her interests are travel, the theatre, reading and cryptic crosswords. To find out more about Liz, visit her website at:

https://lizharrisauthor.com

ALSO BY LIZ HARRIS

Historical novels

The Colonials

Darjeeling Inheritance

Cochin Fall

Hanoi Spring

Simla Mist

Jaipur Moon

The Linford Series

The Dark Horizon

The Flame Within

The Lengthening Shadow

Distant Places

The Road Back

In a Far Place

Three Sisters

The Loose Thread

The Silken Knot

The Woven Lie

The Heart of the West

A Bargain Struck

Golden Tiger

A Western Heart

Contemporary novels

The Best Friend

Evie Undercover

The Art of Deception (2nd edition to be published 2025)

Word Perfect

Translations into German

Eine Erbschaft in Darjeeling

(Darjeeling Inheritance)

Liebe und Verrat in Cochin

(Cochin Fall)

Am Tagesende

(The Dark Horizon)

Die Wiederkehr

(The Flame Within)

Im Dämmerlicht

(The Lengthening Shadow)

Am seidenen Faden

(The Loose Thread)

Translations into Italian

Evie Undercover

(Evie Undercover)

Printed in Dunstable, United Kingdom

.

JAIPUR MOON

LIZ HARRIS

HEYWOOD PRESS